W9-DAU-148

10% Happier

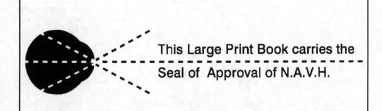

10% HAPPIER

HOW I TAMED THE VOICE IN MY HEAD, REDUCED STRESS WITHOUT LOSING MY EDGE, AND FOUND SELF-HELP THAT ACTUALLY WORKS — A TRUE STORY

DAN HARRIS

THORNDIKE PRESS

A part of Gale, Cengage Learning

GALE
CENGAGE Learning·

Farmington Hills, Mich • San Francisco • New York • Waterville, Maine
Meriden, Conn • Mason, Ohio • Chicago

GALE
CENGAGE Learning®

LIBRARY OF CONGRESS CATALOGING-IN-PUBLICATION DATA

Harris, Dan, 1971–
    10% happier : how I tamed the voice in my head, reduced stress without
losing my edge, and found self-help that actually works—a true story / by
Dan Harris. — Large Print edition.
    pages cm. — (Thorndike Press large print health, home & learning)
    ISBN 978-1-4104-7308-0 (hardcover) — ISBN 1-4104-7308-2 (hardcover)
    1. Mind and body. 2. Stress management. 3. Meditation. 4. Buddhism.
5. Large type books. I. Title. II. Title: Ten percent happier.
    BF161.H29 2014
    158.1'2—dc23   2014024564

Published in 2014 by arrangement with ItBooks, an imprint of
HarperCollins Publishers

Printed in Mexico
1 2 3 4 5 6 7 18 17 16 15 14

For Bianca

We are in the midst of a momentous event in the evolution of human consciousness, but they won't be talking about it in the news tonight.
— Eckhart Tolle, self-help guru

Open up your mind, in pours the trash.
— Meat Puppets, "desert punk" band

CONTENTS

AUTHOR'S NOTE

Conveniently for me, most of the events described in this book were recorded, either by television cameras or the Voice Memos app on my iPhone. When conversations were not recorded, I reproduced the quotes from memory and, in most cases, ran them by the participants. In some places, I cleaned up the dialogue (excising *ums* and *ahs,* etc.) to make it more readable, or to make myself look smarter.

PREFACE

I initially wanted to call this book *The Voice in My Head Is an Asshole.* However, that title was deemed inappropriate for a man whose day job requires him to abide by FCC decency standards.

It's true, though. The voice in my head can be a total pill. I'd venture to guess yours can, too. Most of us are so entranced by the non-stop conversation we're having with ourselves that we aren't even aware we have a voice in our head. I certainly wasn't — at least not before I embarked on the weird little odyssey described in this book.

To be clear, I'm not talking about "hearing voices," I'm talking about the internal narrator, the most intimate part of our lives. The voice comes braying in as soon as we open our eyes in the morning, and then heckles us all day long with an air horn. It's a fever swamp of urges, desires, and judgments. It's fixated on the past and the future, to the detriment of the here and now. It's what has us reaching into the fridge when we're not hungry, losing our temper when we know it's not really in our best interest, and pruning our inboxes when we're ostensibly engaged in conversation with other human beings. Our inner chatter isn't all bad, of course. Sometimes it's creative, generous, or funny. But if we don't pay close attention — which very few of us are taught how to do — it can be a malevolent puppeteer.

If you'd told me when I first arrived in New York City, to start working in network news, that I'd be using meditation to defang the voice in my head — or that I'd ever write a whole book about it — I would have laughed at you. Until recently, I thought of meditation as the exclusive province of bearded swamis, unwashed hippies, and fans of John Tesh music. Moreover, since I have the attention span of a six-month-old yellow Lab, I figured it was something I could never do anyway. I assumed, given the constant looping, buzzing, and fizzing of my thoughts, that "clearing my mind" wasn't an option.

But then came a strange and unplanned series of events, involving war zones, megachurches, self-help gurus, Paris Hilton, the

Dalai Lama, and ten days of silence that, in a flash, went from the most annoying to the most profound experience of my life. As a result of all of this, I came to realize that my preconceptions about meditation were, in fact, misconceptions.

Meditation suffers from a towering PR problem, largely because its most prominent proponents talk as if they have a perpetual pan flute accompaniment. If you can get past the cultural baggage, though, what you'll find is that meditation is simply exercise for your brain. It's a proven technique for preventing the voice in your head from leading you around by the nose. To be clear, it's not a miracle cure. It won't make you taller or better-looking, nor will it magically solve all of your problems. You should disregard the fancy books and the famous gurus promising immediate enlightenment. In my experience, meditation makes you 10% happier. That's an absurdly unscientific estimate, of course. But still, not a bad return on investment.

Once you get the hang of it, the practice can create just enough space in your head so that when you get angry or annoyed, you are less likely to take the bait and act on it. There's even science to back this up — an explosion of new research, complete with colorful MRI scans, demonstrating that meditation can essentially rewire your brain.

This science challenges the common assumption that our levels of happiness, resilience, and kindness are set from birth. Many of us labor under the delusion that we're permanently stuck with all of the difficult parts of our personalities — that we are "hot-tempered," or "shy," or "sad" — and that these are fixed, immutable traits. We now know that many of the attributes we value most are, in fact, *skills,* which can be trained the same way you build your body in the gym.

This is radical, hopeful stuff. In fact, as I discovered, this new neuroscience has led to the flowering of an elite subculture of executives, athletes, and marines who are using meditation to improve their focus, curb their addiction to technology, and stop being yanked around by their emotions. Meditation has even been called the "new caffeine." I suspect that if the practice could be denuded of all the spiritual preening and straight-out-of-a-fortune-cookie lingo such as "sacred spaces," "divine mother," and "holding your emotions with love and tenderness," it would be attractive to many more millions of smart, skeptical, and ambitious people who would never otherwise go near it.

One of the questions I hear most often from skeptics is: If I quiet the voice in my head, will I lose my edge? Some think they need depression to be creative or compulsive worry to be successful.

For the past four years, I've been road testing meditation in the crucible of one of the most competitive environments imaginable, television news. I'm here to tell you, it's totally doable. More than that, it can give you a real advantage — and, not for nothing, it might even make you nicer in the process. Yes, as you will see, I did stumble into a few embarrassing pitfalls along the way. However, with the benefit of my experience, you should be able to avoid them.

What I'm attempting to do in this book is demystify meditation, and show that if it can work for me, it can probably work for you, too. The best way to illustrate this is to give you, as we say in the business, "exclusive access" to the voice in my head. All of us struggle to strike a balance between the image we present to the world and the reality of our inner landscape. This is particularly tricky for a news anchor, whose job is to project calm, confidence, and (when ap-

17

propriate) good cheer. Most of the time, my external presentation is authentic; at baseline, I'm a happy guy who is keenly aware of his good fortune. But there are, of course, moments when my interior reality is a bit more complicated. And for the purposes of this book, I am going to put a magnifying lens directly on the knotty stuff.

The story begins during a period of time when I let the voice in my head run amok. It was during the early part of my career; I was an eager, curious, and ambitious cub reporter who got swept up, and swept away — and it all culminated in the single most humiliating moment of my life.

CHAPTER 1
AIR HUNGER

According to the Nielsen ratings data, 5.019 million people saw me lose my mind.

It happened on June 7, 2004, on the set of *Good Morning America.* I was wearing my favorite new tie and a thick coating of makeup. My hair was overly coiffed and puffy. The bosses had asked me to fill in for my colleague Robin Roberts as the News Reader. The job basically entailed coming on and anchoring brief news updates at the top of each hour.

I was sitting in Robin's spot, at a small, satellite anchor desk inside the second story of ABC's glass-encased studio in New York's Times Square. On the other side of the room was the main anchor desk, home to the show's cohosts, the avuncular Charles Gibson and the elegant Diane Sawyer.

Charlie tossed it over to me: "We're gonna go now to Dan Harris, who's at the news desk. Dan?" At this point, I was supposed to read a series of six "voice-overs" — short news items, about twenty seconds apiece, over which the control room would roll video clips.

It started out fine. "Good morning, Charlie and Diane. Thank you," I said in my best morning-anchor voice, chipper, yet authoritative.

But then, right in the middle of the second voice-over, it hit. Out of nowhere, I felt like I was being stabbed in the brain with raw animal fear. A paralytic wave of panic rolled up through my shoulders, over the top of my head, then melted down the front of my face. The universe was collapsing in on me. My heart started to gallop. My mouth dried up. My palms oozed sweat.

I knew I had four more stories to read, an eternity, with no break and no place to hide — no sound bites or pretaped stories or field correspondents to toss to, which would have allowed me to regroup and catch my breath.

As I began the third story, about cholesterol drugs, I was starting to lose my ability to speak, gasping as I waged an internal battle against the wave of howling terror, all of it compounded by the knowledge that the whole debacle was being beamed out live.

You're on national television.
This is happening now. Right *now.*
Everyone is seeing this, dude.
Do something. DO something.

I tried to fight through it, with mixed results. The official transcript of the broadcast reflects my descent into incoherence:

"Researchers report people who take cholesterol-lowering drugs called statins for at least five years may also lower their risk for cancer, but it's too early to . . . to prescribe statins slowly for cancer production."

It was at this point, shortly after my reference to "cancer production," with my face drained of blood and contorted with tics, that I knew I had to come up with something drastic to get myself out of the situation.

My on-air meltdown was the direct result of an extended run of mindlessness, a period of time during which I was focused on advancement and adventure, to the detriment of pretty much everything else in my life. It began on March 13, 2000: my first day at ABC News.

I was twenty-eight years old, terrified, and wearing an unfortunate double-breasted suit as I walked through the high-ceilinged entryway lined with pictures of such luminaries as Peter Jennings, Diane Sawyer, and Barbara Walters (all now my colleagues, apparently), then took the steep, stately escalator up into the mouth of the building on Manhattan's Upper West Side.

They made me go to the basement that day, to some fluorescent-lit security office to have my picture taken for my new identification card. In the photo, I looked so young that a colleague would later joke that a wider shot might reveal me to be holding a balloon.

That I had made it to ABC at all seemed like a big misunderstanding, or maybe a cruel joke. During the preceding seven years, as I toiled in local news, my dream had always been to "get to the network" — which was how people in the farm leagues referred to it — but I had assumed it wouldn't happen until I was maybe forty and looked old enough to operate a motor vehicle.

I had started in TV news straight out of college, with the vague goal of pursuing a career that had a modicum of glitz and also did not require me to do any math. My parents were doctors, but I didn't have the aptitude or the attention span for med school. So, despite some initial misgivings on the part of my folks, I took a job at an NBC station in Bangor, Maine (one of the smallest television markets in the country — number 154 out of 210). The gig was part-time, paid $5.50 an hour, and involved writing scripts for the anchorwoman, then operating the studio camera during a broadcast called *Alive at 5:30*. On my first day, the producer who was assigned to train me wheeled around from his electric typewriter and matter-of-factly announced, "This is not a glamorous job." He was right. Covering tire fires and snowstorms in rural Maine — not to mention living in a tiny apartment on the first floor of an elderly woman's house and eating mac and cheese nearly every night — was profoundly unsexy. Nevertheless, I loved it immediately.

After a few months of badgering my bosses to put me on camera, they relented, and I became a reporter and an anchor, even though I was barely twenty-two and only had one blue blazer, a hand-me-down from my dad. It didn't take long for me to know that this job was what I would be doing for the rest of my life. I found the craft itself fascinating — especially the challenge of writing stories that were meant to be spoken aloud and matched to pictures. I delighted in the opportunity to get intrigued by an obscure but important subject, and then devise ways to teach viewers something that might be useful or illuminating. Most of all, I took enormous pleasure in the fact that my new position gave me license to march up to important people and ask impertinent questions.

Broadcast news is a tricky beast, though. Aside from the high-minded stuff about holding powerful interests accountable and using the power of the medium for good, there is also something deeply and irrationally affirming about getting your mug on TV. Watch how excited people get at baseball games when their faces flash on the JumboTron. Now imagine doing that for a living.

My colleague in Bangor was correct that much of the actual work of being a TV reporter — sitting through interminable news conferences, spending hours in a news van with an irascible cameraman, chasing down cops for sound bites — was not glamorous, but as I moved to larger markets, first to Portland, Maine, and then to Boston, the pay got better and the stories bigger, and the visceral thrill of being recognized in bars and on line at the bank never got old.

I remember my mother, a repository of wisdom, once telling me offhandedly at some point during my youth that she thought anyone who would run for president must have a hole on their inside that was so big it could never be filled. To the extent that I ever allowed myself to reflect on my drive to be on TV, I always found her comment haunting.

Seven years after that first job in Bangor, I was working at a twenty-four-hour cable news channel in the Boston area when I got a call, seemingly out of nowhere, indicating that I might be on the cusp of landing the big fish. My agent told me that executives at ABC News had seen my tapes and wanted to talk.

They hired me as the co-anchor of ABC's loose and scrappy overnight newscast, *World News Now,* which airs from two to four in the morning, to an audience consisting primarily of insomniacs, nursing mothers, and college students hopped up on ADD drugs. By the time I reported for duty, though, on that day in March of 2000, the guy I was supposed to replace, Anderson Cooper, had decided he didn't want to leave just yet. Not knowing what else to do with me, the bosses gave me a chance to file some stories for the weekend edition of our evening newscast, *World News Tonight.* As far as I was concerned, this was the coolest thing that had ever happened to me. Just a few weeks prior, I'd been reporting for an audience of tens of thousands of New Englanders; now I was broadcasting to millions of people all over the country. Then it got even better: I was asked to file my first story for the weekday edition of the evening news, anchored by Peter Jennings himself.

I idolized Jennings. My whole on-air style was a straight-to-video version of his. I had studied his intricate anchor desk ballet — the masterful mix of slow leans, head nods, and arched eyebrows. I admired his ability to be smooth, and yet emote without being mawkish. He was the epitome of the voice-of-God anchorman, with a personal mystique to boot: the 007 looks, the four wives, the rumored celebrity trysts.

He was the colossus who sat astride ABC News. Internally, his broadcast was referred to simply as "The Show," almost as if we didn't have other major broadcasts like *20/ 20, GMA,* and *Nightline.* He was also the object of bottomless fear. I hadn't met him yet, but I'd already heard the stories about his volcanic temper. Because of his reputation for eating his young, the executives deliberately scheduled my first appearance on his show for July 4, a day they knew he would be on vacation.

I did a feature story about baby boomers going back to work as lifeguards because all the young people were taking jobs with dot-com companies. When it aired, the show's producers seemed satisfied with the piece, but I never heard from Jennings himself. I didn't know if he'd been watching, or if he even knew who I was.

A few weeks later, I was at the apartment I shared with my younger brother, Matt, riding the exercise bike we'd set up in the living room, when my landline, cell phone, and pager went off in rapid succession. I got off the bike and checked the pager. It read, "4040." This was the extension for the *World News Tonight* "rim," the area where Peter and his senior producers spent the day putting together the show. I called in, and the young assistant who answered the phone put me on hold. Then a man picked up and said, "I think we need to start covering Ralph Nader. His campaign is picking up speed. Can you do it?" I looked over at Matt and mouthed, "I think this is Peter Jennings."

The next day, I was on a plane to Madison, Wisconsin, to interview Nader and file a piece for that night's broadcast. It was a hectic, harrowing process, exacerbated by the fact that, late in the day, Peter requested a series of significant changes to the script I had written. We managed to "make air," but just barely. When I got back to my hotel room and dialed into the Internet, I saw that I had a two-word email from Peter: "Call me." So I did. Immediately. I was expecting him to ream me out for writing a subpar script, but the first thing he said was, "Wear lighter-colored shirts." He then proceeded to inform me that he'd been named to *People*'s Best Dressed list based entirely on clothes he ordered from catalogues.

That sealed it. For the next five years, Peter was my mentor and, sometimes, tormentor. Anchoring the overnight show was now off the table. I had, improbably, become a network news correspondent. They gave me a set of business cards and my very first office, on the fourth floor of the building, alongside five other correspondents, all men several decades older than I was. Our offices were arrayed along a catwalk that overlooked the set from which Peter anchored his show. One morning, shortly after I moved in, I got off the elevator and the other reporters were huddled together, chatting. None of them would speak to me. It was awkward and a little bit intimidating, but if this was the price I had to pay for scoring this job a full decade before I thought it could happen, it was totally worth it.

Working for Peter was like sticking your head in a lion's mouth: thrilling, but not particularly safe. He was frightening for a lot of reasons: he was about a foot taller than me, he was subject to sudden and unpredictable mood swings, and — even though he was originally from Canada — he was a bona fide American icon, which made it surreally mortifying when he yelled at you. He seemed to take pleasure in embarrassing me, preferably in front of as many people as possible. Once, his assistant called me down to the rim, saying Peter needed to discuss something. When I arrived, Peter looked up, did a double take, and eyeing my plaid jacket, said, "You're not going to wear that on television, are you?" Everyone laughed uncomfortably. I turned fuchsia, and muttered something about how of course I wasn't. I may have subsequently burned it.

But the real flash point — as with every correspondent — was the script-writing process. Peter was an exacting and irascible editor, and he often made changes at the last minute, sending producers and correspondents into frenzied scrambles minutes before airtime. Even when he affected a more-in-sadness-than-in-anger tone to his revisions, I strongly suspected that he actually enjoyed the power play. He had a set of semi-rational writing rules that every correspondent learned to obey over the course of a particularly rigorous hazing period: don't start a sentence with "but"; don't say "like" when you can say "such as"; never, ever use the word "meanwhile."

By no means were all of Peter's standards arbitrary, though. After observing and interacting with him for a while, it became clear that he cared deeply about this work. He saw his job as a privilege — a sacred trust with the audience, and a vital part of a functioning democracy. He was a congenital contrarian who expected his staff to aggressively question authority (including our own bosses — except, of course, him). Early in my tenure, I pitched him a story about the treatment of mentally ill inmates in prison, which Peter personally helped me produce and gave prominent play on his broadcast. Then he had me launch more investigations, one on the issue of rape in prison, and another into the silencing of conservative voices on American college campuses. It was a journalistic apprenticeship par excellence.

Very often, though, Peter's inspirational

qualities were obscured by his mercurial behavior — and the primary venue for this was at the rim in those frenetic late afternoon hours before airtime, as reporters and producers were desperately vying for him to approve their scripts — which he insisted on doing personally. Some of his signature moves included reordering all of the ideas in a story for no discernible reason, and poaching the best lines from our pieces and using them himself. We correspondents (the older guys on my hall eventually deigned to communicate with me) often commiserated about getting "Petered," inevitably concluding that the level of criticism we received was directly correlated to Peter's mood or his personal feelings about you at that moment. He was, we all agreed, a man fueled by a combustible mix of preternatural talent and crushing insecurity. The first — and only — time I was handed back a script with no marks from his red pen, I saved it.

While I may have been initially stunned by my ascent at ABC News, I was not about to let the opportunity go to waste. I quickly got over my I-can't-believe-they're-letting-me-through-security phase and started focusing on how to navigate what could be a Hobbesian environment where the various broadcasts, anchors, and executives competed fiercely against one another, and where aligning yourself too closely with any particular clique carried risks.

My modus operandi was inherited from my father, whose motto was: "The price of security is insecurity." Dr. Jay Harris, a gifted wringer of hands and gnasher of teeth, used his security/insecurity maxim to advance through the world of cutthroat nebbishes in academic medicine. My mom, a reserved Massachusetts Yankee, was slightly mellower about her equally demanding medical career. The joke around the house was that this was because my dad is Jewish and my mom is not. The other running joke was that I had inherited all of my dad's worrier genes, and my brother had been spared. As Matt once quipped, "Dan makes Woody Allen look like a Buddhist monk."

Kidding — and ethnic stereotypes — aside, I took my dad's maxim very much to heart. Straight from childhood, I was a frequent mental inventory taker, scanning my consciousness for objects of concern, kind of like pressing a bruise to see if it still hurts. In my view, the balance between stress and contentment was life's biggest riddle. On the one hand, I was utterly convinced that the continuation of any success I had achieved was contingent upon persistent hypervigilance. I figured this kind of behavior must be adaptive from an evolutionary standpoint — cavemen who worried about possible threats, real or imagined, probably survived longer. On the other hand, I was keenly aware that while this kind of insecurity might prolong life, it also made it less enjoyable.

Once at ABC, though, any attempts at balance went directly out the window. I was young and out of my league; I had to work triply hard to prove myself in the face of widespread institutional skepticism. (One night, as I was standing in front of the camera waiting to go live on Peter's show, his executive producer got into my earpiece and said, "You look like you're getting ready to pose for Bar Mitzvah pictures.") To compensate, I was pitching stories constantly; I was ruthlessly self-critical; I was willing to work nights, mornings, and weekends — even if it meant skipping important events (such as friends' weddings and family gatherings) in order to get on the air.

The news division was a fertile environment for this kind of intensity. In fact, people here were fond of repeating a famous quote from the legendary White House reporter Helen Thomas, one I embraced with gusto: "You're only as good as your last story." Getting on the air was not easy. On any given night, *World News* ran six or seven taped pieces from correspondents, and most of those slots went to the people covering specific beats such as the White House. Meanwhile, there were about fifty other correspondents vying for what remained. I set up an endless mental tape loop: *How many stories have I had on this week? What is the state of my relationship with Peter right now? What else do I have coming up?*

For the first year or so on the job, my strategy was to focus mainly on producing what we called "back of the book" pieces, stories that aired after the first commercial break. These ranged from investigations to in-depth pieces to fluffy features. I figured that given all the competition to cover the big, breaking news, this was the smart play. Aside from the aforementioned investigations, I reported on the dot-com boom and bust, and did colorful features on the periphery of the Bush-Gore recount battle in Florida.

About a year into my tenure, Peter summoned me to his book-lined office to discuss a new assignment. He was settled behind an imposing dark wood desk as I sank uncomfortably into his overstuffed couch, which was clearly designed by the same person who invented such medieval torture devices as the iron maiden and the pear of anguish. He made an announcement that was both unforeseen and unwelcome. He wanted me to take over ABC's coverage of religion. This beat was a top priority for Peter. He had recently hosted a pair of highly rated, well-reviewed prime-time specials about the lives of Jesus and Saint Paul. He had also personally overseen the hiring of the first full-time religion correspondent in the history of network news, Peggy Wehmeyer. But Peggy, a comely, blond evangelical from Texas, was leaving now, and Peter had decided I was going to take over her responsibilities. I tried to issue some sort of a protest about being a devout atheist (I didn't have the guts to tell him I couldn't care less about the subject), but he was having none of it. This was happening. End of discussion.

Several months later, I was sitting in a puddle jumper on the tarmac in Fort Wayne, Indiana, having just finished shooting a story about church youth groups. A guy in the front of the passenger cabin hung up his cell phone, turned around, and told everyone that the Twin Towers were on fire. It was September 11, 2001, and suddenly every civilian airplane in the country was grounded. I was no longer heading back to New York anyway. My own cell phone rang, and my new marching orders were to get myself to Shanksville, Pennsylvania, where United Flight 93 had been brought down by passengers who stormed the cockpit.

I disembarked, rented a car, and with my producer alongside me, began the four-hundred-mile trek eastward. I spent those seven hours in the car experiencing what was, for me, a new and confusing breed of misery. Like all Americans, I was furious and scared. But there was also an overlay of self-interest. This was, in all likelihood, the biggest story of our lifetimes, and here I was stuck driving a "midsize vehicle" across the breadth of Ohio, helplessly listening to the news unfold on the radio. I knew Peter would be in his element, in full-on clarify-and-comfort mode, and it made me feel physically ill not to be part of the team reporting on — and explaining — this news to the country. I knew now that "back of the book" would no longer cut it for me.

I reported from Pennsylvania that night, and then drove the rest of the way back to New York, where I essentially moved into the Tribeca Grand Hotel, just blocks from

Ground Zero. The police had closed off much of Lower Manhattan, and since I lived and worked uptown, the only way to cover the story was to stay nearby. This boutique hotel, with its tiny rooms, exposed wrought iron elevator shafts, and huge lobby lounge (normally filled with boulevardiers sipping overpriced cocktails — now eerily empty), was an incongruously chic spot from which to cover the deadliest terror attack ever on American soil.

I was right about Peter. His round-the-clock anchoring during those terrible days was nearly universally lauded, and under his guidance, I produced stories about the anguished crowds visiting the rubble at Ground Zero, and also the troubling number of attacks on innocent Muslims around the nation.

A few weeks later, as the maelstrom of Ground Zero coverage began to abate, I was back uptown in my office one afternoon when my phone rang. The caller ID read FOREIGN DESK. The voice on the other end of the line said, "We need you to go to Pakistan." A pint of dopamine was released into my brain. After I hung up the phone, I actually paced around the room, pumping my fist.

This, fittingly, was how I began the most

dangerous and formative years of my life: with a series of douchey gesticulations. I lurched headlong into what would become a multiyear adventure — during which I would see places and things that I never would have had the audacity to imagine as a shaggy twenty-two-year-old reporter in Bangor. I was floating on a wash of adrenaline, besotted with airtime, and blinded to the potential psychological consequences.

Prior to this first trip to Pakistan in October of 2001, I had never been to the Third World, unless you count a visit to Tijuana in the 1980s when I was on a Teen Tour. So when I boarded the flight for Islamabad the day after that call from the Foreign Desk, I had no idea what to expect. I arrived to what my British friends would call a "proper *Star Wars* scene." Baggage claim was teeming with bleary-eyed passengers, bored-looking cops, and greasy, brown jumpsuit–wearing baggage-handling hustlers. I was the only Westerner in the hall. A local driver met me on the other side of customs, holding a sign with my name on it. Outside, the morning air was hazy, warm, and smelled vaguely of burnt tires. The highway was clogged with huge, brightly decorated cargo trucks whose drivers were constantly beeping their tinny, melodic horns. I later figured out that people in places like this didn't honk to get other drivers out of the way so much as to simply alert people of their presence, like a pulse of sonar. I had never felt so far away from home before.

But then we got to the hotel. To my surprise, it was a Marriott, and a nice one at that — much larger and more elegant than the average American version. I dropped off my bags then went straight up to the presidential suite, where the ABC team was working. This was my first time meeting many of these people. They were mostly from our London bureau — swashbuckling types, veterans of places like Bosnia and Rwanda. They seemed completely comfortable with the cognitive dissonance of being in a dangerous, impoverished country where we had uniformed hotel staff bringing us cellophane-wrapped platters of cookies and mixed nuts twice a day. My fellow correspondent Bob Woodruff strolled in and nonchalantly ordered scrambled eggs from room service.

Things got edgier pretty quickly. Within just a few days, I got word that we'd received an invitation from the Taliban, who were still ruling Afghanistan, to come visit their home base in Kandahar. It would be a sort of embed. At first blush, it sounded like a supremely dumb idea — to go behind enemy lines, a guest of the actual enemy — and it provoked a spirited debate among our staff. We had a big meeting and argued it out. I went through the motions of listening to both sides, but it was really a foregone conclusion: there was no way I was going to miss this.

I tried to call my mother to let her know where I was going before she saw it on TV, but I couldn't reach her at the hospital where she worked. So, against my better judgment, I called my father, the far more emotional parent. When I told him the plan, he started to cry. As the line went silent, except for the sounds of my dad catching his breath, the myopia of exhilaration gave way to remorse. Up until this point, I had been thinking only about what was in this trip for me; I hadn't considered the special kind of hell it would create for my family. My dad recovered pretty quickly, engaging in characteristically self-deprecating humor: "You have a Jewish mother — it's just not your mother."

That night, I felt so guilty — and, frankly, scared — that I couldn't sleep. The next day, I was part of a small group of reporters who boarded a bus to the unknown. After a long, spine-rattling ride on the unpaved main road that bisects southern Afghanistan, we arrived in the middle of the night at a complex of squat government buildings on the outskirts of Kandahar. The American air campaign had knocked out power and the whole city was pitch-black. We quickly went to the roof of one of the buildings, established a satellite signal, and taped a report in which Peter Jennings, at the news desk in New York, asked me questions about our journey. After talking to me, Peter — who still had a national newscast to prepare for — took the time to call my parents and let them know I was okay.

The next three days were a surreal, heady blur. We were ferried around town by hirsute, heavily armed men. For the most part, they showed us things they wanted us to see for PR purposes, including bombed-out buildings in which they claimed innocent civilians had been killed by U.S. warplanes. But it was the offscreen demeanor of these Taliban fighters that made the strongest impression on me. Aside from the top commanders, who engaged in the requisite propagandist puffery, the rank-and-file soldiers were actually easygoing and sociable. They were kids, really. They taught us local curse words. (Apparently "donkey"

41

is a serious insult in Pashto.) At one point, one of them whispered to me, "Take me to America."

I included a lot of this kind of color in my reports and received laudatory emails from the home office that were head-swimmingly intoxicating for a young reporter on the make. Peter was referring to me on the air as "our man in Afghanistan." My crew, a pair of Brits, spent many hours ribbing me, predicting that I was going to be "an insufferable twat" when I got home. They would act out imagined scenes of me in New York City bars with friends, interrupting every conversation with, "Yeah, yeah, yeah — did I tell you about the time I was in Afghanistan?"

This trip was my first taste of what I would describe as journalistic heroin: the pure, sick rush of being somewhere you are not supposed to be and not only getting away with it but also getting on TV. I was hooked.

When I got back to New York, though, I didn't have much time to play peacock. I was greeted with a public repudiation in the *New York Times.* Arts critic Caryn James compared my coverage unfavorably to the BBC's, calling mine "warm and fuzzy." It was a hammer blow to my psyche. I bitterly disagreed with her, but many of my colleagues did not. Her article cemented the impression that I was too green to do this job. Around the office, I immediately went from hero to donkey.

A few weeks later, the Foreign Desk decided to give me a second chance, sending me this time to Tora Bora, where Osama bin Laden was holed up and under assault by local Afghan warlords on the American payroll. In the taxi on the way to the airport, I got a call from Peter. He told me the consensus was that I had blown it the first time around, and that now I really needed to prove myself. I spent much of the flight in the fetal position.

There was no Marriott in Tora Bora. Upon arrival, we paid an opium farmer to let us sleep in his ramshackle compound of mud huts in the middle of an iced-over poppy field. There was a large, smelly ox tied up right outside the door, and every day when we came home for dinner, there would be one less chicken running through the yard.

On this assignment, I redeemed myself. Part of what turned things around for me was a scene, captured on video, where I was shooting a "stand-up," the part of a news story where the reporter speaks directly to the camera. I was perched on the side of a mountain, and right in the middle of my spiel, there was a whistling noise overhead. I had never heard gunfire up close before, so it took me a second to realize what was happening and dive to the ground. There was nothing warm or fuzzy about this. My bosses ate it up.

There were, however, two embarrassing things about this moment. First, a close inspection of the videotape revealed that none of the Afghans in the frame behind me ducked, or even looked particularly concerned. Second, my immediate thought as that bullet whizzed over was: *I hope we're rolling on this.*

This was new. If gunshots had gone off in a situation where I was not on the job, I would have wet my pants. I had no record of courage in my personal life. No military service, not even any experience in contact sports. My only prior brush with danger was when I got hit by a cab after wandering into an intersection in Manhattan without looking. When you're covering a news story, however, there's a tendency to feel bulletproof. It's as if there's a buffer between you and the world, an exponentially more dangerous variant of the unreality you feel when taking a stroll while listening to your iPod. In the context of combat, my reflex to worry had been completely overridden by my desire to be part of the big story.

Tora Bora was a military failure — with Bin Laden most likely scurrying along a goat trail into Pakistan — but for me it was a resurrection of sorts. Having regained the trust of my bosses, I spent the next three years shuttling back and forth between New York and places such as Israel, the West Bank, Gaza, and Iraq. I was like a slightly less dorky Zelig, somehow materializing in the backdrop of the world's most important historical events.

These were assignments that entailed repeated exposure to grotesquerie. In Israel, outside a seaside hotel after a suicide bombing, I watched as a gust of ocean breeze sent a bedsheet billowing off the ground, revealing a row of legs. In Iraq, a group of marines and I stared down at a bloated corpse on the side of the road as we collectively realized that what we thought were gunshot wounds in the man's face were, in fact, drill holes. In the West Bank, I stood next to a father, watching bodies being dumped from a forklift into an impromptu mass grave in a hospital parking lot. The man let out a sustained, high-pitched wail as he spotted his own son tumbling into the pit.

While I was unable to hold it together in the face of the crying father, walking out of camera range with a lump in my throat, I was surprised by my overall reaction to the horrors of war — or, more accurately, my lack of reaction. As far as I could tell, I was not that shaken. I convinced myself this kind of psychological distance was a job requirement, like the doctors from M*A*S*H who cracked jokes over the patients on their operating table. I reckoned reportorial remove served a higher purpose, allowing me to more effectively convey urgent information. If I broke down every time I saw something disturbing, how could I function?

Back home, people would ask me whether my experiences overseas had "changed" me. My reflexive answer was: no. The old line "Wherever you go, there you are" seemed to apply. I was still the same; I just had the proverbial front-row seat at history. My parents openly worried about whether I was traumatized by what I'd seen, but I didn't feel traumatized at all. Quite the opposite; I liked being a war correspondent. Loved it, in fact. The bodyguards, the armored cars, being driven around like I was a head of state. I also liked the way flak jackets made my diminutive frame look larger on TV. In a war zone, the rules are suspended. You ignore traffic lights, speed limits, and social niceties. It has an illicit, energizing feel not unlike being in a major city during a blackout or a blizzard. And then, of course, there's the added romance of risk. We used to repeat to one another bastardized versions of an apt old quote from Winston Churchill: "Nothing in life is so exhilarating as to be shot at without result."

It wasn't just the rush I enjoyed. I also genuinely believed in the importance of what we were doing, bearing witness to the tip of the American spear. I felt a sense of purpose — that this was a cause that merited the risk. For both of these reasons — the thrill and the principle — I freely engaged in ABC's notorious intramural battles in order to stay in the game. An outsider might assume that we journalists spend most of our time competing with people from other networks. In actuality, we expend most of our energy competing with our own colleagues. In order to retain my spot on the front lines, I found myself vying against fellow correspondents like David Wright, another young reporter who'd recently arrived from local news. He was aggressive and smart, and I kind of resented him for it.

While I'd once been content to let the

senior folks fight it out for the big stories, I was now much more assertive. This competition mostly took the form of overt lobbying — phone calls and emails to the anchors and executives who make the assignments. While the internal wrangling was, in many ways, a sign of a healthy, vibrant organization, it was also stressful and provoked me to dedicate way too many hours to measuring myself against people I worked with. For example, during a period in which David was kicking ass over in Afghanistan and I was stuck in New York, I could barely bring myself to watch the news.

Fighting over airtime in the middle of a war was perverse, but such was the nature of the gig, it seemed to me. The great blessing of being a journalist is that you get to witness world events — to interface with the players, to experience the smells and tastes of it all. The great curse, though, is that, as I'd learned on 9/11, you come to see these events, at least in part, through the lens of self-interest. *Did I get to go? Did I perform well?* This psychology was not discussed much in all the autobiographies of legendary journalists that I'd read, but it was nonetheless real. Peter had epic rivalries with fellow anchors like Ted Koppel. The news division had been structured by its preceding president, Roone Arledge, as a star system with competing fiefdoms battling over scarce resources like big interviews and the best correspondents. When Wright and I were both angling to be the first into Iraq after the fall of Baghdad, Peter even called me and made approving jokes about my sharp elbows.

In an environment that was permissive of pique, I sometimes let my temper get the better of me, a tendency that dated back to my early twenties. When I was a young anchorman in Boston, I once threw my papers in the air during a commercial break to express my frustration over a technical glitch. Shortly thereafter, my boss called me into his office to warn me, "People don't like you." That meeting sent my heart into my throat and forced me to correct my behavior. But there continued to be room for improvement; as a network correspondent, I was still occasionally snippy with colleagues, and even, on a few occasions overseas, downright stupid. Like the time I was in the middle of a crowded, angry street demonstration in Pakistan and engaged in a supremely unwise shouting match with a protestor who'd just told me the Israelis were behind 9/11. The one situation in which my peevishness remained firmly bottled up was, of course, when dealing with Peter Jennings himself.

On a muggy July day in 2003, I got out of a taxi in front of my apartment building on the Upper West Side, having just wrapped up a five-month stay in Iraq, a posting that stretched from the months before the U.S. invasion all the way up to the beginning of the insurgency. It was strange to be back from the desert, in a world of deciduous trees, a place where I no longer required an entourage. The doormen looked at me with surprise, and I sensed that they were struggling to remember my name. I rolled my bag down the hallway of the fourteenth floor and opened the door to the "home" I'd scarcely visited in two years. The place was pathetic, decorated like a college dorm room, and with stacks of unopened mail all over the place. I'd been away so long that I'd missed the transition to DVDs — I still had one of those big, boxy televisions with a VHS player in it. I hadn't come to the end of my overseas assignments, but the powers that be had decided that now was the time for me to focus more on domestic priorities, like covering the 2004 presidential campaign and trying my hand at the anchor desk.

Meanwhile, my personal life was a blight-scape. While I had been abroad, the already limited social network I'd maintained outside of work had largely evaporated. I was in my early thirties, and my friends had all coupled up and hunkered down. People my age were maturing, nesting, and reproducing. I, by contrast, had just endured an epic breakup after a short, fiery relationship with a Spanish journalist I'd met in Iraq. But I was so focused on work that romantic stability wasn't even on my list of priorities.

Not long after I got home, I developed a mysterious illness with flulike symptoms. I felt tired and achy all the time, I was perpetually cold, and I had trouble getting out of bed. I'd always been a little bit of a hypochondriac, but this was different. It dragged on for months. I convened lengthy, medical symposia over the phone with my parents. I got tested for tropical diseases, Lyme disease, and HIV. There was even talk of chronic fatigue syndrome.

When all the tests came back negative, I latched on to the theory that my apartment had a gas leak, and I paid an exorbitant fee to get the place tested. For a few nights, I slept on the floor at the apartment of my close friend Regina, whom I'd known since college. She was a law school grad who had started a legal headhunting company. Throughout the night, her miniature pinscher would bring his kibble next to my head and chew it in my ear. Ultimately, the test results showed there was no leak. At which point I jokingly said to Regina that if I didn't find a diagnosis soon, I might have to admit that I was crazy.

When I finally broke down and went to see a psychiatrist, he took about five minutes to deliver his verdict: depression. As I sat on the couch in this cozy Upper East Side office, I insisted to the kindly, sweater-wearing shrink that I didn't feel blue at all. He explained that it is entirely possible to be depressed without being conscious of it. When you're cut off from your emotions, he said, they often manifest in your body.

This was humbling. I had always fancied myself to be reasonably self-aware. My mind, a perpetual motion machine of plotting, planning, and evaluating, had apparently missed something essential. The doctor had a couple of theories. It was possible, he said, that the horror of what I had witnessed overseas was too much for my conscious mind to handle. It was also possible that I was subconsciously pining for the adrenaline of war zones — that I was essentially in withdrawal from journalistic heroin. Or perhaps it was a combination of both. He recommended antidepressants. Unfortunately, I had already started self-medicating.

Although many of my friends partook, I had made it through high school, college, and my twenties without experimenting with hard drugs. Alcohol and a little weed, yes, but nothing more. I was never even tempted — or to be more honest, I was scared. On a few occasions, pot had made me so intensely paranoid that I felt like I was incarcerated in an inner Mordor. I figured harder drugs had the potential to be even worse.

However, my psychosomatic illness had left me feeling weak and adrift. One night, I agreed to go to a party with a guy from the office. We were at his apartment, having a quick drink before going to meet his friends, and he shot me an impish look and said, "Want some cocaine?" He had offered before and I had always demurred, but this time, on an impulse, I caved. Here I was crossing what had always been a distinct, bright line, in an utterly haphazard fashion. I was thirty-two years old.

The drug took about fifteen seconds to kick in. At first, it was just a pleasant electric sizzle coursing through my limbs. Then I noticed a disgusting ammonia-flavored post-nasal drip. It didn't bother me, though, because it was accompanied by a triumphant horn flourish of euphoric energy. After months of feeling run-down and ragged, I felt normal again. Better than normal. Rejuvenated. Restored. Logorrhea ensued. I said many, many things over the course of the evening, one of which was: "Where has this drug been all my life?"

Thus began what my friend Regina sardonically called my *Bright Lights, Big City* phase. That night, at the party I went to with the guy from work, I made a bunch of new friends. And those people also did cocaine.

With coke, you never reach satiety. It hits, it peaks, it fades — and before you know it, every cell in your body is screaming for more. It's like that line from the poet Rilke, who referred to the "quick gain of an approaching loss." I chased this dragon with the zeal of the convert. Late one night, I was partying with another new friend, Simon — a man who had, to put it mildly, a great deal of experience with drugs — and when he was ready to go to bed, I insisted we stay up and keep going. He looked over at me wearily and said, "You have the soul of a junkie."

Then I discovered ecstasy. I was with some friends in New Orleans when someone started handing out little blue pills. They said it would take a half hour or more before I felt anything, and as I waited, I strolled through the city's French Quarter. I knew I was high when we passed a piano bar where they were playing Bon Jovi's "Livin' on a Prayer," and it sounded transcendent.

I couldn't believe one pill could make me so happy. I felt as if my torso was swaddled in heated cotton balls. The very act of talking, the mere vibration of my vocal cords, was blissful. Walking was a symphony of sensual pleasure, with waves of euphoria melting all the calcified barriers of self-consciousness. I could even get out of my own way to dance.

Sadly, the pain of the comedown was proportional to the power of the high. Reality reentered the scene with a pickax. The lesson for the neophyte drug taker was that there is no free lunch, neurologically speaking. On the day after ecstasy, my serotonin stores would be utterly depleted. I often found myself overwhelmed by a soul-sucking sense of emptiness, a hollowed-out husk of a man.

It was partly because of the severity of the hangover — cocaine, too, left me cracked-out and colicky for at least twenty-four hours — that I was meticulous about never doing drugs when I had to work the next day. Not only did I largely quarantine my substance abuse to weekends, but there were also long stretches of time when I was traveling for work and completely abstinent — covering the 2004 Democratic presidential primaries, for example. The pull of drugs was powerful, but the tug of airtime was even more so. In fact, during one of the years when I was using drugs, I was ranked as the most prolific network television news correspondent. This only served to compound my master of the universe complex, convincing me I could fool everyone and pull it all off.

On some level, of course, I knew I was taking a massive professional risk. If my partying leaked out I could have been fired. And yet I carried on, impelled forward blindly, my common sense hijacked by the pleasure centers of my brain. I kept using drugs well past the point where I had been diagnosed with depression. I failed — or refused — to connect the dots.

I had always had an addictive personality. It's a lucky thing that the first time I tried cigarettes, at age fourteen, I puked. Otherwise, I might have picked up a lifelong habit. One of my most vivid childhood memories was playing ball one afternoon with my mom and brother on top of a hill near our house. I kept telling them I needed to use the bathroom, and would then sneak back to the kitchen to take slices of cake from the fridge. On the fourth or fifth trip, after realizing I had eaten nearly the whole thing, I came back and tearfully confessed. Not long afterward, I found out where my parents — who were very strict about candy — had hidden a bag of lollipops on a very high shelf in the kitchen. Over the course of several days, I repeatedly weaseled up there and ate them all. The power of craving, the momentum of wanting was always difficult for me to resist.

Now, as a budding drug abuser, it wasn't just the professional risks I shrugged off. I developed persistent chest pains that got so bad that one night I went into the ER to get checked out. A young medical resident told me that the trouble was very likely caused by cocaine, which I had reluctantly admitted to using. Despite her pleading, I left the hospital and pretended the encounter had never happened.

Every drug recovery narrative has to have its bottom, and mine — or at least my first one — came on that warm June morning on the set of *GMA* when I melted down on live TV. Ever since my return from Iraq, I'd been occasionally filling in for Robin Roberts as the News Reader. It was a huge opportunity, one I valued immensely and hoped would turn into something larger. I was used to the routine — I'd been appearing semi-regularly for a few months now — so I had no reason to think this morning would be any different. Which is why I was shaken to my core when that irresistible bolt of terror radiated out from the reptilian folds of my brain.

My mind was in outright rebellion. My lungs seized up in what pulmonary doctors call "air hunger." I could see the words scrolling up in front of me on the teleprompter, but I just could not get myself to say them. Every time I stumbled, the prompter would slow down. I could picture the woman who operated the machine, tucked away in a corner of the studio, and I knew she must be wondering what the hell was going on. For a nanosecond, amid my inner hurricane of thoughts, I really cared what she, in particular, was thinking.

I tried to soldier on, but it wasn't working. I was helpless. Marooned, in front of millions of people. So, at the end of the voice-over about cholesterol-lowering drugs and their impact on "cancer production," I decided to resort to a gambit I'd never used before on TV. I bailed — punted. I cut the newscast short, several full minutes before I was supposed to be done, managing to squeak out, "Uh, that does it for news. We're gonna go back now to Robin and Charlie." Of course, I was supposed to have said "*Diane* and Charlie."

You could hear the surprise in Charlie's voice as he picked up the verbal baton and started to introduce the weather guy, Tony Perkins. Diane, meanwhile, looked genuinely worried for me, making a series of quick, anxious glances in my direction.

As soon as the weathercast began, Charlie shot out of his seat and ran over to see if I was okay. The producers were buzzing in my earpiece. Stagehands and camera operators were crowding around. No one seemed to know what had happened. They probably thought I'd had a stroke or something. I insisted I had no idea what went wrong. But as the panic subsided, humiliation rushed in; I knew with rock-solid certitude that, after having spent the previous decade of my professional life trying to cultivate a commanding on-air persona, I had just lost it in front of a national audience.

My superiors expressed sincere concern over the incident. When they asked what happened, though, I lied and said I didn't know — that it must have been a fluke. I was ashamed, and also afraid. I thought that if I admitted the truth, that I had just had a panic attack, it would expose me as a fraud, someone who had no business anchoring the news. For whatever reason, they seemed to accept my explanation. To this day, I'm not sure why. Maybe it was because it all happened so quickly, or because it was out of character, or perhaps because I managed to get through my next newscast, just an hour later, without a hitch. In the news business, memories are mercifully short; everyone moved on to the next crisis.

I called my mom from backstage. She had been watching, and she knew exactly what was up. She'd always been impossible for me to fool. I was frantic, but her response, a mixture of the maternal and the clinical, was enormously comforting. Within hours, she had me on the phone with a psychiatrist colleague from her hospital in Boston. This was the second shrink I had consulted since returning from Iraq. It never crossed my mind to mention my drug use to him, because I hadn't gotten high in the days or weeks leading up to the incident.

Stage fright seemed like a reasonable enough explanation. Performance anxiety had actually dogged me throughout my entire life, which, of course, made my choice of profession a little odd. One of the only lighter moments in the whole crisis was when I jokingly said to my mom that my career up until this point had been a triumph of narcissism over fear. I had experienced a few minor episodes of panic before this — in Bangor in 1993, I nearly fainted when my boss announced that she wanted me to do my first live shot that night — but a meltdown of this magnitude was unprecedented. I was put on an immediate, steady dose of Klonopin, an antianxiety medication, which seemed to bring things under control. For about a week, as I became habituated to the drug, it gave me a pleasant, dopey feeling. With the Klonopin on board, you could have marched an army of crazed chimps armed with nunchucks and ninja stars into my apartment and I would have remained calm.

Meanwhile, I kept on partying. Which is how, a little over a year later, it happened again. Same basic scenario: I was at the news desk on *GMA*. The terror cut straight through the Klonopin even before I started to read the first story. The anchors tossed it to me, and from the very first word you could hear my voice getting thinner as my throat constricted. I had five stories to get through, and no respite, no lifeline. I was determined, though, to make it all the way.

I had to stop to catch my breath at a few points, but each time I would then physically will my face back up toward the camera and start reading again. This verbal Bataan Death March continued through four stories until I arrived at the "kicker" (news-speak for the requisite light, closing note), which was about the Miracle-Gro company coming out with a plant that blossoms with the words I LOVE YOU on it. As I read the last words off the prompter, I even felt confident enough to attempt a little extemporizing, although it fell flat. "We'll keep tuned — stay tuned on that." (Half-hearted laugh; awkward pause.) "Now to Tony for more on the weather."

This time, there was no crowd hovering around me after it ended. None of my colleagues or friends said anything to me at all. I hid it well enough that I don't think anyone even knew it had happened.

I may have gotten away with it, but once again I knew full well what had gone down, and I went into DEFCON 1. If I couldn't reliably speak on the air — even while taking antianxiety meds — my entire working future was up for grabs. From a professional standpoint, this was an existential issue.

My folks found me a new psychiatrist — now the third shrink I'd seen since returning from Iraq — and purportedly the "best guy" in New York City for panic disorders. He was a tall, sturdy man in his mid-fifties named Dr. Andrew Brotman. He had a twinkle in his eye and an un-ironic salt-and-pepper goatee. In our first meeting, he asked me a series of questions, trying to get to the source of the problem. One of them was, "Do you do drugs?"

Sheepishly, I said, "Yes."

He leaned back in his large office chair and gave me a look that seemed to say, *Okay, dummy. Mystery solved.*

He explained that frequent cocaine use increases the levels of adrenaline in the brain, which dramatically ups the odds of having a panic attack. He told me that what I had experienced on air was an overwhelming jolt of mankind's ancient fight-or-flight response, which evolved to help us react to attacks by saber-toothed tigers or whatever. Except in this case, I was both the tiger and the dude trying to avoid becoming lunch.

The doctor decreed in no uncertain terms that I needed to stop doing drugs — immediately. Faced with the potential demise of my career, it was a pretty obvious call. I agreed then and there to go cold turkey. He did not think I was a heavy enough user to require sweating it out in rehab. He did, however, say I needed to take better care of myself, with a steady regimen of exercise, sleep, healthy food, and temperance. He compared it to the way trainers take good care of racehorses. He also suggested that I come back to see him twice a week.

As I sat there in Dr. Brotman's office, the sheer enormity of my mindlessness started to sink in. All of it: from maniacally pursuing airtime, to cavalierly going into war zones without considering the psychological impact, to using cocaine and ecstasy for a synthetic squirt of replacement adrenaline. It was as if I had been sleepwalking through the entire cascade of moronic behavior.

It was now thunderously clear to me that I needed to make changes — beyond just giving up drugs. Psychotherapy seemed like a reasonable route. This is what people like me did when things got rough, right? I mean, even Tony Soprano had a therapist. So I agreed: I would come back twice a week.

The sessions were held in Brotman's ground-floor office in a cavernous hospital located in an extremely inconvenient part of Manhattan. Initially, the principal topic of our biweekly sessions was, of course, drugs. While I may not have been physically addicted, I was certainly psychologically hooked. I missed getting high so badly that it was the first thing I thought about in the morning and the last thing I fantasized about before I drifted off to sleep. I'd had some of the happiest moments of my life while high, and pulling the plug was wrenching. I worried I might never feel happy again — that I'd shorted out my brain circuitry for pleasure. Certain friendships had to be sacrificed because simply being around some of the people I'd partied with was too powerful a trigger. I went through the various Kübler-Ross stages of grief, including sadness, anger, and a robust phase of bargaining, where I fruitlessly tried to convince the doctor to let me have a big night, like, maybe once a month. Comments like these would inevitably provoke Brotman to pull what I soon learned was a signature move: leaning back in his chair and shooting me a skeptical look that sent the following non-verbal message: *Really, asshole?*

I found a degree of comfort in the fact that my case was not an aberration. I learned of soldiers returning home and attempting to recreate the adrenaline rush of combat by driving at excessive speeds. And while the psychological impacts on veterans were well documented, an underreported study of war correspondents found high rates of post-traumatic stress disorder (PTSD), major depression, and alcohol abuse. The psychiatrist who conducted the research noted that, despite the risks, many journalists insisted on repeatedly returning to war zones. As one veteran reporter put it, "War is a drug."

Despite having this larger context, I still could not get over that I had allowed this whole train wreck to happen, that I had risked everything I'd worked so hard to achieve. I felt disappointed — defective, even. I kept pushing Brotman to produce some sort of blockbuster psychological revelation. I hoped that I would be able to give him some magic set of data points from my past that would lead to an aha moment that would explain not just my mindless behavior, but also my penchant for worry, as well as the fact that I was a thirty-three-year-old with zero propensity for romantic commitment. Approximately a million times, Brotman — who had a pronounced allergy to the dramatic — tried to explain that he didn't believe in such epiphanies and couldn't suddenly conjure some "unifying theory." I remained unconvinced.

Still, the mere fact of having someone smart to talk to — and to make sure I didn't go back to doing coke in the bathrooms of Lower Manhattan bars — was enormously valuable. But there was something else afoot — another development that would also play a role in putting me on the weird and winding path toward finding the antidote to mindlessness. This new X factor was the emergence of an unsought and long-neglected assignment from Peter Jennings.

CHAPTER 2
UNCHURCHED

Seemingly unprovoked, the woman standing next to me erupted in a high-volume stream of feral gibberish.

"Mo-ta-rehsee-ko-ma-ma-ma-ha-see-ta!"

"Ko-sho-toh-toh-la-la-la-hee-toh-jee!"

She was scaring the crap out of me. I wheeled around to gape at her, but she didn't notice because her eyes were closed, with her head and arms inclined skyward. It took me a few beats to put together that this person was speaking in tongues.

I looked around the packed 7,500-seat evangelical megachurch and realized that a whole bunch of these people were also doing it. Others were singing along with the surprisingly good band that was playing strummy, Christian rock up on the stage.

Coming through the crowd, glad-handing and backslapping as he went, was a sandy-haired guy in his forties. He caught a glimpse of me and started heading right in my direction. He thrust out his hand and said, "Hi, I'm Pastor Ted." I took in his toothy grin, his boyish face, and his freshly pressed suit and immediately reached a whole set of conclusions about this man. All of which would eventually explode in spectacular, salacious fashion.

After the 2004 elections, the religion beat didn't look like such a back-of-the-book dead end after all. Evangelicals had just mounted an impressive display of electoral muscle, helping George W. Bush remain in the White House. Questions of faith seemed to be at the core of everything, from the culture wars at home to the actual wars I'd covered overseas.

Even though I could now see the opportunity in the assignment Peter had given me some years before, it did not change my personal attitude about faith, which was one of disinterest bordering on disdain. Technically, I was not an atheist, as I'd told Peter when he'd first asked me to take over for Peggy Wehmeyer. Many years prior, I had decided — probably in some hackneyed dorm room debate — that agnosticism was the only reasonable position, and I hadn't thought about it much since. My private view was quite harsh, and rooted in a blend

of apathy and ignorance. I thought organized religion was bunk, and that all believers — whether jazzed on Jesus or jihad —
must be, to some extent, cognitively im-
paired.

I had grown up in one of the most secular
environments imaginable: the People's
Republic of Massachusetts. My parents met
in medical school (where they shared a
cadaver — true story). This was in the San
Francisco area during the late 1960s, and
they subsequently moved east and raised
my brother and me with a mix of hippie
warmth and left-of-Trotsky politics. Our
childhood featured Beatles records, home-
made tie-dyes, and touchy-feely discussions
about our emotions — but zero faith. When
I was maybe nine years old, my mother sat
me down and matter-of-factly told me that
not only was there no Santa Claus, there
was also no God.

In seventh grade, I managed to convince
my folks to let me go to Hebrew school and
have a Bar Mitzvah, but that had nothing to
do with religion; I was gunning for social
acceptance in our heavily Jewish hometown.
I also wanted the gifts and the party. My
family being mixed, we found a reform
temple that didn't require that my mother
convert. At Temple Shalom, I studied the

basics of the Hebrew language, learned a bunch of Jewish folk songs, and flirted unskillfully with the girls at the annual Purim party. I don't remember there being much God talk. No one I knew, other than maybe the rabbi, actually subscribed to the metaphysics, and since that time I hadn't had a conversation of any significant length with a person of faith until Peter strong-armed me into this assignment.

After a three-year reprieve, during which time I covered the global, post-9/11 convulsions and then John Kerry's failed presidential bid, I now decided the time was right to take a deep dive into religion. Weeks after Bush's reelection, I traveled to a hard-right church in Florida, where I interviewed parishioners who were clearly feeling elated and empowered. One of them told me, "I believe our Lord elected our president." Another said he wanted a Supreme Court that would enable him to take his kids to a baseball game and not have to see "homosexuals showing affection to one another."

I interviewed the pastor, a televangelist by the name of D. James Kennedy, who was straight out of central casting: a tall, imposing man who dressed in robes and spoke with a booming voice. I asked, "What would you say to the people in those states who are really worried about the impact Christian conservatives can have on our government?" I expected him to offer an answer that was at least partially conciliatory. Instead, he issued a mirthless chortle and said, "Repent."

In that moment, I converted happily from war reporter to culture war reporter. When the story aired, Peter and the rest of my bosses loved it, and I realized this beat that I very much hadn't wanted was, in fact, tantamount to a full employment act for me — it got me on the air a lot, which was, of course, the coin of our particular realm.

For several years, I reported on every twitch, every spasm — or, as Jesus said in the Sermon on the Mount, every "jot or tittle" — of the national argument over abortion, gay marriage, and the role of faith in public life. There was a new tempest seemingly every day, from Christians boycotting Procter & Gamble for sponsoring *Queer Eye for the Straight Guy,* to the uproar over a two-hundred-pound, six-foot-tall, anatomically correct sculpture of Jesus made out of chocolate called "My Sweet Lord."

When I wasn't gorging on the culture wars, I was out producing lighter feature stories about evangelicals, feeling like a tourist in an open-air zoo. I filed reports on Christian reality TV shows, Christian rock festivals, Christian financial advisers, Christian plumbers, Christian cheerleaders, Christian health insurance — you name it. During a story about a Christian fitness club in California, I noted, "You can work your thighs while you proselytize." Not my finest moment.

After an extended run of this, the producer who'd been assigned to work with me started to grow weary of my approach. He was a young man with a pleasingly alliterative name: Wonbo Woo. Like me, he was also not an obvious choice for the faith beat. He was a secular, second-generation Korean from Boston. And, he was openly gay. Over long car rides through the Bible Belt, we had some pretty epic debates. Not about the fact that we were interviewing a lot of homophobes — Wonbo was too professional to let that deter him. What he objected to was my proclivity for pieces that revolved around conflict and caricature. He wanted me to stop acting like the Anthony Bourdain of spirituality, feeding on the most bizarre fare I could find. He was tired of the culture wars; he wanted to focus not just on people shouting about their faith but rather on how their faith affected their daily lives. In sum, he wanted to go deeper. I told him he should go work for NPR.

I was in pursuit of another of my fetishistic, look-at-what-the-wacky-evangelicals-are-doing-now stories when I landed in that megachurch filled with people speaking in tongues. My crew and I had traveled to New Life Church in Colorado Springs, a complex of large buildings perched atop a hill with sweeping mountain views. We were here to see the "NORAD of prayer." Our guide was a super-solicitous man of God by the name of Pastor Ted Haggard.

Moments after I was jarred by his noisily reverent congregant, the pastor ushered me and my team out of the main sanctuary, into the brisk Colorado air, and then into a gleaming, new, $5.5 million, fifty-five-thousand-square-foot building about a hundred yards away. We pushed through the glass doors, and walked down a long hallway decorated with religious art, the crew back-pedaling in front of Ted and me, recording our conversation. Then we entered the main room, a rather astonishing space lined with enormous glass windows, at the center of which was a huge, spinning globe. It was meant to be a sort of mission control for human communication with God, outfitted

74

with computers, and piping in news feeds from around the planet. "We're watching the whole world all the time for events that need to be prayed for," he told me with earnest excitement. Ted was what's called a "prayer warrior" — someone who believes in the power of targeted, "intercessory" prayer to effect real-world changes. "If there's any indicator that there's a problem, we notify hundreds of thousands of intercessors immediately."

Ted was really excited about this place — although I got the feeling he could muster equal ebullience while discussing parsnips or annuities. He did, in fact, have the air of a man who could be a top regional insurance salesman. With his short, parted hair and his sparkling eyes, he had the Clintonesque way of locking in on you and making you feel that, at least in that moment, you were the most important person in the world.

He and his wife, Gayle, had started New Life in their basement several decades earlier, with a congregation of twenty-two people. It grew with fevered intensity as Ted led his followers on a sort of siege of the city, praying outside government offices, gay bars, and the homes of suspected witches. He and his troops "prayer-walked" nearly every street in the city, and even prayed over random names in the phone book, all in an attempt to chase the Devil out of town. Undoubtedly, part of Ted's appeal was that he had a way of invoking Satan while remaining ceaselessly chipper.

At the time of our visit, the church had fourteen thousand people on its membership rolls, and Ted was one of the leading lights in Colorado Springs, which, because it was home to many large Christian organizations, such as Campus Crusade for Christ and Focus on the Family, had come to be known as the "evangelical Vatican." He wore his authority lightly, though, insisting that everyone simply call him "Pastor Ted."

By now the congregants had filed out of the sanctuary, so that's where we went to sit down and have our formal interview. As we talked, it became clear that Ted was a different breed from his fiery forebears on the Religious Right, figures like Jerry Falwell, Pat Robertson, and D. James Kennedy. He was part of a new generation of pastors who were trying to broaden the evangelical agenda beyond gay marriage and abortion. In some ways, he was more like a self-help guru. He'd written a series of books on things like making your marriage last and saving your neighbors from going to hell.

He'd even published a weight loss guide, *The Jerusalem Diet*. To be sure, he was against abortion and homosexuality, but he didn't go out of his way to talk about it.

After the interview, as the crew was breaking down their lights and packing up their gear, Ted sat down on the stairs leading up to the main stage and patted the step next to him. My first instinct was to make an excuse, figuring this was going to devolve into some sort of proselytizing session. But to beg off would have been rude, so I plopped down reluctantly, only to be pleasantly surprised by the conversation that ensued. With the cameras off, Ted toned down his eagerness a notch and began speaking with bracing frankness about the state of the evangelical scene in America.

"Can we talk off the record?" he asked.

"Absolutely," I said, thinking, *This could get interesting.*

"There's a huge difference between what I do as a pastor and what people like Jim Dobson do." Dobson was the head of Focus on the Family, whose main office was right down the road and was so large it actually had its own zip code. Dobson was a pillar of old-school orthodoxy, a firebrand, and an avid critic of gays and "abortionists."

"I have an actual congregation that I see

face-to-face every week," Ted added, "so I see what their real issues are, like their marriages, children, and finances. If I'm consistently negative, it doesn't help them. Dobson, on the other hand, runs what's called a 'parachurch ministry.' His ministry grows in the midst of controversy, because that attracts interest and funds."

I was a little surprised to hear a big-time pastor trash-talking another major figure in Evangelicalism. It seemed a little . . . unchristian. But it was certainly intriguing, and I was starting to like this guy. He was a bit of a paradox: overfriendly and yet likable, saccharine but also capable of knowing irony. I sat there on those steps well past the point dictated by politeness, and Ted patiently answered all the questions about Evangelicalism I would have been too embarrassed to ask anyone else. He didn't make me feel inferior for being, as they called it in evangelical lingo, "unchurched," and he didn't try to convert me. He was also not defensive at all when I asked how biblical literalists reconciled the fact that different books in the Bible said different things about key details in the Jesus story. He beamed mischievously and said, "We have our ways."

Sitting there with Pastor Ted, I realized,

with genuine regret, how unthinkingly judgmental I'd been — not only of Ted, but of religious people, generally. It hit me that I'd blindly bought into the prevailing stereotypes. The *Washington Post* had once declared these people to be "poor, uneducated and easy to command." Pastor Ted's story about the inner clashes of the movement put the "easy to command" notion to rest. As for my assumption about all religious people being unintelligent — Ted clearly wasn't. Then again, neither were believers such as Tolstoy, Lincoln, and Michelangelo, not to mention contemporary people of faith like Francis Collins, the evangelical and scientist who led the charge to map the human genome.

Not only had I been unfair to people of faith by prematurely reaching sweeping, uninformed conclusions, but I'd also done myself a disservice. This beat could be more than just a chance to notch more airtime. Most people in America — and on the planet, for that matter — saw their entire lives through the lens of faith. I didn't have to agree, but here was my chance to get under the hood and understand what was going on. More than that, I could approach faith coverage as a way to shed light instead of heat. At a time when religion had become

so venomously divisive, thoughtful reporting could be a way to take audiences into
worlds they'd never otherwise enter, and in
the process demystify, humanize, and clarify.
It was why I'd gotten into this business in
the first place — to both get on TV *and* do
meaningful work.

Shortly thereafter, I admitted to Wonbo
that he was right; we could start covering
this beat with more nuance without having
to move to public radio.

I became so gung ho about improving my
faith coverage that, in the spring of 2005, I
packed a Bible in my luggage as I headed
off for a reporting trip to Israel, Egypt, and
Iraq. I figured if I was going to be a proper
religion reporter, I should at least read the
source material.

It was right before I left on this trip to the
Middle East that I had my last encounter
with Peter Jennings. We met in his office,
ostensibly so he could brief me on what my
reporting priorities should be. He opened,
characteristically, with an insult. "There's a
perception," he said, "that you're not very
good at this sort of overseas coverage." Even
though I was reasonably sure this was
untrue — and probably just part of Peter's
never-ending psyops campaign — I felt

compelled to defend myself. As soon as I started to stammer out some sort of objection, though, he cut me off and lectured me about the various stories he wanted me to produce for his broadcast while I was abroad. Then he abruptly took a call from his wife, Kayce. After cooing into the phone for a few minutes, he hung up and looked at me and said, "I have a piece of advice for you, Harris: Marry well — at least once."

A few weeks later, I was sitting out on the veranda of our Baghdad bureau, Bible in hand, struggling to get through Leviticus, with all of its interminable discussions of how to slaughter a goat. I stood up in frustration to go back into the office to check my computer, and that's when I spotted the message from Peter. It was a group email announcing that he had lung cancer.

I never saw him again. By the time I got home, he had taken medical leave. Just a few months later, he was gone. Despite the fear and frustration he had provoked in me over the preceding five years, I felt enormous affection for him, and the night he died was one of the few times I could remember crying as an adult.

Perhaps more than any other single person outside of my immediate family, he had genuinely altered the course of my life. He built me into a better journalist than I had ever imagined I could be, sending me all over the world, giving me the chance to get a taste of the same gritty, global education that he, a high school dropout, had gotten during his years as a foreign correspondent. He could be a massive pain in the ass, but he was, in his own funny way, very generous. He was a restless soul, an idealist, and a perfectionist — a man who definitely followed my dad's "price of security" maxim. No matter how hard he was on me, I always knew he was exponentially harder on himself.

Interestingly, during the entire time I knew Peter, the subject of his personal faith never came up. It wasn't until years after his death that I learned that Peter himself was not particularly religious at all. He hadn't needed faith in order to see that religion was a vital beat for us to cover; he was simply an insatiably curious reporter with a peerless instinct for what would interest the audience.

Peter's death set off a ripple of reassignments among the on-air staff. The network's first choice to replace him was the anchor duo of Elizabeth Vargas and Bob Woodruff, the correspondent I'd met in the presidential suite in the Islamabad Marriott. Only weeks after his ascent to the Big Chair, however, Bob was hit by a roadside bomb in Iraq and nearly died, which sent the news division reeling. Charlie Gibson from *GMA* was then tapped to move to the evenings, while Robin Roberts was elevated to be Diane Sawyer's cohost.

Meanwhile, Ted Koppel had stepped down from *Nightline* and was replaced by the troika of Cynthia McFadden, Martin Bashir, and Terry Moran. I was then tapped to replace Terry on the Sunday edition of *World News* — a promotion I considered to be incalculably awesome.

In no way, however, did this step up the ladder reduce my neuroses about work. Quite the opposite, in fact. Yes, it was insanely great to be given the steering wheel of the news division every Sunday night — to pick the stories we'd cover, frame how they were presented, and then deliver it all right from the chair that Peter Jennings once occupied. Whenever anyone asked me, I told them I had the best job on the planet. And I meant it. But perversely, my good fortune meant I now had that much more to lose, and thus that much more to protect.

And the competition all around had intensified. I'd been at the network for five years, and the ranks of younger people had filled out dramatically. It wasn't just David Wright I had to watch out for. There was also: Chris Cuomo, the charismatic, strapping son of the famous former governor of New York, who had replaced Robin Roberts on *GMA;* Bill Weir, the hilariously funny and wildly creative former local sports anchor who'd been named as cohost of the newly created weekend edition of *GMA;* and David Muir, the eminently likable, ferociously hardworking anchorman who had been lovingly profiled in *Men's Vogue* and was now helming the Saturday edition of *World News.*

My relationships with these newer additions were great — they were friends — but that didn't change the fact that we were locked in a zero-sum competition for a scarce resource: airtime. Specifically, assignments to cover the big stories, as well as fill-in slots for when the A-list anchors were away.

The mental loop (*How many stories have I had on this week? etc.*) that began when I first arrived from local news went into hyperdrive, only with an even more personal tinge. It was one thing, back in the day, to be big-footed by a veteran correspondent — but to be beat out by someone my own age, now that stung. Like almost all correspondents, every day I would check the "run-downs" for various shows — the computer-ized lists of stories the broadcasts would be covering — to see who was doing which ones. If someone scored an assignment I wanted, I'd experience a brief rush of re-sentment.

I'd collect data points (*Weir gets to cover the election of the new pope? Muir is filling in for Cuomo?*), and immediately extrapolate to far-reaching conclusions (*This means that* x *or* y *executive or anchor dislikes me* → *My career is doomed* → *I'm going to end up in a flophouse in Duluth*). Sometimes, before I'd even thought it through, I'd find myself on the phone with an executive producer of one of our broadcasts, saying impolitic things.

I would occasionally complain about all of this to Dr. Brotman, who applied his perfect shrink-y mix of sympathy and skepticism. He had a competitive job, too, negotiating the executive ranks at his hospital, but often he thought I was blatantly overreacting to intramural developments at ABC. In fact, his theory was that, just as I had used drugs to replace the thrill of combat, I was now inflating the drama of the office war zone to replace drugs.

Maybe. I was conflicted. I was absolutely

aware that worrying could be counterproductive. Furthermore, I did not enjoy harboring competitive feelings toward people I liked and admired. But I still firmly believed that a certain amount of churning was unavoidable, especially in this business, and I had no intention of abandoning the whole "price of security" thing.

During this period, as I continued to deal with the aftermath of my panic attacks, my residual drug cravings, and the intensifying competitive pressures of work, it never once occurred to me that any aspect of the religious traditions I was reporting on could be relevant or useful to me personally. Faith was proving an increasingly interesting beat to cover for journalistic reasons, but it wasn't serving the same purpose for me as it did for all the believers I was meeting: answering my deepest questions, or speaking to my most profound needs.

That said, I continued with my plan for broadening our coverage beyond the hot buttons of the culture wars. I went to Salt Lake City to profile the Apostles of the Mormon Church; I interviewed the head of a Wiccan coven in Massachusetts; I even covered the annual American Atheists convention. On Wonbo's urging, we launched a series called "Tests of Faith," which included stories about a Unitarian congregation in California agonizing over whether to accept a registered sex offender, and also about an Episcopal priest who claimed that, after a profound conversion experience, she now believed in both Christianity and Islam.

I kept covering the born-again scene, of course. It was too juicy — and too newsy — to ignore. And with Ted Haggard, I now had a terrific inside source to make sure my coverage was more accurate and nuanced. He became my first stop when I was looking for candid answers about evangelicals. He was always willing to respond to questions off the record, returning emails instantaneously from his private AOL account.

When Pat Robertson publicly suggested that the United States send "covert agents" to assassinate Venezuelan dictator Hugo Chávez, Ted was the only major evangelical figure to go on the record about it, saying, "Pat was not speaking for Christianity." I did the interview from an edit room at our offices in New York City, where I could see Ted on a monitor, beamed in via satellite from Colorado. When it was over, we exchanged a few pleasantries and Ted goodnaturedly made fun of me for having worn an ugly green tie on television the night before.

Not long afterward, he and his top lieutenant, a crisp young guy named Rob, came to New York, and I took them out to a fancy restaurant for lunch. Ted seemed impressed by the whole Manhattan scene. Over the gentle clinking of silverware and with a view of Central Park, he continued to pull back the curtain on the inner workings of American Evangelicalism. He told me how he and Jim Dobson had clashed over Ted's desire to focus evangelicals on issues like global warming. In Ted's account, the behind-the-scenes maneuvering included behavior that was surprisingly ruthless.

It was fun to talk to Ted. You might think that the yawning cultural and philosophical gap between us — he was a guy who believed that he had a running dialogue with Jesus, after all — would make a genuine connection impossible, but that clearly wasn't the case.

While I liked Ted, it was also pretty obvious that he had a dual agenda: to promote the faith — and to promote himself. I was by no means the only reporter Ted was working. In fact, he played the media like a fiddle, doing interviews with Tom Brokaw and Barbara Walters — and all that exposure worked. Since we'd met, Ted had been elected head of the National Association of Evangelicals, which had twenty-seven million members at forty-three thousand churches. Every Monday, he joined a conference call with the White House and other high-ranking Christians. *Time* put him on their list of the 25 Most Influential Evangelicals.

Sometimes he pushed his shtick a little too far. He made a memorably creepy cameo in an HBO documentary about the American faith scene, in which he said, seemingly off-the-cuff, "You know, all the surveys say that evangelicals have the best sex life of any other group." In one interview with me, after I'd just asked him a series of questions about hot-button social issues, he stopped short in the middle of an answer. Then, while the cameras rolled, he said, "I hope I'm not coming across here as too harsh. Am I coming across as too harsh? I'm just going to focus on how cute Dan is, and then I won't seem so harsh." I had no idea how to deal with this comment other than to laugh and shift uncomfortably in my chair.

Notwithstanding Ted's foibles, he'd helped me become utterly at ease around people who said "God bless you" when I hadn't sneezed. Increasingly, I even now found myself in the position of defending evangelicals to my friends and family. Once, when I made a passing reference to "evangelical intellectuals," a relative quipped, "Isn't that a contradiction in terms?" Another stereotype I spent a lot of time batting down: that Christians were all spittle-spewing hatemongers. I met a few of those in my travels, of course, but they struck me as a distinct minority. Wonbo and I — two nonreligious New Yorkers, one of them gay, the other gay-friendly — were never treated with anything short of respect. Often, in fact, what we found was kindness, hospitality, and curiosity. Yes, people would always ask whether we were believers, but when we said no, there were never gasps or glares. They may have thought we were going to hell, but they were perfectly nice about it.

Then early one November morning in 2006, I was groggily rooting around the Internet, looking for stories. I started each day with an email to the senior producers of *World News,* pitching pieces I could do for that night's show. And there it was on Drudge: an article saying that Ted Haggard had been accused by a male escort of paying for sex as well as for crystal meth. I immediately assumed it must be a mistake, or a smear. I was so convinced it couldn't be true that I didn't even include it in my pitch email. A short while later, when one of the senior producers from *Good Morning America* called to ask me about it, I confidently assured her it must be false.

But then the story took on real legs. The male escort, a beefy, incongruously soft-voiced man named Mike Jones, seemed pretty credible. He said he'd had repeated encounters with a man who called himself "Art." In an interview with our ABC affiliate in Denver, Jones said, "It was not an emotional relationship. It was strictly for sex." He explained that this had gone on for years, but that when he saw Ted/Art on television backing a ballot initiative that would ban gay marriage, he decided he had to come forward. "He is in the position of influence of millions of followers and he's preaching against gay marriage," he said, "but behind everyone's back doing what he's preached against." Making matters worse for Ted, Jones had voice mails, on which he claimed Ted could be heard arranging assignations and drug deals. On one of them, a male voice said, "Hi, Mike, this is Art, just calling to see if we can get any more supply." It was unmistakably Ted.

I was thunderstruck. No one I knew had

ever taken me by surprise quite like this. The clean-cut, Indiana-raised, God-fearing Ted Haggard — a father of five and the spiritual shepherd to thousands — had been leading a double life. I had been in contact with the guy for years and had never had even the slightest inkling. In hindsight, there might have been a few signs: that all of his lieutenants were young and male; that time he called me "cute." But really, none of that would have foretold the panoramic collapse that was now playing out.

The unmasking of Ted Haggard became a massive national story. There are few things the media loves more than a self-appointed paragon of virtue falling from grace. Local reporters captured Haggard leaving his house in an SUV, with his wife by his side and several of his children in the car. To me, he looked like a child caught dead to rights but still hoping against hope that he could talk his way out of it. He leaned over the wheel and told the assembled reporters, "I've never had a gay relationship with anybody, and I'm steady with my wife."

"So you don't know Mike Jones?" one reporter asked.

"No, I don't know Mike Jones," he said.

Moments later, in a flagrant bit of bad acting, Ted asked, "What did you say his name was?"

Days later, the charade crumbled. He stepped down from his positions at the National Association of Evangelicals and at New Life Church. In a statement read aloud to his followers, he said, "There is a part of my life that is so repulsive and dark that I've been warring against it all of my adult life."

The affair gave birth to a thousand snarky blog posts, and it confirmed Americans' lowest opinions about evangelicals. This was, after all, a man who described homosexuality as a sin, as a "life that is against God." My gay friends were eating it up — Wonbo being one notable exception. He never once crowed. Like me, he seemed surprised and a little saddened. We both agreed that, while Ted was clearly guilty of towering hypocrisy, there was also some poignancy to the fact that the moral teachings associated with his faith had forced him to suppress a fundamental part of who he was. We covered the story aggressively, but we also took pains to point out that Haggard was much less strident than many of his co-religionists on the issue of homosexuality. In fact, he had once assured Barbara Walters in a prime-time interview that gays, too, can go to heaven.

Throughout the crisis, I had been calling and emailing Ted repeatedly. No reply. The guy who used to get back to me within seconds had gone completely dark.

After a few days, the story died down, as it always does. America, as then senator Barack Obama had noted after Hurricane Katrina, "goes from shock to trance" faster than any other nation on earth.

As Ted's world fell apart, mine was getting much better. Just weeks later, Bob Woodruff told me he wanted to set me up on a date. Not two years after surviving a bomb blast to the head in Iraq, Woody — as he was known to his friends — was playing matchmaker.

At first I was skeptical. I wasn't enthusiastic about being set up — to me it seemed slightly pathetic — but it was hard to say no to an American hero, a guy whose story was turned into a bestselling book, and who was greeted by Jon Stewart during an appearance on *The Daily Show* with the question, "Why are you still more handsome than me?"

Bob's wife, Lee, an effervescent and hilarious blonde, was hard to refuse as well. Here's how she laid out the whole setup situation: "Her name is Bianca. She's beautiful, she's a doctor, and you're an idiot if you don't do this." This Bianca was, per Bob and Lee, an internal medicine resident at Columbia University. The Woodruffs were friends with her parents, and what could I do? I said yes.

On the night prearranged for the date, I was walking out of the gym on my way to the restaurant when my phone rang. It was Bob, calling to make sure I wasn't flaking out. "Dude," he assured me, "she's hot."

We were meeting at an Italian spot on the Upper West Side. Pathologically punctual, I showed up early and staked out a spot at the bar, near a pair of bankers from New Jersey doing shots. It was mid-December and the place had festive decorations and a holiday feel. My plan was to lean against the bar, staring at my BlackBerry, so that when Bianca walked in, she could come over and tap me on the shoulder and I could look up all cool and nonchalant. Of course, I was too nervous to pull that off and ended up staring anxiously at the door.

Minutes later, when she appeared, my internal reaction was similar to the one my cousin Andy described the first time he met his future wife: "I'll take this one." Bob had not exaggerated; she was beautiful, with golden hair and piercing, light blue eyes — like a husky's, but much softer. As I did whenever I was confronted with anyone I found intriguing, I peppered her with biographical questions. She was raised in Manhattan. Her dad was a doctor, her mom an artist. She was six months out of medical school and in the hellishly stressful first year of residency. She was also, as I learned over the course of the evening, smart, passionate about medicine, humble, optimistic, quick to laugh, and a lover of animals and dessert. Pretty soon, we were doing tequila shots with the bankers.

Drinks turned into dinner. The first date turned into a second. Three months later, Bianca moved into my apartment. (On the day we brought her stuff over, I marveled at the affable yet unyielding diplomatic skills she employed to convince me to give up 60 percent of my closet space.) Two months after that, we adopted cats. When we called my parents to ask them to provide a character reference for the assiduous pet-vetters at the ASPCA, my father — who aside from being a worrier is also a wiseass — asked whether we were also going to have a commitment ceremony. The cats immediately became the butt of jokes among my male friends at work, who automatically associated felinity with femininity (ignoring historical cat-loving avatars of machismo such as Ernest Hemingway, Winston Churchill, and Dr. Evil). When Chris Cuomo heard about our pet adoptions, he sent me an email that read, "Do u sit when u pee?"

As a man who was a mild hypochondriac, it was handy to have a doctor around. More significantly, after living alone in my apartment for nearly a decade, I found it wonderfully strange to get back into bed after a middle-of-the-night trip to the bathroom and see three cats and a human form lying there, all of whom now had equal claim to the territory.

Bianca truly brought out the fool in me. I had never been this comfortable around anyone before. I would march around the apartment, a displeased feline under each arm, singing songs. I would make up ridiculous nicknames for them. When she was in the living room trying to work, I'd use the Remote app on my iPad to blast Steppenwolf and then lie there with a stupid, twisted-up grin as she burst into the room, tut-tutting about the interruption.

I was beguiled by the contrasts. This was a woman who subscribed to *The New England Journal of Medicine,* and also *Us Weekly.* She looked great in both scrubs and cocktail dresses. She could work a thirty-hour shift — during which she would perform chest compressions, manage ornery colleagues, and comfort grieving families — then come home, take a nap, and cook her grandmother's sauce and meatballs. When I went away on work trips, I often arrived at my destination to find that she had packed snacks and a mash note in my suitcase.

I'd never been in love before. I'd long had a nagging fear that maybe I was too self-centered to ever get there. Everyone always said you'd "know," but I never "knew." Now, all of a sudden, I did. It was a giant relief to sincerely want what was best for Bianca — to worry about her life and her career, rather than just fixate inwardly. Selfishly, I felt she was both a smarter and kinder person than I was, and that being by her side might make me better.

Sorting out my romantic life after decades of often aimless bachelorhood was like scratching a huge existential itch. On the downside, though, it left me free to concentrate all of my neurotic powers on work. Bianca pointed out that I would sometimes come through the door at night scowling. "What's wrong?" she'd ask. "Nothing," I'd mutter, then make a beeline for the couch, turn on the television, and launch into a harsh postgame analysis of my latest story. It was hard for her not to take my occasional gruffness a little personally. More than that, she hated seeing me gloomy; she had a doctor's urge to cure and a sense of sadness and frustration that she couldn't.

It was not as if she didn't understand and sympathize with the "price of security" stance. This was a woman who had graduated at the top of her med school class, was in an elite residency program, and who still felt she had more to prove than anyone else. She, too, would come home frayed, but — fairly or unfairly — the very nature of Bianca's anxiety would make me feel superficial by comparison. She would cry over her patients' pain or loss, whereas my complaints often involved a colleague getting a story I wanted, or questions about whether I'd handled myself well during a contentious on-air interview.

From Bianca's point of view, though, perhaps the most annoying part of my work fixation was my unnatural attachment to my BlackBerry, which I kept within reach during dinner, on the couch as we watched TV, and on my bedside table all during the night. She'd catch me glancing at it in the middle of conversations and shoot me a *j'accuse* look. She did eventually convince me to at least move the offending instrument, and its charger, to the other side of the bedroom while we slept.

One of the things I was often doing with that BlackBerry was sending emails to Ted Haggard. I'd hit him up every month or so, desperately seeking that exclusive interview whenever he emerged from seclusion. Journalism aside, I also was massively curious about where he was and what he was doing.

Nearly a year went by before he wrote me back. When at last I got him on the phone, he had an incredible story to tell: *Time*'s 11th most influential American evangelical was now living with his family in a dingy apartment in Arizona, barely scraping by, selling insurance. Remarkably, his wife, Gayle, had decided to stand by him.

Several months later, on a frigid January morning in New York City, Ted and I sat down for his first network news interview since the scandal.

I was nervous — and it showed. I have a very obvious tell when I'm anxious: my face looks tired. And on this day I looked exhausted. I tried jumping up and down, slapping my cheeks, and standing out in the cold, but I couldn't fix it. I was simply uncomfortable doing what was sure to be a tough interview with someone I knew and liked.

For the shoot, Wonbo had rented a studio downtown, and I was sitting in a cushioned chair opposite Ted, who was on a couch. Unlike me, he seemed entirely at ease with the inquisition that was to ensue. He was leaning back, legs crossed, wearing a blazer but no tie.

I dove right in. "Is it fair to describe you as a hypocrite and a liar?" I asked.

"Yes. Yes, it is," he said, almost enthusiastically, as if he couldn't wait to get this off his chest.

"Do you think you owe gay people an apology?" I asked.

"Absolutely. And I do apologize," he said. "I'm deeply sorry for the attitude I had. But I think I was partially so vehement because — because of my own war."

Amazingly to me, he insisted he wasn't gay. Months of psychotherapy, he said, had cleared everything up. "Now I'm settled in the fact that I am a heterosexual, but with issues," he said. "So I don't fit into a neat little box."

He said it was no problem to stay faithful to his wife. "It's not a struggle at all now."

"Why not just live as a gay man?" I asked.

" 'Cause I love my wife. I love my intimate

relationship with my wife. I'm not gay."

"Can you hear people watching this, though, and thinking to themselves, 'This guy is just not being honest with himself?' "

"Sure, but everybody has their own journey. And people can judge me. I think it's fair if they judge me and that they think I'm not being real with myself."

The toughest moment in the interview came when I surprised him by playing him a damning piece of videotape we'd obtained. It was an interview with a former parishioner, a young man who said he'd been sexually harassed by Ted. On the tape he described, in graphic terms, how one night Ted had hopped into bed with him in a hotel room and began to masturbate.

When the video ended, Ted said, "It is true. We never had any sexual contact, but I violated that relationship and it was an inappropriate relationship."

"What's it like to watch that?" I asked.

"It's embarrassing. That was very embarrassing. I mean, I am . . . I am a failure."

When it was all over, Ted didn't seem at all resentful that I'd blindsided him. I had coffee with him and his wife and we chatted as if none of it had ever happened. We talked a lot about what Ted's next move might be. The one thing he swore he'd never do again was pastor a church. (A couple of months later, he asked me to meet him and Gayle for lunch at a midtown hotel because they wanted advice on how to pitch a reality show they were dreaming up. When that didn't take off, they started a church.)

What struck me most from the interview was not Ted's slipperiness or his eyebrow-raising claims about the nature of sexuality or even his wife's decision not to file for divorce; it was something else. For all of Ted's hypocrisy and deception, there was one issue on which he did not waver: his faith. "I never fell away from God," he told me. When I pointed out that it was his religious beliefs that forced him to live a lie for so many years, he countered that it was the "culture of hatefulness" in the modern church that did that, not the core teachings of Jesus himself. In his darkest moments, when he was living in that apartment in Arizona, crying every day for a year and a half and actively contemplating suicide, his faith was his main source of comfort. It gave him the sense that his travails were part of a larger plan, that even if everyone on earth hated him, his creator did not. "I knew with assurance," he said, "that God cared for me."

In the weeks and months after the interview, I kept coming back to this. I, too, had endured my own self-created crisis, albeit of a less public and less intense variety. Ted's involved doing drugs and cheating on his wife; mine involved doing drugs and having a nationally televised freak-out. On this score, I envied Ted — and not in a patronizing, I-wish-I-were-stupid-enough-to-believe-this-stuff way. It would have been enormously helpful to have had a sense that my troubles had a larger purpose or fit into some overarching plan. I had read the research showing that regular churchgoers tended to be happier, in part because having a sense that the world is infused with meaning and that suffering happens for a reason helped them deal more successfully with life's inevitable humiliations.

Up until my interview with Ted, I had derived a smug sense of self-satisfaction that, unlike the believers I was covering, I did not have a deep need for answers to the Big Questions; I was comfortable with the mystery of how we got here and what would happen after we died. But I now realized that a sort of incuriosity had set in; my sense of awe had atrophied. I might have disagreed with the conclusions reached by people of faith, but at least that part of their brain was functioning. Every week, they had a set time to consider their place in the universe, to step out of the matrix and achieve some perspective. If you're never looking up, I now realized, you're always just looking around.

Ted Haggard, who had taught me to see people of faith in a different light, had also taught me something else: the value of a viewpoint that transcended the mundane. Of course, I wasn't forsaking ambition — and I wasn't planning to magically force myself to believe in something for which there was, in my opinion, insufficient evidence. However, I was about to cover a story that, for the first time since Peter Jennings ordered me to start reporting on spirituality, would actually penetrate my defenses. The message came in a deeply weird and extremely confusing package.

CHAPTER 3
GENIUS OR LUNATIC?

The man sitting across from me and completely blowing my mind favored a style, both verbal and sartorial, so monochrome that it was as if he wanted to vanish like a chameleon into the barf-colored wallpaper of this hotel room in Toronto. He was elfin, rheumy-eyed, and, as the cameras rolled, droning on in a gentle Teutonic lilt. Superficially, at least, he was the type of person who, if you met him at a cocktail party, you would either ignore or avoid.

And yet he was saying extraordinary things. Life-altering things. He was making points that were forcing me to rethink my whole "price of security" modus operandi. Not just rethink it, but think above it, beyond it — and possibly go beyond *thought* altogether.

The real mindfuck, though, was this: almost as soon as he said something brilliant, he would say something else that was totally ridiculous. The man was toggling seamlessly between compelling and confusing, incisive and insane.

He would go like this:

Zig: a spot-on diagnosis of the human condition.

Zag: a bizarre, pseudoscientific assertion.

Zig: a profound insight into how we make ourselves miserable.

Zag: a claim that he once lived on park benches for two years in a state of bliss.

He said he had a way for me to be happier, too, and despite the fog of folderol, I half suspected he actually might be right.

Weeks before I first heard the name Eckhart Tolle, I was staring, unhappily, in the mirror of an airplane bathroom. I was on my way home from shooting a *Nightline* story in Brazil, where we'd spent a week living with an isolated Amazon tribe. It had been amazing. These people still lived exactly as their ancestors had in the Stone Age. They'd barely met any outsiders. They let my producer and me sleep in hammocks in their huts. I returned the favor by entertaining them with my video iPod. Leaning over the metallic counter in this lavatory, I was neither savoring the incredible experience I had just had nor strategizing about how to write my story, which was set to air a few weeks hence. Instead, I had my forelock pushed back and was scrutinizing a hairline that seemed to me about as stable as the Maginot Line.

Bianca had busted me doing this on more than one occasion in our bathroom at home. She pointed out that, other than some thinning in the back and a receding divot near my part, I basically had a full head of hair. But every now and again, a stray glance in a reflective surface would send me down the rabbit hole. Here in this cramped airplane bathroom, I was flashing on a future that looked like this:

Baldness → Unemployment → Flophouse in Duluth

Inevitably, this led to a nasty rejoinder from some other, more reasonable part of my brain:

Get over yourself, Harris.

When I brought the hair thing up with Dr. Brotman, he leaned back in his chair and beamed skepticism at me from across his desk.

"You don't understand," I said to him. "If I go bald, my career is screwed."

"*You* don't understand," he replied, eyeing my hairline. "You're not going bald."

By any rational measure, things were

otherwise going extremely well in my life. Nearly three years had passed since my panic attacks. I was off the Klonopin and down to seeing Brotman only once a month or so. Occasionally I'd be ambushed by waves of longing for drugs, but the cravings were vastly diminished. (Although I tried to always keep in mind something a friend had once told me: "Your demons may have been ejected from the building, but they're out in the parking lot, doing push-ups.") At home, the situation was even better: after living together for more than a year, Bianca and I had gotten engaged and were planning a wedding in the Bahamas. At work, my gig anchoring the Sunday edition of *World News* continued to be a joy. And even though public interest in the wars in Iraq and Afghanistan was on the wane, a new opportunity had emerged. The post-Koppel *Nightline* had moved away from live interviews and more toward lengthy taped stories from all over the world. The producers had allowed me to launch major investigations, such as tracking rhino poachers in Nepal, and posing as a customer in order to expose child slave traders in Haiti. This was a new type of reporting for me. It had a crusading spirit. Corny or not, I found that old journalistic injunction to "comfort the afflicted

109

and afflict the comfortable" inspiring.

Nevertheless, my worrying over work had grown worse, and the hair issue was just the leading indicator. Increasingly, I was waking up to the fact that the whole industry rested on such an uncertain foundation. In my eight years at the network, I had witnessed seemingly immovable fixtures of broadcast news fade or simply disappear. Among the missing were Peter Jennings, Tom Brokaw, and Dan Rather. When I had arrived at ABC News back in 2000, I was the youngest correspondent on the fourth floor. Suddenly, at age thirty-seven, I was nearly the oldest. All but one of those more senior correspondents had departed, often unceremoniously. These were guys who had given their lives to a profession that could be lavishly kind or capriciously cruel. I'd seen so many careers soar or sour based on seemingly random things, such as changing physical appearance, the personal whim of a specific anchor or executive, or the emergence of a more eye-catching rival. In discussing the unpredictability of my profession with my brother recently, he told me about scientific studies where lab rats were rewarded with food pellets at random, illogical times. Those rats went crazy.

To make matters worse, the country was

in the most severe recession since the Great Depression. Bear Stearns had just collapsed, along with Lehman Brothers. The stock market was in free fall. It felt like the world had gone off a cliff no one had seen coming. ABC News went through a wrenching round of layoffs. While my job seemed safe at the moment, I felt bad for my colleagues and fretted about the future. When I thought about alternative careers, I drew a blank. What other marketable skills did I have besides wearing makeup and bellowing into cameras? This was a bit maudlin, but there were a few times where I found myself lying on the couch in my office, staring at a picture on my wall of the ocean, thinking about the word *impermanence.*

On one such occasion there was a knock on my door. It was David Muir popping by to chat. We had a lot in common. We'd both worked in local news in Boston, arrived at the network before the age of thirty, and loved to travel the planet doing stories. Just a couple months earlier, David had filed some amazing reports from Chernobyl. He had the office down the hall from me and we'd sometimes get together to talk about our latest stories — or just gossip. In the spirit of misery looking for company, I asked him what he would do if the whole TV news business imploded. He shrugged his shoulders with enviable insouciance and said, "Eh, I'd find something else."

Back in the toilet on the airplane coming home from Brazil, I replayed that scene in my mind as I continued to stare at my faltering hairline.

Easy for you to say, Muir — with your full head of hair.

I'd been in this position in front of the mirror for at least ten minutes. I realized, with a twinge of embarrassment, that there was probably a line outside by now. I let my hair fall back down onto my forehead and returned, sheepishly, to my seat.

About a month later, on a sunny Saturday in September, I was at a block party in New Jersey. There was a cookout, a bounce castle for the kids, and a band with a bassist wearing a do-rag. When the music stopped, a pastor took the mic and declared, with his voice echoing off the brightly colored vinyl siding of the surrounding row houses, "There's room for everyone at the cross today."

I was here for a story about Sarah Palin, recently plucked from obscurity to become John McCain's running mate. A video had just hit the web showing Palin praying for

God's help to get a gas pipeline built in her home state of Alaska. That had sparked a lot of discussion about the fact that she was a Pentecostal, a strain of Christianity sometimes described as "Evangelicalism on steroids." I wanted to do a piece that would explain to viewers exactly what Pentecostals believed. The closest church was here in Jersey City, and they just happened to be throwing a party.

To be away from the noise, our cameraman, soundman, and producer had set up for the interviews a little farther down the street. The three of them were in the middle of an animated discussion led by Felicia, the producer, a petite, apple-cheeked mother of two with whom I'd worked for many years. She was telling the others about a book she'd just read by someone named Eckhart Tolle. As I approached, she turned toward me: "Have you read him? You might like him. It's all about controlling your ego."

The crew burst out laughing. Like me, they took it as a joke about the anchorman's inevitably inflated sense of self-importance. Felicia, earnest and unfailingly polite, flushed and, speaking rapidly now, assured us that she wasn't making a joke. Her point was that she had read Tolle's books and found them personally useful. More than that, Oprah had been heavily promoting his latest volume, and she thought Tolle might make a good story.

Fair enough. I was always looking for stories, and this one — featuring an Oprah-approved self-help swami — sounded like it might include the requisite exotica. So when I got home later that day, I went online and ordered the book.

By the time his book arrived at my apartment a few days later, I had almost forgotten about Eckhart Tolle. I saw the cheesy orange cover shining dully through Amazon's irrationally excessive bubble wrap. It bore the rather overwrought title *A New Earth: Awakening to Your Life's Purpose,* as well as the seal of Oprah's Book Club.

I propped it on my chest that night, an unsuspecting Bianca sleeping to my left, blissfully unaware that her future husband was being sucked into a strange vortex.

At first, the book struck me as irredeemable poppycock. I was put off by the strained stateliness of Tolle's writing, as well as its nearly indecipherable turgidity. How could Oprah fans stand to drink from a fire hose of jargon like "conditioned mind structures" and "the one indwelling consciousness"? What's more, the guy was stunningly grandiose. He referred to his book as a "transformational device," and promised that, as you read, a "shift takes place within you."

I lay there rolling my eyes, quietly cursing Felicia for inflicting this upon me. But just when I thought I'd been defeated by all the porridge about "inner opening" and the impending "shift in planetary consciousness," a clearing appeared in the spiritual thicket. Tolle began to unfurl a fascinating thesis, one that made me think he must have somehow spent an enormous amount of time inside my skull.

Our entire lives, he argued, are governed by a voice in our heads. This voice is engaged in a ceaseless stream of thinking — most of it negative, repetitive, and self-referential. It squawks away at us from the minute we open our eyes in the morning until the minute we fall asleep at night, if it allows us to sleep at all. Talk, talk, talk: the voice is constantly judging and labeling everything in its field of vision. Its targets aren't just external; it often viciously taunts *us,* too.

Apparently Felicia was right when she got all flustered on that little side street in Jersey City: Tolle wasn't using the term "ego" the way most of us normally do. He wasn't referring solely to pride, conceit, or amour propre of the variety often displayed by people who appear on television for a living. Nor was he using it in the Freudian sense, as the psychological mechanism that mediates between our id and our superego, our desires and our morality. He meant something much larger. According to Tolle, the ego is our inner narrator, our sense of "I."

Certainly Tolle had described *my* mind to a T. While I had never really thought about it before, I suppose I'd always assumed that the voice in my head was me: my ghostly internal anchorman, hosting the coverage of my life, engaged in an unsolicited stream of insensitive questions and obnoxious color commentary.

Per Tolle, even though the voice is the ridgepole of our interior lives, most of us take it completely for granted. He argued that the failure to recognize thoughts for what they are — quantum bursts of psychic energy that exist solely in your head — is the primordial human error. When we are unaware of "the egoic mind" (*egoic* being a word he appears to have invented), we blindly act out our thoughts, and often the results are not pretty.

I began to recall some of the many brilliant suggestions the voice in my head had made to me over the years.

You should do cocaine.

You're right to be angry at that producer. Throw your papers in the air!

That Pakistani protestor is way out of line. Even though he's surrounded by a thousand angry friends, you should have a shouting match with him.

I'd been reading for an hour now, and Tolle had my full attention. As I turned the pages, he began to list some of the ego's signature moves, many of which seemed to be grabbed directly from my behavioral repertoire.

The ego is never satisfied. No matter how much stuff we buy, no matter how many arguments we win or delicious meals we consume, the ego never feels complete. Did this not describe my bottomless appetite for airtime — or drugs? Is this what my friend Simon meant when he said I had the "soul of a junkie"?

The ego is constantly comparing itself to others. It has us measuring our self-worth against the looks, wealth, and social status of everyone else. Did this not explain some of my worrying at work?

The ego thrives on drama. It keeps our old resentments and grievances alive through compulsive thought. Is this why I would sometimes come home to Bianca, scowling over some issue at the office?

Perhaps the most powerful Tollean insight into the ego was that it is obsessed with the past and the future, at the expense of the present. We "live almost exclusively through memory and anticipation," he wrote. We wax nostalgic for prior events during which we were doubtless ruminating or projecting. We cast forward to future events during which we will certainly be fantasizing. But as Tolle pointed out, it is, quite literally, always Now. (He liked to capitalize the word.) The present moment is all we've got. We experienced everything in our past through the present moment, and we will experience everything in the future the same way.

I was a pro, I realized, at avoiding the present. A ringer. This had been true my whole life. My mom always described me as an impatient kid, rushing through every-thing. In eighth grade, an ex-girlfriend told me, "When you have one foot in the future and the other in the past, you piss on the present." Now, as a grown-up in the deadline-dominated world of news, I was always hurtling headlong through the day, checking things off my to-do list, constantly picturing completion instead of calmly and carefully enjoying the process. The unspoken assumption behind most of my forward momentum was that whatever was coming next would definitely be better. Only when I reached that ineffable . . . *whatever* . . . would I be totally satisfied. Some of the only times I could recall being fully present were when I was in a war zone or on drugs. No wonder one begat the other.

It finally hit me that I'd been sleepwalking through much of my life — swept along on a tide of automatic, habitual behavior. All of the things I was most ashamed of in recent years could be explained through the ego: chasing the thrill of war without contemplating the consequences, replacing the combat high with coke and ecstasy, reflexively and unfairly judging people of faith, getting carried away with anxiety about work, neglecting Bianca to tryst with my BlackBerry, obsessing about my stupid hair.

It was a little embarrassing to be reading a self-help writer and thinking, *This guy gets me.* But it was in this moment, lying in bed late at night, that I first realized that the voice in my head — the running commentary that had dominated my field of consciousness since I could remember — was kind of an asshole.

119

This is where things got confusing, though. Just as I was coming to the conclusion that Tolle was a sage who perhaps held the key to all of my problems, he started saying some ludicrous shit. It was no longer his rococo writing style that was throwing me; I was getting used to that. No, now what was sticking in my craw was his penchant for making wild, pseudoscientific claims. He argued that living in the present moment slowed down the aging process and made the "molecular structure" of the body "less dense." He asserted that "thoughts have their own range of frequencies, with negative thoughts at the lower end of the scale and positive thoughts at the higher." Sometimes in the course of a single sentence, he would say something lucid and compelling, and then veer straight into crazy town. I honestly could not figure out if he was a genius or a lunatic.

Then I learned more about who this guy actually was. After several nights of reading his book well into the wee hours, I padded over to the computer to do a little Googling. I don't know what I was expecting, but certainly not this: a small, sandy-haired

German man who appeared to be at some indeterminate point north of middle age. His presentation style was totally at odds with the voice-of-God tone he affected on the page. In YouTube videos, he spoke softly and slowly, excruciatingly so, as if someone had forced him to ingest a large dose of my leftover Klonopin. His wardrobe appeared to consist solely of sweater-vests and pleated khakis. One observer described him as looking like a "Communist-era librarian." Another called him a "pale, kindly otter."

The seminal event of his personal history was an experience he claimed to have had as a severely depressed graduate student at Oxford University. He said he was lying in bed when he was overcome with suicidal thoughts. Suddenly, he felt himself being "sucked into a void." He heard a voice telling him to "resist nothing." Then everything went dark. He woke up the next morning and the birds were chirping, the sunlight was a revelation, and his life was a shiny, sparkly thing. It was, quite literally, an overnight panacea. Bingo. Done. Sorted. After that is when he spent two years living on park benches "in a state of the most intense joy." This was his spiritual awakening, of which he would later say, "The realization of peace is so deep that even if I met the Buddha and the Buddha said you are wrong, I would say, 'Oh, isn't that interesting, even the Buddha can be wrong.' "

Eventually, he moved to Canada, which had the right "energy field" for his first book "to be born." That book, *The Power of Now,* became a celebrity sensation. Meg Ryan gave it to Oprah, who put copies on the nightstands in the guest rooms of all of her homes. Jim Carrey and Jenny McCarthy produced videotaped testimonials (before they broke up). Paris Hilton carried the book through a gauntlet of paparazzi on her way into jail over a driving violation.

When his follow-up, *A New Earth,* came out, Oprah put on an unprecedented, eleven-part "webinar." Millions of people tuned in to watch her and Tolle sit at a desk, deconstructing the book, chapter by chapter. Their personal styles were almost comically mismatched: Oprah would whoop and holler as Tolle looked on placidly; Tolle would prattle on about "energy fields" as Oprah *mmm*ed and *aah*ed credulously. At one point she threw up her arms for a double high five, and Tolle, clearly not knowing what such a thing was, awkwardly clasped her hands.

Sitting there in my underwear in front of

my computer in the middle of the night, I put my head in my hands. My whole life, I'd prided myself on being a skeptic. I'd spent nearly a decade interviewing spiritual leaders, and none of them had penetrated my defenses. Now this guy — who looked like a character from *The Hobbit* — was the one who had punched through?

I was looking in the mirror again — this time at an angry red hole, the size of a quarter, smack in the middle of my right cheek.

When the dermatologist first discovered the milky patch on my cheek — basal cell carcinoma, a nonlethal form of skin cancer — I was tempted to just leave it there. Face surgery was an unappetizing prospect for a guy who went on TV for a living. The doctor, however, along with Bianca, argued that inaction was not an option. If I let it spread unchecked, they told me, it could get into my eye socket and blind me. For a nanosecond, I considered whether I might prefer partial blindness to a scar, even though the doctor promised that, if everything went well, said scar would be a small one.

The surgery was Chinese water torture. The surgeon — a crisp young woman — made an initial incision, using a microscopically guided scalpel to remove the cancer. After that first stab, she sent me out to the waiting room as she ran some tests to see if she'd gotten it all. I joined Bianca at a bank of chairs, where I pulled out my copy of *A New Earth,* which I was now reading for the third time.

After a half hour or so, the doctor called me back and said they needed to dig a little deeper. So I went under the knife again, and then back to the waiting room, where I read more of the book. Another half hour passed, and then the nurse came back and told me they still hadn't gotten every last teeny bit; they'd need to take a wider slice.

When I arrived back in the procedure room this time, the doctor explained that the cancer was bigger than she had thought — and she still didn't know how big. I pressed her for worst-case scenarios and she admitted that there was a danger that it might have spread up into the lower part of my eyelid. If that were true, closing the wound would likely involve a scar that permanently pulled down my right eye.

I could feel my heartbeat accelerate as the following movie instantly played out in my mind:

Scar the size of Omar Little's from *The Wire* → Fired from *ABC* News → Seeks career in radio

But then a funny thing happened. After all my reading about the empty nattering of the ego, I realized: These fearful forecasts were just thoughts skittering through my head. They weren't irrational, but they weren't necessarily true. It was a momentary glimpse of the wisdom of Tolle's thesis. It's not like I'd never been aware of my thoughts before. I'd had plenty of experience with being scared and knowing I was scared. What made this different was that I was able to see my thoughts for what they were: just thoughts, with no concrete reality. It's not that my worry suddenly ceased, I just wasn't as taken in by it. I recognized the truth of this situation: I had no idea what was going to happen to my face, and reflexively believing the worst-case scenarios coughed up by ego certainly wasn't going to help.

The doctor made her third slice, and then sent me back out into the waiting room. Bianca remarked that I was staying surprisingly calm. I didn't want to give the credit to Tolle, lest she think I was going crazy. She already thought it was weird that I'd been reading this book for so long.

125

Ultimately, I had to go back in for four facial slices before the tumor was fully removed. They came within a millimeter, but the lower part of my eyelid was spared. Before they sewed me up, the doctor showed me the wound in a mirror and I nearly fainted. I could see well into the side of my cheek — blood, fat, and all. Bianca took out her phone and snapped a picture.

I had done surprisingly well in the crucible of face surgery, but you can't carry an Eckhart Tolle book around with you everywhere you go.

A couple of weeks later, I was checking *TVNewser,* an addictive website that tracks the doings of the broadcast news industry, and I came across a list of the anchors and correspondents who would be covering the inauguration of President Barack Obama. My name was not mentioned. I was, to put it mildly, displeased.

Unlike my experience with the surgery, here I was unable to achieve any distance from the angry thoughts caroming through my head. Instead, I took the bait dangled by my ego, which was yammering on in high dudgeon: *You're getting screwed here, dude.* I shoved back my chair and started pacing around my office in tight circles, like a Chihuahua doing dressage. Over the next twenty-four hours, I buttonholed every executive I could find and voiced my complaints. Instead of winning me a role in the coverage, however, the whining earned me a reprimand. One of my bosses took me aside and told me that the decision wasn't personal, and then advised me to stop "bleeding all over the place."

This was my major beef with Tolle. Setting aside my qualms about his flowery writing, questionable claims, and bizarre backstory, what I truly could not abide was the lack of practical advice for handling situations like this. He delivered an extraordinary diagnosis of the human condition with basically no action plan for combating the ego (never mind for achieving living-on-a-park-bench superbliss).

How do we do a better job of staying in the Now? Tolle's answer: "Always say 'yes' to the present moment." How do we achieve liberation from the voice in the head? His advice: simply be aware of it. "To become free of the ego is not really a big job but a very small one." Yes, right. Easy. But if it were this uncomplicated, wouldn't there be millions of awakened people walking around?

Then there was an even larger question:

Even if I had been able to recognize that my umbrage over not being included in inauguration coverage consisted of mere thoughts, should I have simply ignored them? I could see the value of recognizing thoughts for what they are — fleeting, gossamer, unsubstantial — but aren't some thoughts connected to concrete realities that need to be addressed?

In his books, Tolle repeatedly denigrated the habit of worrying, which he characterized as a useless process of projecting fearfully into an imaginary future. "There is no way that you can cope with such a situation, because it doesn't exist. It's a mental phantom," he wrote. But, while I understood the benefit of being in the Now, the future was coming. Didn't I have to prepare? If I didn't think through every permutation of every potential problem, how the hell would I survive in a competitive industry? Furthermore, wasn't the restless ego the source of mankind's proudest achievements? Sure, it was probably responsible for ills such as war, child abuse, and Pauly Shore movies, but hadn't human striving also given us the polio vaccine, Caravaggio's paintings, and the iPhone?

And yet, and yet . . . I was aware, of course, that my chattering mind was not

128

entirely working in my favor. I was pretty sure that staring at my hairline or brooding on my couch was not time well spent. I used to think pressing the bruise kept me on my toes. Now I realized those moments mostly just made me unhappy.

Tolle was forcing me to confront the fact that the thing I'd always thought was my greatest asset — my internal cattle prod — was also perhaps my greatest liability. I was now genuinely questioning my own personal orthodoxy, my "price of security" mantra, which had been my operating thesis since, like, age eight. All of a sudden, I didn't know: Was it propulsive — or corrosive?

I wanted to excel, yes — but I also wanted to be less stressed in the process. This strange little German man seemed to raise the tantalizing possibility of doing both, but the books were not at all explicit about how to do so — at least not in a way that I understood.

So I decided: I needed to meet this guy.

I ran into Felicia in the hallway at work. "Let's book Eckhart Tolle for an interview," I said. "We could do it as a 'Sunday Profile,' " a weekly feature we'd recently decided to launch.

It was as if I'd told her that she'd hit the

Powerball, or been chosen for beatification. She was beaming. Unlike me, she did not harbor suspicions that Tolle might be a fruitcake. She was all in.

A couple of days later, she reported back that Tolle, who apparently rarely granted interviews, had said yes. He'd be in Toronto in a few weeks hence, giving a sold-out speech, and we'd been granted a one-hour audience. "They're being really strict about the time limit," she said, but she was still giddy.

I flew in from New York on the morning of the interview. When I arrived at the hotel room where we'd be shooting, Felicia was there with the camera crew and a clean-cut young Australian guy named Anthony who appeared to be Tolle's right-hand man. I'd expected a larger staff, but it was just this one guy.

As we awaited the arrival of the Great Man, Anthony told me his story. He'd read some of Tolle's books, called him up, and asked for a job. When Tolle said yes, Anthony packed all his stuff and moved from Australia to Vancouver, where Tolle lived. Anthony struck me as reasonably normal, with his neatly gelled blond hair and pressed shirt. He discussed his boss with genuine admiration but not adulation;

nothing in his bearing screamed "cult" to me.

Shortly thereafter, there was a knock on the door, and Tolle entered. The first thing I noticed was that he was small. Smaller than me, and I'm about five-foot-nine on days when I've used Bianca's volumizing shampoo. No entourage, just him. He had none of the swagger of a man who'd sold tens of millions of books and had a one-man industry of speaking gigs, CDs, and "inspiration cards." He walked up and introduced himself with a handshake. He was unassuming, but not shy. Not unfriendly, but not especially warm. Just as he had on Oprah's webinar, he seemed pleased to be there, but not particularly eager. He was wearing an astoundingly bland, brown blazer over a tan sweater and a pale blue dress shirt. He had a scraggly beard that covered just his chin and neck.

After the exchange of pleasantries, we took our seats for the interview. There were two cameras: one trained on Tolle, the other on me. I was mildly self-conscious about my mottled cheek, but mostly I was just excited. Here I was, finally face-to-face with the man who had come out of nowhere and so thoroughly intrigued and confused me. This was the first interview since I'd started covering spirituality where I actually felt like I had some skin in the game.

"How on earth do you stop thinking?" I began. "How do you stop the voice in your head?"

I had a momentary surge of optimism as he shifted in his chair in clear preparation to give the practical advice I'd been yearning for.

"You create little spaces in your daily life where you are aware but not thinking," he said. "For example, you take one conscious breath."

Un-break my heart, Eckhart. That's all you've got?

"But," I said, "I can hear the cynics in the audience saying, 'This guy's saying I can awaken by taking a deep breath. What is he talking about?' "

"Yes — that's the mind talking. Of course, many people will have their mind commenting on what I'm saying — and saying, 'That is useless.' "

In fact, that was exactly what *my* mind was saying: *That is useless.*

My mind started saying things that were even less charitable as he rolled out his second, allegedly practical suggestion. "Another very powerful thing is to become

132

aware of the inner energy field of your being."

Aware that I had a camera aimed at me, I hammed it up, again using that old journalistic trick of channeling a third-party "cynic," who could really be no one other than me.

" 'Energy field.' Those are two words that, when put together, will fire off cynics' antennae very, very quickly."

"Yes, now those are people who are very much in their mind. So they are not even willing to try out something new."

I mentioned that my efforts to stay in the Now had been frustrating, adding another layer of guilt on top of the normal churn of my mind. "Because I'm thinking all the time," I said, "I can't be in touch with the Now, so now I'm feeling guilty about not being in touch with the Now."

"Yes, as you rightly put it, that's another layer of thinking — and that layer of thinking says, 'You see, it doesn't work. I can't be free of thinking.' Which is more thinking," he said, laughing gently.

"So how do you break out of that?"

"You simply observe that it's another thought. And by knowing that it's another thought, you're not totally identified with the thought."

This made my head hurt. Clearly this line of questioning was going nowhere. Keenly aware that Tolle's assistant, Anthony, had his eye on the clock, I decided to move on — which is when we came to the part of the interview where Tolle made what I considered to be his most ludicrous claim yet.

"Don't you ever get pissed off, annoyed, irritated, sad — anything negative?"

"No, I accept what is. And that's why life has become so simple."

"Well, what if somebody cuts you off in your car?"

"It's fine. It's like a sudden gust of wind. I don't personalize a gust of wind, and so it's simply what is."

"And you're able to enjoy every moment, even if I start asking you a ton of annoying questions?"

"Yes. That would be fine."

"Don't tempt me."

Here he let out a real laugh — from the diaphragm, leaning forward in his chair, eyes almost closed. He recovered and picked right up: "It's becoming friendly just with the is-ness of this moment."

The is-ness of this moment? Who was this guy kidding? Was he really saying that he was never in a bad mood? That nothing ever bothered him? How could he sit there on camera and claim that? It sounded great, of course. But so did learning how to fly.

"I don't fully understand that, because I sometimes think about change — either innovation or social activism — like that little bit of sand in an oyster that creates the pearl."

"Yes, well . . ."

"Is it a clam or an oyster? I can't remember. Anyway, you know what I'm talking about."

Laughing again, he continued. "The most powerful change comes actually out of that different state of consciousness. This is why people so admire what Gandhi did, because he was bringing about change from a state of consciousness that was already at peace. And people sometimes believe that if you're already at peace you're never going to do anything. But that's not the case. Very powerful actions come out of that."

"So, you're not saying sit around, let everything wash over you, let people cut you off in your car. You're saying understand that it is what it is right now —"

"And then do what you need to do," he said, interrupting me this time, and speaking with uncharacteristic brio. "Make the present moment your friend rather than your enemy. Because many people live habitually as if the present moment were an obstacle that they need to overcome in order to get to the next moment. And imagine living your whole life like that, where always this moment is never quite right, not good enough because you need to get to the next one. That is continuous stress."

Okay, now this made a ton of sense to me. For example, in the case of inauguration coverage, I could have accepted that my exclusion was already a reality, and then simply had a series of calm conversations with my bosses about whether it was possible to change things — instead of firing off a spray of footbullets.

Sitting with Tolle was like watching the movie version of his books. Both in person and on the page, he moved with total ease between tremendously useful insights, and head-scratching, grandiose claims about perfect imperturbability.

By this point, the interview had run long. Felicia was visibly anxious. She apologetically explained to Tolle and Anthony that we really needed a "walking shot" — a picture of me and Tolle walking down the street or something. Everyone agreed this request could be accommodated.

We took the elevator down to the lobby,

where I chatted with Tolle while Felicia and the crew went outside to find a suitable spot for the shot. Sometimes, after an interview, people are warmer; they're relieved it's over and they feel they've gotten to know their interviewer a bit. Tolle's affect, however, was utterly unchanged. He exuded the same pleasant unflappability. Making small talk, I asked him his age, and he told me he was sixty-two. When I remarked that he looked much younger than that, he told me matter-of-factly that he basically hadn't aged since he'd had his spiritual awakening, which happened when he was twenty-nine. Yet another sharp left turn into crazy town.

The story aired a few weeks later on both Sunday *World News* and *Nightline.* The reactions from my colleagues were interesting. A few of them wrote Tolle off as a whack-job. Several others said they found him oddly compelling. My friend Jeanmarie, for example, described him as being like a Yule log — initially boring, but ultimately mesmerizing.

Personally, the encounter had left me in a funny spot. I definitely didn't think Tolle was a fraud. I'd interviewed hucksters — prosperity preachers, child slave dealers, Saddam Hussein flunkies who vowed to turn back the U.S.-led invasion — but this guy didn't give off the I'm-full-of-shit-and-I-know-it vibe at all. Maybe he was simply deluded? Impossible for me to tell.

Essentially, I was right back where I was the first time I peered into the pages of his strange little book: fascinated yet frustrated. Tolle had opened something up for me — a window into the enfeebling clamor of the ego. But he had not answered my most pressing questions. How do you tame the voice in your head? How do you stay in the Now? Was it really possible to defeat the gray Stalinism of self-absorption without ending up on a park bench? I was not about to let this drop. It was as if I'd met a man who'd told me my hair was on fire, and then refused to offer me a fire extinguisher.

CHAPTER 4
HAPPINESS, INC.

The first thing you notice is the rhinestone glasses. Then the fragrance — like he's just stepped out of a two-hour massage.

I met Deepak Chopra six weeks after my interview with Eckhart Tolle. While I had thought of little else other than the ego and its discontents during those weeks, my encounter with Chopra, another self-help superstar, was entirely unplanned. I called it serendipity; Chopra almost certainly would have called it karma.

I had been asked to fly to Seattle to moderate a *Nightline* debate (or "Face-Off," in the preferred rebranding of the show's executive producer) with the extremely subtle title "Does Satan Exist?" Chopra — who was always, as we say in the business, "TV-friendly" — had been booked to argue the "no" case, alongside a Pentecostal bishop who'd lost most of his congregation after publicly reconsidering the existence of the Devil. The "yes" side was made up of a hip, young local pastor as well as a former prostitute who ran an evangelical group called Hookers for Jesus.

I was only vaguely familiar with Chopra. I knew, of course, that he was probably the most famous guru on earth and that he'd written truckloads of bestselling books. I had seen his cameo in the movie *The Love Guru.* He struck me as the Golden Arches or Nike Swoosh of spirituality — a globally recognized icon next to whom celebrities could pose when they wanted to signal "depth."

I was also aware that while he preached good vibes and serenity, Chopra enjoyed wading into controversies over politics, science, and faith — sometimes even going on Fox News to mix it up with conservative hosts like Sean Hannity.

It was that combination of spiritual star power and zeal for rhetorical combat that had motivated my producers to book Chopra for this Face-Off, which we were filming in a church in downtown Seattle. The house was packed with a thousand people, all invited by the four debaters. The plan was to have the participants go at it for two hours, while we recorded with a battery of cameras strategically located throughout the room. We would then cut it down to the juiciest moments, and air it as a full half-hour broadcast of *Nightline* several weeks later.

Before the main event, the producers asked me to tape preinterviews with the combatants, goading them into talking smack like boxers before they go in the ring. After chatting with the ex-hooker and the two pastors, my crew and I found Deepak in one of the church's back rooms. In addition to blinged-out glasses, he wore jeans, bright red sneakers, and a blazer the likes of which I had never seen — charcoal gray, knee-length, with an elaborate mandarin collar. He had a fleshy face; pleasant, latte-colored skin; and a soft, chocolate baritone, with just enough of an Indian accent to sound exotic.

In the interview, he exuded bravado, as befitted an event such as this. He dismissed Satan as a construct of people who needed an "irrational, mythical explanation" for evil in the world. As for his debate performance, he vowed, "I am not going to do anything to offend anyone, but I still have to speak my own truth."

Clearly, Chopra was "with the program," the one envisioned by *Nightline,* but he also presented an irresistible opportunity for me

141

to pursue my own agenda. I wanted to get his take on Eckhart Tolle. So I told him my story — that I had been intrigued by Tolle's description of the ego but bemused by his lack of actionable advice.

Right off the bat, Chopra dismissed Tolle as "not a very good writer." (*Apparently self-help gurus talk smack about one another, just as some evangelicals do,* I realized.) Then, when I asked him if he knew how to stay in the moment, he allowed that he did. In fact, he insisted that he was permanently present.

Our bosses had been encouraging the on-air types to produce more content for ABCNews.com. I thought talking to Deepak about the notion of the Now might make a good little video, so I whipped out a Flip camera and popped a few more questions.

"So your mind doesn't wander?" I asked. "You don't find yourself thinking about things that are in the past or in the future?"

"I have no regrets about the past," he said, "and I don't anticipate the future. I live in the moment."

"Okay, so what if the moment is horrible? What if you really have to go to the bathroom and there's no toilet nearby? Or what if you're super hungry and there's no food?"

"Then I separate myself from the situation surrounding the moment. The moment

142

is always free."

"Run that by me again," I said. "It's a sort of mind trick?"

"It's not a mind trick. When you're totally present, whatever the situation is, good or bad, it's gonna pass. The only thing that remains is the moment. It's the transformational vortex to the infinite."

Apparently when one lives in the moment, one becomes unafraid of using terms like "transformational vortex to the infinite."

He still wasn't giving me specifics, so I pushed again. "How do you do that? Because while I'm talking to you right now, sometimes my mind wanders, and I think, 'Wow, those are nice glasses,' or 'What am I going to ask next?' "

"If you stay in the moment, you'll have what is called spontaneous right action, which is intuitive, which is creative, which is visionary, which eavesdrops on the mind of the universe."

I had no idea what he was talking about, but we were out of time. The sound tech arrived and began wiring Chopra with his lapel microphone for the debate.

"I still think you make it sound easier than it is," I said.

He looked at me and gave a good-natured shrug that seemed to say, *What can I say,*

143

you unlucky schmuck?

"For me it is," he said.

"How do I become more like you?"

"Hang around with me," he said. And then, moving in closer as the sound guy struggled to keep up, he asked for my mailing address, which I somewhat reluctantly gave him.

After all that fancy talk of living in the moment and "eavesdropping on the mind of the universe," as soon we hit the stage and got into the heat of the debate, Chopra was raising his voice, gesticulating wildly, and arguing in a way that certainly did not signal serenity. When he didn't have the floor, he would slouch back in his chair, feet stretched out in front of him, looking entirely nonplussed. To me, at least, he didn't seem to be present at all — certainly not in the Eckhart Tolle, blissed-out way. But maybe he was? What did I know? Maybe, I thought to myself, I shouldn't reach reflexive conclusions as I did with Ted Haggard. Perhaps Deepak Chopra represented the twinning of passionate striving and ego subjugation. Is it possible this guy had it all figured out?

I wasn't optimistic.

But I was surprised by the reaction when I

posted my Chopra video on the ABC News website. First, it generated so much traffic that it landed in the "Most Viewed" column. Then, I got an email from the last person I expected: my boss.

David Westin, the president of the news division, was not the type of man I thought likely to be searching for a transformational vortex to the infinite. Formerly a corporate lawyer, he'd run the news division for more than a decade. He was sharply handsome, with boyish Midwestern features and a full head of slightly blond hair that seemed to stay firmly in place without any discernible application of product. He favored Brooks Brothers suits, striped ties, and loafers, and his personal style was commensurately crisp, earnest, and affable. He easily could have been a politician — or an anchorman.

Westin's email said he was curious, on a personal level, about my conversation with Chopra. He suggested we meet to discuss.

His assistant set an appointment, and a few days later I found myself walking up one flight of stairs from my office to the executive suite, referred to simply by its geographic designation, the Fifth Floor. The air was different up here, as if it were pumped in from the Sierra Nevada. It was a wide-open room, with offices lining the periphery, and assistants stationed outside of each. The heavy hush was devoid of the clack and clamor that characterized the rest of the news division. In the middle of the space was a kitchen island, perennially stocked with snacks and free-flowing Starbucks.

Westin's secretary ushered me in, and the man himself got up from his neatly organized desk to give me a firm handshake and a courtly, enthusiastic, "Hi, Dan!"

After a bit of small talk, he brought up Chopra. In his diplomatic way, he said he was surprised to see me taking the guy so seriously. "I respect your opinion on these things, Dan — and Deepak is somebody I've only ever seen on daytime television. Is there really something to him?"

As he spoke, I began to suspect that there must be more to my boss's interest than he was letting on. Here was a man with a supremely stressful job, managing both the outsized personalities within the news division and the demands of his corporate overlords. Once, over lunch, he'd admitted to me that his real personality was at times significantly less sunny than his persona.

"There is something there," I said, "although I'm not sure Chopra is the best example of it."

Then I launched into an unsuccessful and overly emphatic soliloquy about Eckhart Tolle, the ego, the present moment, and God knows what else. The longer I yammered on about the "thinking mind" and the "voice in the head," the more I realized that I wasn't making much sense. This was the first opportunity I'd had to discuss this material with anyone, aside from actually interviewing Tolle and Chopra themselves, and it suddenly hit me that I didn't really know what I was talking about. Which made me even more anxious and, by turns, even more talkative. Finally, seeing I'd lost my audience, I swallowed the flood of saliva in my mouth and concluded by saying that maybe Westin should just read Tolle's book.

The next day, I slinked back upstairs and dropped it off with his secretary, all the while thinking: *This is what it's come to. I'm the crazy guy handing out religious tracts on the street.*

I still wanted to talk about this stuff, though, to people I liked and trusted. It wasn't that I felt compelled to convert anyone; I just wanted a sounding board. Figuring that this would be easier with someone who wasn't my boss, I broached the subject at a dinner with my friend Regina. For a decade, Regina and I had been having no-holds-barred debates about everything from TV shows to New York real estate to my sometimes questionable, pre-Bianca romantic decisions. I figured the machinery of the ego would be terrific fodder. Moments after I started blathering about Eckhart Tolle, however, Regina cut me off. "Whatever, Dan. If you need this, fine." Then she changed the subject to which soups we should order. The verdict was rendered with such offhand ferocity that it made me realize that this topic I thought so alive with potential could come off as merely fuzzy and embarrassing. She wasn't engaged enough to even needle me about it.

My losing streak continued at a family brunch, when I floated Tolle past my younger brother. I should have seen this one coming. Matt's mission in life since emerging from the womb had been to torment me. Even though he was now a venture capitalist and the father of a beautiful baby girl, his devotion to puncturing my balloon had not diminished. As soon as I finished my spiel, he just stared back at me with a satisfied smirk. The knife inserted with nary a word. (Not long afterward, he gave me an Eckhart Tolle calendar for Christmas. I unwrapped it, looked up, and saw him on the other side of the room, wearing the same smirk.)

What made this series of failures especially frustrating was the realization that the expressions on the faces of my interlocutors were probably not dissimilar to the way I must have looked when confronted with some of the fringier religious people I'd interviewed over the years.

Even with people who weren't reflexively hostile to the material, I wasn't making terrific inroads. At a group dinner downtown, I cornered my friend Kaiama, an open-minded professor of French Lit at Columbia. As I concluded my discourse on the Now, she asked, "But how do you really stay in the moment when it's always slipping away?" I had no answer.

Perhaps the most meaningful exchange I had on the subject was a completely random discussion with my uncle Martin at my parents' annual summer pool party. Martin, a former entrepreneur who was now in the early stages of Alzheimer's, turned to me and asked an intriguing question: "Which is more exciting to you? Reality or memory?" I paused, considered it, and said, "I wish I could say reality, but it's probably memory." And then I asked, "What about you?" At which point Martin stared blankly back at me and asked, "What was the question?"

Bianca was mildly receptive to my new-found area of interest. Mostly, she was intrigued by the notion of having a less stressed husband-to-be. Then again, I had just come through a yearlong obsession with climate change. It was reasonable to assume that this was just another of my transient fixations, only kookier.

I was stuck in the same place I'd found myself at the end of my Tolle interview, knowing my hair was on fire but lacking an extinguisher. With Tolle having failed to answer my questions, and struggling with an ongoing inability to explain what intrigued me about all of this in even the most basic, comprehensible terms, I was at my wit's end. I didn't know where to turn. I recalled what Chopra had said to me at the end of our interview: "Hang around with me." Just days after I met him, he'd sent a whole stack of his books to my office, with titles like *The Book of Secrets* and *Reinventing the Body, Resurrecting the Soul.* He'd been texting and emailing me, and even forwarding me a Google Alert he'd set on himself, in which Kim Kardashian sang his praises. Warily, I figured: *What do I have to lose?*

■ ■ ■ ■

Deepak was wearing a black T-shirt emblazoned with a peace sign made out of sequins as he enthusiastically showed me around the Manhattan outpost of the Chopra Center. Located in a chichi midtown hotel, the Center offered spa treatments, medical consults, yoga, and astrological readings. We were in the gift shop. As I let my eyes fall on his vast array of personally branded products (Ayurvedic Cold & Allergy Remedies, Antioxidant Supplements, "Harmonizing" necklaces, shirts printed with the word ABUNDANCE, and books (fifty-five or fifty-six of them, he couldn't remember exactly — on everything from God to golf to cooking) I was thinking about Jay Z, who once rapped, "I'm not a businessman . . . I'm a business, man."

Felicia and I had decided to profile Deepak for Sunday *World News.* It didn't take a lot of convincing to get him on board, and it became readily apparent how this man had landed on the *Forbes* list of richest celebrities, with an estimated income of $22 million a year. His itinerary was a manic, many-splendored thing. In just a few days I personally saw him host a satellite radio show, hold meetings with video game developers for a project based on his spiritual teachings, and discuss a Broadway show with a man who claimed he could bend spoons with the power of his mind.

On many levels, Deepak seemed like a walking contradiction. He claimed to be perennially present, and yet we filmed him pounding down the street while furiously typing on his BlackBerry, and then voraciously devouring articles on his Kindle while ostensibly working out on an elliptical machine. He claimed to live in a state of "flow" and "effortless spontaneity," but he seemed pretty focused on mundane self-promotion to me. While publicizing his latest book, he lobbied a reporter to follow him on Twitter, and when shooting a promotional video, he told the cameraman, "Make sure I don't look fat." These didn't strike me as the actions of a man living in perfect harmony with himself; this was the type of shit *I* did.

We did an interview at a picnic table in Central Park, and I challenged his self-proclaimed imperturbability. Thinking back to his performance at the Face-Off, I said, "Sometimes I've seen you worked up."

"But even though I was worked up," he responded, "did you find that there was

152

anger, resentment, or hostility in that?"

"I can't read your mind, but judging from your body language, you weren't pleased."

"Without passion, you'd be a walking dead person," he said. "Even though you're dynamically engaged, you're not stressed."

Was it really just "dynamic engagement" and not stress? Deepak insisted that, in fact, he hadn't experienced stress in decades. He told me that, years ago, when he was a frazzled young medical resident in suburban Massachusetts he smoked two packs of cigarettes a day and drank too much. "We used to take care of a cardiac arrest and then we'd go outside and smoke a cigarette," he said. But then, quite suddenly, he changed everything. "It was dramatic," he told me. "I finally one day made a decision that that part of my life was over. I said, 'I've been there, done that.' "

He quit his day job and went to work for the Maharishi Mahesh Yogi, the bearded Indian holy man perhaps most famous for his stint as the official guru of the Beatles. (After a brief stay at his ashram, John Lennon left in a huff over allegations that the Maharishi had tried to fondle Mia Farrow. On his way back to London, Lennon wrote the song "Sexy Sadie," featuring the lyric, "What have you done? You've made a fool of everyone.") Deepak climbed to the rank of the Maharishi's top lieutenant. But he and the Maharishi grew apart. Deepak started feeling like the group had become too cultish; the Maharishi thought Deepak too ambitious. So Deepak left.

Unleashed from hierarchical constraint, Deepak spread his wings. He'd become intrigued by "spontaneous remissions," those dramatic and inexplicable recoveries, where people bounce back from serious illnesses. When he couldn't get any reputable medical journals to publish his research, he paid a vanity press five thousand dollars to put it out as a book. It was a hit. Scores more followed. He became friends with Michael Jackson, who introduced him to Oprah, who put him on television. The rest was history. By the time I met Deepak, he was sixty-three years old. He'd recorded an album of freaky New Age music with Martin Sheen, Madonna, and Demi Moore; Lady Gaga had called him the most influential person in her life; *Time* had dubbed him "the poet-prophet of alternative medicine." He had fierce critics, though. The publisher of *Skeptic* magazine put Deepak on the cover, lampooning his medical conclusions as "mostly wild speculations based on only the slimmest of evidence."

So was he full of shit? I couldn't tell. As with Tolle, I found him to be a baffling mixtape of the interesting and the incomprehensible — like a DJ toggling between the Rolling Stones and Rick Astley, the Band and Dokken. I liked it when he said things like, "The fact that you exist is a highly statistically improbable event, and if you are not perpetually surprised by the fact that you exist you don't deserve to be here." But too often, he reverted to a seemingly involuntary, impenetrable spiritual patois that had a certain *je ne sais pas pourquoi.* His memorable assertions to me included "The universe is a nanotechnology workshop in the mind of god," and "Don't call it God, call it a-causal, non-local, quantum-mechanical inter-religiousness."

Chopra was infinitely more fun to hang out with than Tolle — I preferred Deepak's rascally *What Makes Sammy Run?* style to the German's otherworldly diffidence — but I left the experience more confused, not less. Eckhart was befuddling because, while I believed he was sincere, I couldn't tell if he was sane. With Deepak it was the opposite; I believed he was sane, but I couldn't tell if he was sincere. It was intriguing that someone could strive so nakedly and yet claim to be without stress. That would have answered many of my questions about defeating the ego without killing your edge — if only I believed him.

My next move was motivated by sheer desperation. It was mercifully brief, but unrelentingly absurd. Felicia and I decided to launch a whole series of stories on self-help for Sunday *World News.* We called it "Happiness, Inc." The idea was to delve into an unregulated, $11 billion industry that had attracted a growing number of followers as Americans moved away from organized religion. With no answers forthcoming from Tolle or Chopra, this was the only thing I could think to do. What I found in this distinctly American subculture was beyond crazy — a parade of the unctuous and the unqualified, preaching to the desperate and, often, destitute.

One of the leading players in this questionable game was Joe Vitale, who had risen to prominence after landing a cameo in what would become a monster cultural phenomenon called *The Secret.* This was a high-gloss book and DVD that came out in 2006 and featured a whole crew of self-help gurus expounding on the "Law of Attraction," which offered the prospect of getting anything you wanted — health, wealth, love —

simply by thinking about it in the right way. It was essentially a slick repackaging of an old idea that had been sent up the flagpole by such pioneering turkeys as Napoleon Hill, who produced the 1930s bestseller *Think and Grow Rich,* and Norman Vincent Peale, author of the canonical turd, *The Power of Positive Thinking.*

As I slid into the backseat of Vitale's Rolls-Royce, it truly hit home to me how far Deepak was on the benign end of the self-help spectrum. Vitale had a doughy face and a large, hairless head, which gave the impression of a vastly overgrown baby. He was giving my crew and me a free taste of what would normally cost $5,000: something he called the "Rolls-Royce Phantom Mastermind" session. As his driver squired us through the Texas countryside, Vitale explained that people paid to come to his home in exurban Austin and take a ride with him, during which he helped them "mastermind ideas that change lives."

With the camera pointing back at us from the front seat, I said, "This is an amazing car, but five grand is a lot for three hours with you."

"Well, there are people who think I should charge a lot more than that. They think that's giving it away."

The Rolls was just one of many sources of income for "Dr." Vitale. Homeless just thirty years ago, Vitale had earned his PhD in "metaphysics" through a correspondence course from the University of Sedona. He now lived in a large house with many cars, purchased with the proceeds from dozens of books, with titles like *Expect Miracles* and *Attract Money Now.* He also sold products like margarita mix, a health drink called YouthJuice, and stickers with pictures of Russian dolls on them that, for reasons I couldn't quite understand, Vitale insisted would help the owner meet his or her life goals. (List price: $39.)

In an interview in Vitale's home office, I asked, "You never wake up in the middle of the night thinking, 'I can't believe I'm getting away with this'?"

"No, never," he said, laughing as if this were the last thing that would have ever occurred to him.

While, in theory, I could see the appeal of positive thinking — especially as a man who unquestionably spent too much time ruminating — when I scratched the surface of this "philosophy," I quickly encountered gale force inanity. On the DVD version of *The Secret,* Vitale pops on-screen to utter such memorable chestnuts as "You are the

Michelangelo of your own life. The David that you are sculpting is you — and you do it with your own thoughts." Under questioning in our interview, though, Vitale admitted that it was not that easy. In fact, he folded like a cheap lawn chair.

"So, what if I want a diamond necklace for my wife?" I asked. "Can I get that by thinking about it?"

"Not just by thinking about it. That's one of the biggest misconceptions of all time. You have to take action. It's not just thinking — it's thinking coupled with action."

"Isn't that a statement of the glaringly obvious? You think it's news to most people that if you want something you have to try to get it?"

"You know, when you put it that way, it sounds silly," he said, laughing sheepishly. "Pretty brainless."

The more worrisome message of *The Secret* phenomenon was not the preposterousness of its primary sales pitch, but instead its destructive undercurrent. "The inverse of your logic," I argued to Vitale, "seems to blame the victim. Because if you aren't getting what you want, it must be your fault."

"This is not a blame game," he insisted. "Our unconscious thoughts is [*sic*] what's creating our reality — and many of our

159

unconscious thoughts are not very positive; they are negative. They actually attract problems."

So this would be true of kids with cancer? Victims of genocide? "It strains credulity," I said, "to say that everybody who got hit by the earthquake in Haiti had some unconscious thinking going on that led to them being victims."

"None of those people are being victimized. In other words —"

"In an earthquake, you're victimized, aren't you?"

An awkward pause. A stutter. And then he conceded, "In an earthquake you're victimized."

The other star of *The Secret* I covered managed to push the absurdity level directly into the truly dangerous range. James Arthur Ray was a fit, fifty-something, divorced junior college dropout who oozed smarmy overconfidence. An oily character, he looked like he always had a thin sheen of sweat covering his face. He promised his followers that he could help them achieve "harmonic wealth" in all areas of their life. He claimed that, using his own techniques, he'd not only gotten rich, but that he also no longer so much as caught a cold.

There was clearly some sort of error in his

thinking, however, because in October of 2009, at a "Spiritual Warrior Retreat" in Arizona, which cost nearly ten grand per person, three of Ray's followers died in a sweat lodge ceremony over which he personally presided. It was an imitation of a Native American ritual that Ray promised would be a "re-birthing exercise."

As the sweat lodge story began to gain national traction, the producers of *Nightline* sent me to Arizona to check it out. Sedona, a city known as the New Age Vatican, set amid dramatic red rock cliffs, was a mecca for spiritual tourists who were catered to by a legion of self-proclaimed healers, mystics, wind whisperers, and intuitive counselors who offered such services as "soul-retrieval," "energy healing," and "aura photos." The downtown shopping district echoed with the sounds of wind chimes and the low hum of didgeridoo.

For me, the most pathetic part of the entire story was talking to the survivors who still claimed to believe in Ray. We went to the home of Brian Essad, an unassuming employee at an event production company. He showed us his "visioning board," on which he had a picture of Alyssa Milano, who he was hoping to meet. He also showed us the books and handouts he'd collected from all the Ray retreats he'd attended. Then he revealed all the unpaid bills that were mounting on his kitchen table — bills he might have been able to pay if he hadn't given so much money to Ray. "It's like right now, I don't actually have enough cash in my account to pay all these bills. So I'm just kind of putting out there that I need to attract money that I need to pay all these."

After investigating for four months, police in Arizona charged Ray with manslaughter. The man who once told viewers of *The Secret* that they should treat the universe as if it were Aladdin's lamp was perp-walked in front of news cameras, wearing handcuffs and leg irons, looking mortified. Even though he'd authored a book called *Harmonic Wealth,* he said he didn't have enough money to make bail. In another delicious twist, investigators released documents that seemed to explain how Ray maintained his robust physical appearance. It wasn't the Law of Attraction. After the sweat lodge, police found a suitcase in Ray's room, filled with diet supplements and prescribed steroids.

That discovery in the hotel room crystallized everything that I found most absurd and hypocritical about the self-help industry. To tell the truth, it hadn't taken long for me to figure out that this scene was not for me. Luckily, with an assist from my future wife, I'd found something more promising.

CHAPTER 5
THE JEW-BU

I was back at the Tribeca Grand, the self-consciously hip hotel in downtown Manhattan where I'd stayed in the days after 9/11. The place had now been restored to its natural state, with mood lighting, techno music, and well-dressed people sipping foreign beers on fluffy chairs. Hardly the environment in which I would have expected to find the kind of guru I was looking for. Until this moment, in fact, I hadn't quite realized that looking for a guru was what I'd been doing all along.

The guy standing here with me at the bar certainly would not have embraced the title, which was, of course, part of his appeal. He was totally reasonable and utterly uncheesy, a man with actual credentials, including a medical degree from Harvard, which conferred a sort of legitimacy that, say, an online degree from the University of Sedona did not.

His basic message was that the best self-help program was developed 2,500 years ago — a worldview that, oddly enough, held that there is actually no "self" to "help."

The seeds of this encounter had been planted one evening at home as I was changing out of my suit and tie and into sweatpants, shucking sartorial detritus — pants, socks, belt — all over the floor. I enjoyed doing this not only because it appealed to both my laziness and my constant desire to rush to the next thing (*The sooner I get these clothes off, the sooner I'll get dinner*), but also because it annoyed Bianca, who sometimes playfully called me Hurricane Harris. On this night, though, she was not taking the bait. She was coming at me with a gift, in fact.

In her hands she had a pair of books written by someone named Dr. Mark Epstein. She told me that, after months of listening to me alternately rhapsodize or carp about Eckhart Tolle et al., it had finally clicked with her why the ideas I was yammering on about with varying levels of cogency sounded so familiar. About ten years prior, she had read some books by Epstein who, she explained, was a psychiatrist and a practicing Buddhist. His writing had been useful for her during a difficult time in her twenties, a quarter-life crisis when she was struggling with family issues as well as the decision about whether to embark on the interminable training necessary to become a doctor.

I flipped over one of the paperbacks to get a look at this Epstein character, and there on the back cover was a kind-faced, middle-aged guy wearing a V-neck sweater and wire-rimmed glasses, sitting on the floor against the type of white backdrop you often see in photography studios. Even though he looked infinitely less weird than either Eckhart Tolle or Deepak Chopra, I still found myself thinking, *Not my kind of guy.*

That mild, momentary spasm of aversion was assuaged by the little bio next to Epstein's picture, which said he was a trained psychiatrist with a private practice in Manhattan.

Thus began another night of delayed sleep and revelatory reading, with Bianca quietly dozing by my side. It was like my first evening with Tolle, only less embarrassing. What I found in the pages of Epstein's book was thunderously satisfying. Like scratching an itch in an unreachable area. Like finally figuring out why Luke Skywalker and Princess Leia's sexual tension never felt right.

Very quickly, it became blazingly clear: The best parts of Tolle were largely unattributed Buddhism. Tolle had not, as I'd assumed when I'd first read *A New Earth,* made up his insights out of whole cloth. Apparently he'd appropriated them, and then effected a sort of intellectual elephantiasis, exaggerating their features in the most profitable of ways. Two and a half millennia before Eckhart Tolle started cashing his royalty checks, it was the Buddha who originally came up with that brilliant diagnosis of the way the mind works.

In Epstein's writings, it was all there: the insatiable wanting, the inability to be present, the repetitive, relentlessly self-referential thinking. Here was everything that fascinated me about Tolle, without the pseudoscience and grandiloquence. To boot, the good doctor could actually write. Compared to Tolle, in fact, this guy was Tolstoy. After months of swimming against the riptide of bathos and bullshit peddled by the self-help subculture, it was phenomenally refreshing to see the ego depicted with wry wit.

"We are constantly murmuring, muttering, scheming, or wondering to ourselves under our breath," wrote Epstein. " 'I like this. I don't like that. She hurt me. How can I get that? More of this, no more of that.' Much of our inner dialogue is this constant reaction to experience by a selfish, childish protagonist. None of us has moved very far from the seven-year-old who vigilantly watches to see who got more." There were also delightful passages about the human tendency to lurch headlong from one pleasurable experience to the next without ever achieving satisfaction. Epstein totally nailed my habit of hunting around my plate for the next bite before I'd tasted what was in my mouth. As he described it, "I do not want to experience the fading of the flavor — the colorless, cottony pulp that succeeds that spectacular burst over my taste buds."

Prior to reading Epstein, my most substantial interaction with Buddhism was when, as a fifteen-year-old punk kid, I stole a Buddha statue from a local gardening store and put it my bedroom because I thought it looked cool. Despite the fact that I was now a religion reporter, I still had only a glancing understanding of this faith. With Buddhists comprising only about 1/300 of the U.S. population and not being in the habit of taking strident political stands, they didn't attract much coverage. What I knew of Buddhism was limited to the following: it was from Asia somewhere; the Buddha was overweight; and his followers believed in things like karma, rebirth, and enlightenment.

Epstein made clear, though, that you didn't have to buy into any of the above to derive benefit from Buddhism. The Buddha himself didn't claim to be a god or a prophet. He specifically told people not to adopt any of his teachings until they'd test-driven the material themselves. He wasn't even trying to start a religion, per se. The word *Buddhism* was actually an invention of the nineteenth-century Western scholars who discovered and translated the original texts. As best I could tell, the whole thing appeared to be less a faith than a philosophy, and one that had been intriguing psychologists since the days of Freud, when his early Viennese followers studied those newly translated texts. In recent decades, the mental health community had come to embrace Buddhism in an increasingly thoroughgoing way. According to Epstein, the Buddha may well have been the "original psychoanalyst." To my surprise, Epstein seemed to be arguing that Buddhism was better than seeing a shrink. Therapy, he said, often leads to "understanding without relief." Even Freud himself had conceded that the best therapy could do was bring us from "hysteric misery" to "common unhappiness."

Epstein's frank admissions about the limitations of therapy tracked with my personal experiences. I was, of course, grateful to Dr. Brotman for getting me to quit drugs and then steadfastly but affably making sure I stayed the course. I was also fond of him personally — especially for his ability to point out my idiosyncrasies and hypocrisies. However, I still had that nagging and perhaps naive sense of disappointment that he had failed to come up with some sort of "unifying theory" to explain my entire psychology. Now Epstein seemed to be saying that even if Brotman had ripped the cover off some primordial wound, it wouldn't have left me better off. The limitation wasn't my therapist, Epstein seemed to be arguing — it was therapy.

So what exactly was this not-quite-religion that could purportedly do a better job of salving the tortured soul? I attacked the question the way I would a major investigative news story, learning everything I could. I bought a ton of books, adding them next to the already precarious stack of self-help tomes on my bedside table. (A tableau Bianca often insisted on covering up when

170

we had company.)

According to the official story, the Buddha was born about five hundred years before Christ in northeast India, in what is now Nepal. As legend has it, his mother was spontaneously impregnated, in what sounded like the Buddhist version of the Immaculate Conception. She died seven days after the birth, leaving the boy, whose name was Siddhartha, to be raised by his father, a regional king.

The king had been advised by a local wise man that Siddhartha would grow up to either be a powerful monarch or a great spiritual leader. Eager to ensure that the boy would one day take the throne, the king arranged to have him confined to the palace walls, protected from the outside world and anything that might trigger his mystical tendencies.

At age twenty-nine, however, Siddhartha grew curious, ran away from home, and became a wandering monk. This was a pretty common practice back in those days. Penniless renunciates with shaved heads, bare feet, and tattered robes would roam the forests, seeking spiritual awakening. The prince did this for six years, until one night he sat under a bodhi tree, vowing not to get up until he'd achieved enlightenment. At

171

dawn, the man formerly known as Siddhartha opened his eyes and gazed out at the world as the Buddha, "the awakened one."

For a skeptic, there was obviously a lot not to like in this story. However, the substance of what the Buddha allegedly realized beneath the bodhi tree — and then began disseminating to his followers — was fascinating, illuminating, and once again appeared to have been crafted by someone who had spent a great deal of time inside my brain.

As best I could understand it, the Buddha's main thesis was that in a world where everything is constantly changing, we suffer because we cling to things that won't last. A central theme of the Buddha's "dharma" (which roughly translates to "teaching") revolved around the very word that had been wafting through my consciousness when I used to lie on my office couch, pondering the unpredictability of television news: "impermanence." The Buddha embraced an often overlooked truism: nothing lasts — including us. We and everyone we love will die. Fame fizzles, beauty fades, continents shift. Pharaohs are swallowed by emperors, who fall to sultans, kings, kaisers, and presidents — and it all plays out against the backdrop of an infinite universe in which our bodies are made up of atoms from the very first exploding stars. We may know this intellectually, but on an emotional level we seem to be hardwired for denial. We comport ourselves as if we had solid ground beneath our feet, as if we had control. We quarantine the elderly in nursing homes and pretend aging will never happen to us. We suffer because we get attached to people and possessions that ultimately evaporate. When we lose our hair, when we can no longer score that hit of adrenaline from a war zone we so crave, we grow anxious and make bad decisions.

Unlike many of the faiths I'd come across as a religion reporter, the Buddha wasn't promising salvation in the form of some death-defying dogma, but rather through the embrace of the very stuff that will destroy us. The route to true happiness, he argued, was to achieve a visceral understanding of impermanence, which would take you off the emotional roller coaster and allow you to see your dramas and desires through a wider lens. Waking up to the reality of our situation allows you to, as the Buddhists say, "let go," to drop your "attachments." As one Buddhist writer put it,

the key is to recognize the "wisdom of insecurity."

That phrase — "the wisdom of insecurity"
— really struck me. It was the perfect
rejoinder to my "price of security" motto. It
made me see my work worries in an entirely
different light. If there was no such thing as
security, then why bother with the insecurity?

For 2,500 years, the Buddhists had been
comprehensively mapping the mind — that
tasteless, odorless, formless thing (or, more
accurately, no-thing) through which we
experience our entire lives. They compiled
meticulous lists: The Three Characteristics
of All Phenomena, The Four Noble Truths,
The Four Highest Emotions, The Seven
Factors of Enlightenment, etc. They also
came up with names for so many of the
mental habits I'd come to notice in myself,
such as "comparing mind," and "wanting
mind." They had a term, too, for that thing
I did where something would bother me and
I would immediately project forward to an
unpleasant future (e.g., *Balding → Unemployment → Flophouse*). The Buddhists
called this *prapañca* (pronounced pra-PUN-
cha), which roughly translates to "proliferation," or "the imperialistic tendency of
mind." That captured it beautifully, I

thought: something happens, I worry, and that concern instantaneously colonizes my future. My favorite Buddhist catchphrase, however, was the one they used to describe the churning of the ego: "monkey mind." I've always been a sucker for animal metaphors, and I thought this one was perfect. Our minds are like furry little gibbons: always agitated, never at rest.

As compelling as the Buddhist view was for me, though, it once again threw me back up against the same old questions I'd been wrestling with since the days of Eckhart Tolle. Wasn't the Buddhist emphasis on "letting go" a recipe for passivity? Was the denigration of desire another way of saying we shouldn't bother to strive? Furthermore, shouldn't we be "attached" to our loved ones?

There were other things I did not get. If Buddhism was about being happier, why was the Buddha's signature declaration "Life is suffering"? Then, of course, there was still the issue of enlightenment. The Buddha's claim — which, as far as I could tell, modern Buddhists, including Dr. Epstein, still believed — was that it was possible to achieve "the end of suffering," to reach Nirvana. I couldn't very well mock Tolle for his claims of "spiritual awakening" and give the Buddhists a pass on enlightenment.

Notwithstanding my confusion, the more I learned about the 2,500-year-old historical figure known to me previously as a lawn ornament, the more intrigued I grew. I felt like I was finally onto something truly substantial. This wasn't just the doctrine of one weird German dude, but an ancient tradition that was given serious credence by smart people like Epstein. My hitherto haphazard quest suddenly felt infinitely more directed.

Right in the middle of our wedding reception, I decided to make a conscious effort to put everything I was learning about Buddhism to work. Dinner had been served and consumed, and the dancing was under way. That's when we heard it: the swell of horns in the distance. Marching in were about eight Bahamians, all dressed in elaborate local costumes and playing trumpets, trombones, tubas, and drums. It was what islanders call a "Junkanoo Rush." It took me a minute to recognize the song, U2's "I Still Haven't Found What I'm Looking For." *Perhaps not the best sentiment for a wedding,* I thought. But never mind: the music was beautiful, and our guests were going wild. I grabbed Bianca, who was looking incandescent in her dress, and we formed a conga line behind the band. I was fully present, totally in the moment. No clinging: I knew this wouldn't last and I was wringing every bit of pleasure out of it while I could.

I had always kind of assumed that I might not enjoy my own wedding. These events were all about the bride, I thought; the groom was just supposed to stand there, smiling. I also feared that after a lifetime of avoiding commitment, I would experience some significant last-minute jitters. As usual, my powers of prognostication were completely off. It turned out to be the best weekend of my life.

Admittedly, this was a hard place to be unhappy. We were getting married on Harbour Island, a magical spot where most people drove around in golf carts instead of cars, and where free-range chickens were given right-of-way in the streets.

The wedding was a small affair: just fifty people, our nuclear families and our closest friends. Everyone came for three days. During the day, people lounged on the beach, where the sand was literally pink, and every night we threw a party. Instead of the usual flybys that most newlyweds do on receiving lines and at guests' tables, Bianca and I got plenty of face time with everyone.

I was also buoyed by my confidence that I was making the right decision. I couldn't imagine marrying anyone other than Bianca. As my friend Regina had quipped, "For a person with terrible judgment, you did a great job with the most important decision of your life."

But there was something else at work here, too. My consumption of Buddhist books was paying off. Throughout the weekend, I made a deliberate effort to pause, look around, and savor things while they lasted. There were little moments, like running errands for Bianca — for example, putting her carefully curated gift bags in people's rooms — and actually enjoying it. Or when I babysat my adorable, big-eyed baby niece Campbell in my room while everyone else was out having lunch. She sat on my lap and cooed contentedly while I ate a cheeseburger, trying not to drip ketchup on her head.

There were big moments, too, like the ceremony itself, where I watched Bianca walk down the aisle and wondered how I'd gotten so lucky.

As soon as I got back home from the honeymoon, though, my penchant for worry reasserted itself — provoked by a conundrum at work that I simply could not figure out how to handle in a Buddhist way.

One Friday evening, I looked up at the TV in my office and saw David Muir anchoring *World News* — the weekday version, the Big Show. He was doing a fantastic job, which threw me into a Triple Lindy of "comparing mind," "monkey mind," and *prapañca. Muir is kicking ass right now. I'm going down.*

I was feeling bad — and then, on top of that, feeling bad about feeling bad. I liked the guy, after all. This incident again crystallized all of my nagging questions about Buddhism. Doesn't competitiveness serve a useful purpose? Is the "price of security" simply incompatible with the "wisdom of insecurity"?

It was time for me to play my trump card. Despite the fact that more than 50 percent of Americans tell pollsters they don't trust the media, generally speaking, people return our calls. I found Mark Epstein's office number and left him a message saying I was a reporter and also a fan. I asked if he'd be willing to meet up, and he called me back right away to say he was game.

So, about a week later, roughly eight months after I'd first discovered Eckhart

Tolle, I took a cab downtown for my man-date with the Buddhist shrink at the Tribeca Grand, just a few blocks from his office — the same chichi hotel where I'd stayed in the days after 9/11.

It was an oddly cool spot for two guys meeting to discuss Eastern spirituality. When I arrived, Epstein was already at the bar, located in the atrium, with seven floors looming overhead. He'd aged a bit since the picture on the back of his books, but I still recognized him, and he still looked consid-erably younger than his fifty-five years. His hair, which he wore combed back, was gray-ing, but his hairline was robustly intact. (I notice these things.) He was about my height and lean, wearing a slightly oversized blazer with a T-shirt underneath. He greeted me warmly, with a voice that had a soft quality to it, perhaps the product of decades in a confined space, discussing people's most private and painful issues.

After the preliminaries — the ordering of beers, my annoying habit of telling anyone who has a medical degree about the educa-tional pedigrees of my wife and parents — we got down to business.

Conditioned as I was by my time with the self-help gurus, I started by asking Epstein flat out whether his life had been radically

180

and grandly transformed by his embrace of Buddhism. For a nanosecond he looked at me like I was crazy, but then he caught himself. He didn't quite laugh at me; he was too polite for that. Instead, he explained that he, like everyone else, got sad, angry, obsessive, you name it — the entire range of emotions, negative and positive.

"Are you always able to stay in the moment?"

"Eh, I try to remain aware of my surroundings," he said, but he admitted he didn't always succeed.

I pushed him on some of the Buddhist metaphysics. "Do you believe in reincarnation?" I asked.

"It's nice," he said, shrugging his shoulders. This was not a dogmatic individual.

It hit me that what I had on my hands here was a previously undiscovered species: a normal human being. Epstein, it appeared to me, was the anti-Tolle, the anti-Chopra. Not a guru in the popular sense of the word, just a regular guy with whom I was having a drink on a Friday night.

We started to talk about his background. He, too, had grown up in the Boston area. His dad was also a doctor. He didn't have some fancy backstory, à la Tolle or Chopra. No sudden, late-night spiritual awakening, no hearing of voices. He'd discovered Buddhism after signing up for an Introduction to World Religion course during his freshman year in college because a girl he liked was also in the class. His fling with the girl didn't last (although he did end up dating her roommate), but he did develop an immediate and abiding interest in the dharma, which resonated with him after a lifelong struggle with feelings of emptiness and unreality, and questions about whether he really mattered.

I explained to him that I was drawn to Buddhism for the exact opposite reasons. Perhaps unsurprisingly for a man who appeared on television for a living, the question of whether I mattered had never occurred to me. I did not struggle, as Mark did, with feelings of being empty or unreal. "On the contrary," I said, only half-jokingly, "I feel all too real. I still kinda have a residual suspicion from childhood that the whole world is laid out for my benefit and nothing happens out of my line of sight. Does that place me at a disadvantage in terms of being a Buddhist?"

He thought this was hilarious. "Absolutely not," he said, laughing. "Your personality and mine are really different. When I'm thinking about it, it's from a much more introverted place. You're talking from an extroverted place. There's an energy there, an enthusiasm there, a rambunctiousness there." Buddhism, he said, could be helpful for both personality types.

I asked what a beginner should do to get deeper into this world. I didn't want to be a Buddhist, per se; I just wanted to better manage my ego. He told me how, after that initial religion class at Harvard, he had fallen in with a bunch of young people who were also interested in Eastern spirituality. Many of these people had gone on to become influential teachers and writers, who'd helped popularize the dharma in America. He suggested I read some of their books, and he started ticking off names. As I madly typed notes into my BlackBerry for future reference, it was impossible not to notice that nearly all of these names were Jewish: Goldstein, Goleman, Kornfield, Salzberg. "This is a whole subculture," he said. The little cabal even had a nickname: the "Jew-Bus."

It sounded like a remarkable group. They had all met at elite Northeast universities and also while taking exotic, druggy romps through the subcontinent. Mark theorized that many of these young Jewish people, having been raised in secular environments, felt a spiritual hole in their lives. He also acknowledged that the Jewish penchant for anxiety probably played a role in their collective attraction to Buddhism. Over the ensuing decades, the Jew-Bus had been a major force in figuring out how to translate the wisdom of the East for a Western audience — mostly by making it less hierarchical and devotional. Mark mentioned that he and some of his peers taught Buddhist-themed seminars around town, where they gave talks and answered questions. "Go to some events," he advised, "until you get bored."

I laughed. I liked this guy. This man whose picture I had reflexively rejected turned out to be somebody with whom I could see myself being friends. We were a bit of an odd pair, to be sure, but there was a certain compatibility, too. He was a professional listener; I was a professional talker. We both had the whole Boston–New York–Jewish cultural affinity thing. He didn't feel foreign, like Tolle and Chopra. He could have been one of my uncles. I wanted to be his friend, but what I really wanted was to figure out how to get what he appeared to have. Not some self-conscious, allegedly unbreakable equanimity, but a quiet confidence, an easy charm. There was no denial of his neuroses;

he seemed to find them amusing rather than enervating.

Normally at this point in the conversation — at least with a Tolle or a Chopra — I'd have been asking for practical advice and in return getting a blizzard of nonanswers. Mark, however, had a very explicit prescription. This is where the Buddhists diverged quite dramatically from self-help: They had an actual, practical program. It wasn't expensive gimcrackery. No spendy seminars, no credit cards required. It was totally free. It was a radical internal jujitsu move that was supposed to allow you to face the asshole in your head directly, and peacefully disarm him. Problem was, I found what they were proposing to be repellent.

Chapter 6
The Power of Negative Thinking

My abiding distaste for anything associated with hippies or the New Age dates back to the mid-1970s when I was about five years old. My parents, still not having sloughed off the cultural residue of the Age of Aquarius, sent me to a children's yoga class at a local elementary school. I showed up wearing Toughskins, the indestructible children's jeans that had been recently introduced by Sears. The teacher, who looms in my memory like an airy-fairy praying mantis, pronounced my pants to be insufficiently flexible for the exercises we'd be doing. In front of all the other little kids, she made me strip down and do sun salutations in my tighty-whities.

My early childhood traumas — which also included compulsory camping trips and visits to musty health food stores — were compounded by my years at Colby College, a small liberal arts school in central Maine, where I was repeatedly forced to listen to Jerry Garcia's interminable guitar noodling by hacky sack–playing, do-rag-and Teva-wearing Deadheads from the suburbs of Massachusetts and Connecticut.

All of which left me in a tricky position vis-à-vis Buddhism. Epstein et al. argued that the only way to tame the monkey mind, to truly glimpse impermanence and defeat our habitual tendency toward clinging, was to meditate — and I had absolutely no intention of following their advice. Meditation struck me as the distillation of everything that sucked hardest about the granola lifestyle. I pictured myself seated in an unbearable cross-legged position (my disavowal of yoga having left me less limber than I would have liked) in a room that smelled like feet, with a group of smug "practitioners" ringing bells, ogling crystals, intoning *om,* and attempting to float off into some sort of cosmic goo. My attitude was summed up nicely by Alec Baldwin's character on *30 Rock,* who said, "Meditation is a waste of time, like learning French or kissing after sex."

Compounding my resistance was my extremely limited attention span. (Another of the many reasons I went into TV.) I assumed there was no way my particular mind

— whirring at best, at worst a whirlwind — could ever stop thinking.

This stalemate between the dharma and me might have dragged on indefinitely, but then a month after my man-date with Epstein, I happened to go see my shrink. I was reluctant to tell Dr. Brotman about my budding interest in Buddhism because, like me, he had an aversion to sloppy sentimentality; it's part of why we were simpatico. But when I fessed up, he responded by telling me about a former colleague of his from Harvard who had written a bestselling book about the health benefits of meditation. Brotman seemed to think it might do me some good.

"Yeah, I'm pretty sure that's not for me," I said. Then, as I sat there absorbing his surprising response, I recalled aloud how, on the first day we met, he had used an animal analogy to explain how someone like me needed to not only refrain from drugs but also engage in careful mental and physical upkeep in order to stay balanced.

"When you say you think meditation might be good for me, is that because of the time you told me I needed to treat myself like a stallion?"

He started laughing and shaking his head. "I never said stallion. I said *thoroughbred.*"

Whatever: semantics. I went ahead and read the book he was referring to by Brotman's friend. The doctor's theory was that, in modern life, our ancient fight-or-flight mechanism was being triggered too frequently — in traffic jams, meetings with our bosses, etc. — and that this was contributing to the epidemic of heart disease. Even if the confrontations were themselves minor, our bodies didn't know that; they reacted as if they were in kill-or-be-killed scenarios, releasing toxic stress chemicals into the bloodstream. The doctor had done studies showing that meditation could reverse the effects of stress and lower blood pressure — which the hypochondriac in me found deeply appealing.

I then read a few books about what Buddhist meditation actually involved, and learned that you didn't need to wear robes, chant Sanskrit phrases, or listen to Cat Stevens. Perhaps my attitude on this matter was yet another example of my reaching hasty conclusions. My resistance was starting to crack.

Saint Paul, the notorious murderer of Christians, had a conversion experience on the road to Damascus. Nixon, the devout anti-Communist, electrified the world by traveling to China. The sudden renunciation of everything one has previously stood for is a well-established part of the human repertoire. Mine came in a stolen moment on the floor of a beach house.

It was the last weekend in August, and Bianca and I were sharing a big, old, converted barn with a group of friends. The people we were leasing it from, a pair of retired college professors, had rather idiosyncratically decorated the place with antique farm equipment, including sickles, axes, and pitchforks, which were hanging precariously from the rafters and from pretty much every inch of wall space. In addition to the elaborate arrays of saws, scissors, and hammers, there was a barrel filled with wooden rakes.

One afternoon, I was out by the pool, after having just finished reading yet another book about Buddhist meditation. The thought popped into my head: *Should I try this?* I was in a weakened state. Tenderized by the scientific evidence, and with my reference points for normalcy scrambled by months of marinating in Buddhism, I decided: *Damn it, let's give it a shot. Carpe diem, and whatnot.*

While my housemates clearly had a high tolerance for kitsch — given their willingness to live in a house named "Barn Again" — I was not at all sure they were open-minded about meditation, and I had no desire to find out. I sneaked off to our bedroom to give it a try.

The instructions were reassuringly simple:

1. Sit comfortably. You don't have to be cross-legged. Plop yourself in a chair, on a cushion, on the floor — wherever. Just make sure your spine is reasonably straight.

2. Feel the sensations of your breath as it goes in and out. Pick a spot: nostrils, chest, or gut. Focus your attention there and really try to *feel* the breath. If it helps to direct your attention, you can use a soft mental note, like "in" and "out."

3. This one, according to all of the books I'd read, was the biggie. Whenever your attention wanders, just forgive yourself and gently come back to the breath. You don't need to clear the mind of all thinking; that's pretty much impossible. (True, when you are focused on the feeling of the breath, the chatter will momentarily cease, but this won't last too long.) The whole game is to catch your mind wandering and then come back to the breath, over and over again.

I sat on the floor with my back up against the bed and my legs sprawled straight out in front of me. I set the alarm on my Black-Berry to go off in five minutes and let rip.

In.

Out.

In.

Shrubbery. *I like that word.*

Why, from an evolutionary perspective, do we like the smell of our own filth?

Get in the game, dude.

In.

Out.

My butt hurts. Let me just shift a little bit here.

In.

Idea for old-school hip-hop show: Rap Van Winkle.

Now I have an itch on the ball of my left foot.

Where do gerbils run wild? Would I describe myself as more of a baller or a shot caller? What was the best thing before *sliced bread?*

And so it went until the alarm went off. By which point it felt like an eternity had passed.

When I opened my eyes, I had an entirely different attitude about meditation. I didn't like it, per se, but I now respected it. This was not just some hippie time-passing technique, like Ultimate Frisbee or making

God's Eyes. It was a rigorous brain exercise: rep after rep of trying to tame the runaway train of the mind. The repeated attempt to bring the compulsive thought machine to heel was like holding a live fish in your hands. Wrestling your mind to the ground, repeatedly hauling your attention back to the breath in the face of the inner onslaught required genuine grit. This was a badass endeavor.

I resolved to do it every day. I started getting up a little early each morning and banging out ten minutes, sitting on the floor of our living room with my back up against the couch. When I was on the road, I meditated on the floor of hotel rooms.

It didn't get any easier. Almost immediately upon sitting down, I'd be beset by itches. Then there was the fatigue: a thick ooze, a sludge-like torpor sliding down my forehead. Even when the itches and fatigue lifted, I was left contending with the unstoppable fire hose of thoughts. Focusing on the breath as a way to temporarily stop the thinking was like using a broom to sweep a floor crawling with cockroaches. You could clear the space briefly, but then the bugs came marauding back in. I knew I was supposed to just forgive myself, but I found that to be extremely difficult. Every time I got lost in thought, I went into a mini shame spiral. My wanderings were so tawdry and banal. Is this really what I was thinking about all the time? Lunch? Whether I needed a haircut? My unresolved anger at the Academy for awarding Best Picture to *Dances with Wolves* instead of *Goodfellas*?

When I wasn't lost in random musings, I was obsessing about how much time was left, dying for the ordeal to be over. It was like that *Simpsons* episode where they showed the world-record holder for longest consecutive case of the hiccups. In between hiccups, she would say, "Kill me." By the end of ten minutes my jaw was often gritted from the effort. It reminded me of how one of our cats, Steve, who had a serious gum disease, would sometimes literally try to run away from himself when he was in pain. Similarly, when the alarm would go off at the end of a meditation session, I often would bolt out of my seated position, as if I could somehow physically escape the commotion of my own mind.

There were always happy, round-faced statues of the Buddha out front at airport spas and Chinese restaurants. (Although, I had come to learn that the "laughing Buddha" is actually a medieval Chinese monk who somehow became conflated in the

Western imagination with the historical Buddha, who only ate one meal a day and was most likely a bag of skin and bones.) His image was bedazzled onto T-shirts sold in the gift shop at my gym. The word *Zen* had become synonymous with "mellow." But this was all false advertising. Buddhist meditation was diabolically hard. Despite its difficulties, though, meditation did offer something huge: an actual method for shutting down the monkey mind, if only for a moment. It was like tricking the furry little gibbon, distracting it with something shiny so it would sit still. Unlike Tolle, who offered very little by way of actionable advice, meditation presented a real remedy, a temporary escape route from the clammy embrace of self-obsession. It may have been miserable, but it was the best — and only — solution I'd heard yet.

Pretty quickly, my efforts began to bear fruit "off the cushion," to use a Buddhist term of art. I started to be able to use the breath to jolt myself back to the present moment — in airport security lines, waiting for elevators, you name it. I found it to be a surprisingly satisfying exercise. Life became a little bit like walking into a familiar room where all the furniture had been rearranged. And I was much better at forgiving myself out in the real world than while actually meditating. Every moment was an opportunity for a do-over. A million mulligans.

Meditation was radically altering my relationship to boredom, something I'd spent my whole life scrambling to avoid. The only advice I ever got from my college adviser, a novelist of minor renown named James Boylan (who later had a sex change operation, changed his name to Jenny, wrote a bestselling book, and appeared on *Oprah*) was to never go anywhere without something to read. I diligently heeded that guidance, taking elaborate precautions to make sure every spare moment was filled with distraction. I scanned my BlackBerry at stoplights, brought reams of work research to read in the doctor's waiting room, and watched videos on my iPhone while riding in taxicabs.

Now I started to see life's in-between moments — sitting at a red light, waiting for my crew to get set up for an interview — as a chance to focus on my breath, or just take in my surroundings. As soon as I began playing this game, I really noticed how much sleepwalking I did, how powerfully my mind propelled me forward or backward. Mostly, I saw the world through a scrim of skittering thoughts, which created a kind of buffer between me and reality. As one Buddhist author put it, the "craving to be otherwise, to be elsewhere" permeated my whole life.

The net effect of meditation, plus trying to stay present during my daily life, was striking. It was like anchoring myself to an underground aquifer of calm. It became a way to steel myself as I moved through the world. On Sunday nights, in the seconds right before the start of *World News,* I would take a few deep breaths and look around the room — out at the milling stage crew, up at the ceiling rigged with lights — grounding myself in reality before launching into the unreality of bellowing into a camera with unseen millions behind it.

All of this was great, of course, but as it turns out, it wasn't actually the main point.

Buddhism's secret sauce went by a hopelessly anodyne name: "mindfulness." In a nutshell, mindfulness is the ability to recognize what is happening in your mind right now — anger, jealousy, sadness, the pain of a stubbed toe, whatever — without getting carried away by it. According to the Buddha, we have three habitual responses to everything we experience. We want it, reject it, or we zone out. Cookies: I want. Mosquitoes: I reject. The safety instructions the flight attendants read aloud on an airplane: I zone out. Mindfulness is a fourth option, a way to view the contents of our mind with nonjudgmental remove. I found this theory elegant, but utterly unfeasible.

On the cushion, the best opportunities to learn mindfulness are when you experience itches or pain. Instead of scratching or shifting position, you're supposed to just sit there and impartially witness the discomfort. The instruction is simply to employ what the teachers call "noting," applying a soft mental label: *itching, itching* or *throbbing, throbbing.* For me, this was infernally difficult. A daggerlike tingle would appear under my thigh, a little pinprick portal to Hades, and I would grit my teeth and question the choices I was making in life. I couldn't suspend judgment; I hated it.

The idea is that, once you've mastered things like itches, eventually you'll be able to apply mindfulness to thoughts and emotions. This nonjudgmental noting — *Oh, that's a blast of self-pity . . . Oh, that's me ruminating about work* — is supposed to sap much of the power, the emotional charge, out of the contents of consciousness.

It was easy to see how scalable mindfulness could be. For instance, it'd be late in the day, and I'd get a call from the *World News* rim telling me the story I'd spent hours scrambling to produce was no longer going to air in tonight's show. My usual response was to think to myself, *I'm angry.* Reflexively, I would then fully inhabit that thought — and actually *become* angry. I would then give the person on the other end of the line some unnecessary chin music, even though I knew intellectually that they usually had a very good reason for killing the piece. In the end, I was left feeling bad about having expended energy on a story that didn't air, and also feeling guilty for having been needlessly salty. The point of mindfulness was to short-circuit what had always been a habitual, mindless chain re-action.

Once I started thinking about how this whole system of seemingly spontaneous psychological combustion worked, I realized how blindly impelled — impaled, even — I was by my ego. I spent so much time, as one Buddhist writer put it, "drifting un-aware on a surge of habitual impulses." This is what led me on the misadventures of war, drugs, and panic. It's what propelled me to eat when I wasn't hungry or get snippy with Bianca because I was stewing about something that happened in the office. Mindfulness represented an alternative to living reactively.

This was not some mental parlor trick. Mindfulness is an inborn trait, a birthright. It is, one could argue, what makes us human. Taxonomically, we are classified as *Homo sapiens sapiens,* "the man who thinks and knows he thinks." Our minds have this other capability — a bonus level, to put it in gamerspeak — that no one ever tells us about in school. (Not here in the West, at least.) We can do more than just think; we also have the power simply to be aware of things — without judgment, without the ego. This is not to denigrate thinking, just to say that thinking without awareness can be a harsh master.

By way of example: you can be *mindful* of hunger pangs, but you *think* about where to get your next meal and whether it will involve pork products. You can be *mindful* of the pressure in your bladder telling you it's time to pee, but you *think* about whether the frequency of your urination means you're getting old and need a prostate exam. There's a difference between the raw sensations we experience and the mental spinning we do in reaction to said stimuli.

The Buddhists had a helpful analogy here.

Picture the mind like a waterfall, they said: the water is the torrent of thoughts and emotions; mindfulness is the space behind the waterfall. Again, elegant theory — but, easier said than done.

There were many areas of my life in which I badly needed this mindfulness thing. Eating, for example. After quitting drugs, food became my replacement dopamine rush. Once I met Bianca, the situation got worse, because I was also happy and homebound. She would cook large meals of pasta followed by fresh-baked cookies. For a bantamweight, I could crush plate after plate. I would tell myself I would be moderate, but once the frenzy started, I couldn't stop. I was feeding the pleasure centers of my brain rather than my stomach, and I was particularly bad with dessert. The fact that my parents never let me have sugar when I was a kid produced a lifelong obsession. (The same thing happened with television, ironically.) I could eat piles of cookies, my teeth scything through the chewy goodness. Airports were particularly dangerous. Auntie Anne, that seductress, would lure me in with a bouquet of Cinnamon Sugar Stix. As my paunch grew, it became the source of nearly as much angst as the recession of my hairline. Neither vanity nor mindfulness helped, though. It wasn't uncommon for me to get directly up from meditating and stuff my face, enter into a postprandial remorse jag, and take a nap.

But where I really could have used a nice dose of mindfulness was in dealing with the events set in motion after I received a call from Amy Entelis, the senior vice president for talent development. Amy was in charge of recruiting and managing all the anchors and correspondents. She reached me when I was on my way to the airport for a story. This was in early September of 2009, about a month after I'd started meditating. She had big news. Later in the day, she told me, management would announce that Charlie Gibson had decided to step down as the anchor of *World News.* They would simultaneously announce that Diane Sawyer would be leaving *Good Morning America* to take over the evenings. This was huge. I was happy for Diane. She'd initially agreed to host *GMA* a full decade ago on a temporary basis, but she'd performed so well that the bosses repeatedly cajoled her into sticking around. Now the brightest star in our news division would be ascending to the Big Chair, a promotion many of us felt she richly deserved.

It didn't take long, though, for me to shift into what-does-it-all-mean-for-me mode. This announcement would surely set off an avalanche of a magnitude akin to what happened after Peter Jennings died. Many dominoes were about to fall. Diane's departure from the mornings meant the brass would probably have to remake the anchor team on *GMA,* which would have ripple effects throughout the on-air ranks. What was coming was a radical reshuffling of the dramatis personae. I had been anchoring *World News* on Sundays for about four years now and still loved it, but if new jobs were going to be opening up, I wanted in. My desire for forward momentum — even when the lack thereof was illusory — roughly resembled that of Woody Allen in that classic scene from *Annie Hall* where he breaks up with Diane Keaton. "A relationship, I think, is like a shark," he says. "It has to constantly move forward or it dies. And I think what we got on our hands is a dead shark."

Not long after the Gibson-Sawyer news, the situation intensified. We got word of two other departures: John Stossel, the co-anchor of *20/20,* and Martin Bashir, one of the three anchors of *Nightline.* The latter development was of especial interest to me. After years of working as a correspondent on *Nightline,* I had begun making it known that I would love to join the staff as an anchor. It seemed like the perfect job for me, the type of gig I could ride all the way to retirement. I genuinely enjoyed the rush of "crashing" short pieces for *GMA* and *World News* — especially in breaking news situations — but these stories were basically haikus: 90- to 120-second-long recitations of the day's events. On *Nightline,* the pieces ran anywhere from four to eight minutes. If the story was really good, they might give you the entire half hour.

It wasn't just the length of the stories that I liked, but also the variety. The show matched my catholic interests. On any given night, they were as likely to do a hard-hitting investigation as they were a profile of a movie star or a story about doggy fat camps. In recent months, *Nightline* had given me even more chances to slake my thirst for comforting the afflicted and afflicting the comfortable. I'd gone off searching for endangered tree kangaroos in Papua New Guinea, hunting down American sex tourists in Cambodia, and confronting pastors in the Congo who made money by convincing parents to submit their children to painful exorcisms.

Problem was, there was another contender. Bill Weir, the weekend *GMA* anchor. Bill had joined ABC News in 2004 from the local affiliate in Los Angeles, where he was the sports guy. He exuded an old-school and sometimes brooding cool. Notwithstanding his lack of hard-news pedigree, Bill very quickly established himself as an excellent journalist, covering major breaking news as well as producing amazingly inventive feature stories.

My favorite example of the latter was Bill's profile of Don LaFontaine, the guy who did all the voice-overs for movie trailers. LaFontaine's voice was so deep that when he delivered his classic lines ("In a world . . ."), it sounded like he had a third testicle. Instead of just doing a traditional sit-down interview, Bill had LaFontaine follow him around L.A., narrating his life through a handheld microphone. The best scene took place at an outdoor café, where Bill was nonchalantly eyeballing the menu.

LaFontaine: *"He's the world's deadliest assassin. His identity is a secret — even from himself. This summer, love . . . gets lethal."*
Weir: *"I'm thinking about getting an omelet."*

LaFontaine: *"I'm thinking about getting a salad."*
Weir: *"Is it too early for a salad?"*
[cut to a close-up of LaFontaine] *"It's never too early . . . for a salad."*

It was gingerly suggested to me by the bosses that perhaps I should also consider the possibility of moving into Bill's spot on weekend *GMA* if he got the nod for *Nightline*. Initially, I dismissed this as a lateral move, but was ultimately convinced to reconsider. This assignment, I came to realize, would not only quadruple my airtime (from a half hour on Sundays to two full hours on Saturdays and Sundays) but it would also provide me with a chance to try a different type of broadcasting, to break out of the mold of the staid, Jennings-esque anchorman. Morning television wasn't just one guy and a teleprompter; it was live, loose, and largely unscripted. Moreover, mornings were where the action was in network news. *GMA* had the younger viewers that advertisers wanted to reach, which made the show the profit center for the entire news division.

I said I was up for it, but made it clear that my first choice was still *Nightline*. I was now in the tricky position of arguing for both jobs simultaneously — and neither was a lock. I kept picturing the worst possible outcomes. *Prapañca,* in full effect: *No promotion → Eventually lose my hair and, as a consequence, all future job prospects → Flophouse in Duluth.*

I was granted an audience with David Westin, where I would be given a chance to plead my case. At the appointed hour, I walked one flight up from my office to the Fifth Floor. After the requisite wait on the couch outside his office, I was whisked inside by his secretary, and greeted by David's wide grin and firm handshake.

He listened politely as I made my case, first for *Nightline,* then for *GMA.* He asked some smart questions, which I answered to the best of my ability. I thought I did okay, but it was hard to tell; like all skilled managers, David was a master at uttering a lot of words without actually committing himself to a position. I knew not to push too hard, to minimize the displays of plumage. Anyone's affability can turn brittle under too much pressure.

Our business concluded, the rest of the meeting moved on to non-work issues. Here things became very relaxed. There was banter and badinage, and I left feeling deceptively buoyant. This lasted about ninety seconds. By the time I'd made it downstairs to my office, I had thoroughly soured. Given a moment to reflect, I realized that David had said absolutely nothing concrete or reassuring. In fact, I came away with the vague sense that he was going to pass me over. Worse, I knew it was possible that he wouldn't make his decision for quite a while.

If ever there was a good time to see if I could summon some mindfulness, this seemed like it. I tried meditating on the couch in my office, but it didn't work. I just couldn't clamber up behind the waterfall. Every time I tried to watch my thoughts, to nonjudgmentally observe my frustration over this professional limbo, I didn't know what to look for — or how to look at it. Wasn't "noting" just another form of thinking? *What the hell am I supposed to be seeing here?*

And wait a minute — wasn't there a practical value to disquiet? Just because my thoughts didn't have any inherent reality didn't preclude them from being connected to real-world problems that need to be dealt with.

Here I was back at square one, pondering the same questions I'd been pondering since first reading Eckhart Tolle. I was still unshakably certain that looking at a problem from all angles and searching for the right move gave me an edge. And yet I was also still concerned that too much worrying was driving me nuts.

I spent the ensuing weeks in a bit of a funk. I tried to "note" it, but I didn't know if I was being mindful or just indulging it. I decided it was time to follow a piece of advice from my new friend Mark Epstein.

The event was held in a huge, nondescript function hall at the Sheraton Towers in midtown Manhattan, and as soon as I got there I regretted it. The place had all the charm of an offtrack betting parlor. It was packed with mostly middle-aged women wearing dangly earrings and intricately arranged scarves. Any one of them could have been the yoga teacher who made me strip down to my underwear as a child.

I'd seen worse, of course, in the self-help trenches, but this was different. I was here at this three-day Buddhist conference not as a journalistic observer, but as a paying customer who'd come for his own personal purposes, a thought that propelled just the tiniest bit of vomit into my mouth.

Making matters worse, this was proving to be very embarrassing in front of a new friend of mine, who I'd roped into coming along. His name was Jason. He was the drummer for one of my favorite bands, Mates of State. They were a husband-and-wife indie act who wrote infectious pop songs about suburban angst. I had done a feature story on them for Sunday *World News,* focusing on how they took their two young children on tour and wrote a blog about it, called *Band on the Diaper Run.* After the story aired, Bianca and I struck up a friendship with Jason and his wife, Kori. Jason was one of the few people to whom I had successfully evangelized about Buddhism. Interestingly, he voiced a concern about meditation that seemed to be a corollary to my ongoing security/insecurity conundrum. He worried that if he became too happy, it would defang his angst and disable his ability to write music. A comedy writer friend of mine had said something similar — that he was worried meditation would make him less "judgmental," and therefore less funny.

Here in the hall, Jason — who was six-foot-three, had fashionably long bangs, and could pull off wearing skinny jeans — stood out like a sore thumb. I was having a mild freak-out. I had been talking up Mark Epstein to Jason for months, and now Mark was up on the stage, seated alongside two other Buddhist teachers, presiding over this horror show.

The opening speaker was a woman in her fifties named Tara Brach. She had long brown hair and pleasant Semitic features. She was holding forth in a creamy, cloying tone. The style was astonishingly affected — artificially soft and slow, as if she were trying to give you a Reiki massage with her voice. She exhorted us to love ourselves, "invited" us to close our eyes and "trust in the ocean-ness, in the vastness, in the mystery, in the awareness, in the love — so that you could really sense, 'Nothing is wrong with me.' " I couldn't bear to look over at Jason, who I imagined must be silently cursing my name. Brach closed with a poem, then a dramatic pause and, finally, a self-serious, sotto voce "Thank you."

Then Mark jumped in and saved the night. "Well, I'm gonna give you a slightly different perspective," he said, with a mischievous glint in his eye, "which is that, actually, there's plenty still wrong with me." People started laughing, and a tight smile came over Tara's face. Jason, who'd seemed oddly detached — but not in a Buddhist way — sat up in his seat.

"People come to me a lot feeling like they

ought to be loving themselves, and I actually counsel against it," he said. His delivery was off-the-cuff and shtick-free. In stark contrast to Brach, he argued that we needed to actively get in touch with our ugly side. "Mindfulness gives us a way to examine our self-hatred without trying to make it go away, without trying to love it particularly." Just being mindful of it, he said, could be "tremendously liberating."

The idea of leaning into what bothered us struck me as radical, because our reflex is usually to flee, to go buy something, eat something, or get faded on polypharmacy. But, as the Buddhists say, "The only way out is through." Another analogy: When a big wave is coming at you, the best way not to get pummeled is to dive right in. This jibed with what I had learned through my own painful, public experience after returning from Iraq, using drugs, and losing my mind on television; when you squelch something, you give it power. Ignorance is not bliss.

Mark's thesis was a direct response to the fears Jason and my comedy writer friend had about meditation leaving them without an edge. If anything, mindfulness brought you closer to your neuroses, acting as a sort of Doppler radar, mapping your mental microclimates, making you more insightful, not less. It was the complete opposite of the reckless hope preached by the self-helpers. It was the power of negative thinking.

As I sat there in the audience, I was feeling proud of Mark, increasingly enthralled with the theory of mindfulness — and hopelessly frustrated by my inability to put it to work.

To my profound surprise, the person who unlocked this mystery for me was Tara Brach.

Driven by some unfathomable masochistic urge, and even though I knew Mark wouldn't be speaking, I had dragged myself back to the ballroom for the second day of the conference. At first, Brach was driving me nuts with all of her ostentatious head-bowing, bell-ringing, and Namaste-saying. But then she redeemed herself.

She nailed the method for applying mindfulness in acute situations, albeit with a somewhat dopey acronym: RAIN.

R: recognize
A: allow
I: investigate
N: non-identification

"Recognize" was self-explanatory. Using my David Westin example, in those moments after our — even in the best light — quite ambivalent meeting, job number one was simply to acknowledge my feelings. "It's like agreeing to pause in the face of what's here, and just acknowledge the actuality," said Brach. The first step is admitting it.

"Allow" is where you lean into it. The Buddhists were always talking about how you have to "let go," but what they really meant is "let it be." Or, as Brach put it in her inimitable way, "offer the inner whisper of 'yes.' "

The third step — "investigate" — is where things got truly practical. Sticking with the Westin example — after I've acknowledged my feelings and let them be, the next move would be to check out how they're affecting my body. Is it making my face hot, my chest buzzy, my head throb? This strategy sounded intuitively correct to me, especially given that I was a guy whose undiagnosed postwar depression had manifest itself in flulike symptoms.

The final step — "non-identification" — meant seeing that just because I was feeling angry or jealous or fearful, that did not render me a permanently angry or jealous person. These were just passing states of mind.

The Brach Plan seemed eminently workable to me. And as grating as she'd seemed at first, I now found something comforting about her manner. She was, after all, a trained professional — in both Buddhism and psychotherapy — who had spent her life helping people. I realized, with a hot blast of self-directed opprobrium that, yet again, I had been unfair.

Just a few weeks later, I put her advice to work, and got behind the waterfall.

I was having a bad day. I was worrying again about whether I'd get the promotion — and then beating myself up for said worrying. I hit the couch in my office again, but this time I tried Brach's RAIN technique, especially the bit about investigating how my inner turmoil was playing out physically.

Noting: chest buzzing.

Head pounding.

Flophouse in Duluth in six months, guaranteed.

Noting: worrying.

Chest buzzing, pounding.

Earlobes hot.

I didn't try to stop it; I just felt it. I was "allowing," "letting be," and "investigating."

215

Buzzing. Tension. Buzzing.
I'm doing it! I'm being mindful of my angst!
Noting: self-congratulation.

The effect was something like the picture-in-picture feature on a television. Normally, my mental clatter dominated the whole screen. When I pressed the mindfulness button, though, I had some perspective. My thoughts were playing out in a larger space, and while they still burned, they burned a little less. The process felt, in a sense, journalistic. (Or at least it conformed to what we reporters tell ourselves we are: objective, dispassionate — fair and balanced, if you will.)

It was a revelation: the voice in my head, which I'd always taken so seriously, suddenly lost much of its authority. It was like peering behind the curtain and seeing that the Wizard of Oz was a frightened, frail old man. Not only did it ease my agita in the moment, but it suddenly imbued me with a sense of hope about better handling whatever garbage my ego coughed up going forward.

A success, yes — but I still had questions. While mindfulness was clearly very powerful, it nonetheless did not erase my real-world problems. So what had really changed? I added a new entry into a file I had created on my BlackBerry, labeled "Questions for Mark."

We were back at the Tribeca Grand, where I had talked Mark into meeting me for another beer summit. As he kicked off his man-clogs and folded his legs up under his butt on his chair, I was reminded of what an odd pair we made. Before I could even get to my questions, I noticed that he had an eager look on his face that clearly signaled he had something he wanted to tell me.

He then mentioned with a conspiratorial grin that he'd just come from a prescheduled phone meeting with Tara Brach. She'd requested they talk; she was not happy with his contradicting her onstage. Mark managed to relate this juicy little nugget without seeming mean-spirited. I argued strenuously that his obligation was not to her but to the audience. He seemed appreciative. In any event, he and Brach had apparently smoothed it all out in the end.

When I launched into my question about whether mindfulness left you flaccid in the face of life's thorny problems, he circled right back to the Brach incident.

"That's the same thing," he said.

Up on that stage in the Hilton ballroom,

Mark had disliked what Brach was saying. Instead of mindlessly criticizing her, though, he calmly and tactfully disagreed. Seeing a problem clearly does not prevent you from taking action, he explained. Acceptance is not passivity. Sometimes we are justifiably displeased. What mindfulness does is create some space in your head so you can, as the Buddhists say, "respond" rather than simply "react." In the Buddhist view, you can't control what comes up in your head; it all arises out of a mysterious void. We spend a lot of time judging ourselves harshly for feelings that we had no role in summoning. The only thing you can control is how you handle it.

Bingo: respond not react. This, it struck me, was the whole ball of wax. This was why, as I'd recently learned, so many surprising people had become meditators. Basketball coach Phil Jackson, Supreme Court Justice Stephen Breyer, Ford CEO Bill Ford, Weezer frontman Rivers Cuomo. Even the rapper 50 Cent. Even Tom Bergeron. A successful dotcom friend of mine said that once he started meditating he noticed he was always the calmest person in the room during heated meetings. He called it a "superpower."

Mark said this had a direct bearing on my

ongoing work situation. "Sitting with your feelings won't always solve your problems or make your feelings go away," he said, "but it can make you stop acting blindly. Maybe you won't be sullen with your boss, for example."

As I sipped my beer in the swank hotel bar with the shrink who I'd forced into doing bespoke guru work for me, I realized that the smart play in my current professional circumstances was to just sit tight. I had made my case; the only thing I could do now was put my head down, work hard, and hope for the best. In other words: respond — don't react.

Mark also pointed out that mindfulness was a skill — one that would improve as I got more meditation hours under my belt. In that spirit, he said I should consider going on a retreat. The type of thing Mark was talking about was much more demanding than the Buddhist seminar with Tara Brach. He was recommending a silent, ten-day slog, where I would be cloistered at a Buddhist retreat center with dozens of other meditators. No talking, no television, no beer — just meditation, all day. When I indicated that I would rather lie down in traffic, he reassured me, saying it would be hard but worth it. Specifically, he recommended that I sign up for a retreat led by someone named Joseph Goldstein, who Mark referred to as "his" meditation teacher. He spoke about this Goldstein character in the most glowing of terms, which intrigued me. I figured if a guy I revered revered another guy, I should probably check that other guy out.

As we were paying the bill, I said, "If you're up for it, I'd love to get together every month or two."

"Sure," he said, looking up from the remains of his drink and meeting my gaze. With uncontrived sincerity he said, "I want to know you." That was one of the nicest things anyone had ever said to me. After we'd finished, as we said good-bye, he gave me a hug. It was touching, and I appreciated his willingness to be my friend, but there was no way in hell I was going on a retreat.

Then Deepak reentered the scene. Via an aggressive email and text campaign, he had convinced me and the executives at *Nightline* to produce another Face-Off. This time, the debate would be between Chopra and his longtime nemesis, Michael Shermer, a former fundamentalist Christian turned militant atheist and professional debunker of pseudoscience. Shermer was the one who, as the head of the Skeptics Society, had decided to plaster Deepak on the cover of *Skeptic* magazine several years prior, with the headline "Doctor Woo Woo."

The subject of the debate was whether God and science were compatible, which would be an interesting twist on the usual is-there-a-God debate, since Deepak didn't believe in what he called the "dead white man" God of the Bible, but rather in an indescribable intelligence at the heart of the universe, a view he believed science could support. In true *Nightline* fashion, we gave the event an understated title: "Does God Have a Future?"

One of the first people I ran into when I got to the debate site — an auditorium at the California Institute of Technology in Pasadena — was Sam Harris, who'd published a pair of acerbic, bestselling anti-religion books, making him one of the heroes of a budding atheist movement. We had actually met back in 2007, when I was shooting a story at the American Atheists convention in Washington, D.C. His writings were so controversial that he lived in an undisclosed location and often traveled with security. I had a visual memory of interviewing him amid vendors of bumper stickers with slogans like JESUS, SAVE ME FROM YOUR FOLLOWERS. I recalled liking the guy; he was much more pleasant than his prose would have suggested.

He was here now, backstage in this auditorium, because Michael Shermer had chosen Sam as his debating partner. (Deepak had chosen a religious scholar named Jean Houston, perhaps best known for helping then first lady Hillary Clinton commune with the spirit of Eleanor Roosevelt.) My positive impression from that first encounter was quickly reaffirmed. Sam and I had the immediate rapport that two semi-Semites with the same last name are bound to have. With his close-cropped Jewfro and a face with just a touch of the shtetl, he reminded me a little bit of my brother. His affect was crisp and serious, but affable. He was dressed in a dark suit and nicely pressed blue shirt. His elegant and clearly very bright wife, Annaka, was with him. As the three of us chatted in Sam's narrow little dressing room, it somehow came up that I was interested in meditation. They both perked up, then admitted that they were, too.

This I wasn't expecting. It turned out that Mr. Atheist had a whole groovy past. As an undergrad at Stanford, Sam had experimented with ecstasy and LSD, had his mind blown, dropped out, and then spent eleven years traveling back and forth between the United States and Asia, where he lived in monasteries and ashrams, studying with various meditation teachers. During that time, he accumulated an aggregate total of roughly two years on silent retreats, meditating for twelve to eighteen hours a day. (Annaka, too, had years of meditation experience, and even worked as a volunteer teaching mindfulness to kids.)

Sam had never tried to hide this part of his past. In fact, as he reminded me, just moments after I had interviewed him at that convention back in 2007 he delivered a controversial speech in which he told the assembled atheists that denying the potential of "spiritual" experiences (he put the word in quotes, arguing it was an embarrassing term, but there were no real alternatives) made them just as ignorant as people who believed in Jesus. "It was the only time I've ever given a speech," he said, "that started with a standing ovation and ended with boos."

Sam truly did not mind pissing people off, though — and that rhetorical bloodlust was on full display at the debate. The hall was packed with partisans from both camps, a thousand people in all. Deepak's opening statement was a vintage Choprian word salad. It included lines like this: "Today, science tells us that the essential nature of reality is nonlocal correlation." As he spoke, our cameras captured Shermer and Harris rolling their eyes. Deepak wrapped up by calling the people at Caltech the "jihadists and Vatican of conservative and orthodox science."

To which Sam responded, "I would never be tempted to lecture a room full of a thousand people at Caltech about physics. I'm not a physicist, you're not a physicist — and basically every sentence you have uttered demonstrates that." The crowd roared in approval.

As the debate ground on, Deepak made his points while gesticulating and shouting. When others talked, he slumped in his chair, looking annoyed, like he had somewhere better to be, even though he was the one who initiated this whole thing.

When it was over and the audience cleared out and I prepared to take off, I made sure to circle back to Sam and Annaka, who once again raised the subject of meditation. They had a suggestion for me: I should go on a retreat. Recognizing the look of dread on my face, they acknowledged it could be a little tough, but assured me it would be worth it. They knew an amazing teacher, they said. His name: Joseph Goldstein.

It was hard to ignore two brilliant people recommending the same meditation teacher. (Turned out, Sam, too, was old friends with Goldstein, although Sam and Mark had never met.) So when I got home, I promptly read a few books by this purported meditative genius. While the books provided terrific explications of how to employ mindfulness as a way to create space between stimulus and response in everyday life, there was also a lot of talk about reincarnation, psychic powers, and "beings on other planes of existence." I wondered how Sam handled assertions like this one: "There are those even today who have developed the power of mind to see karmic unfolding through past and future lifetimes." Charitably, Goldstein did say if you don't find this stuff credible, it wouldn't affect your chances for "liberation."

Still, I had Mark's and Sam's advice ringing in my ears like a taunt. My curiosity was piqued; a little bit of pride was on the line. If I was in this meditation thing now, I might as well go the distance. I went online and saw that Goldstein was leading a retreat in California, called simply the "July Insight Meditation Retreat." Certainly less grandiose than James Ray's "Spiritual Warrior Retreat." Less expensive, too: about a thousand bucks for ten days.

When I tried to sign up, though, I found to my wonderment that it wasn't so easy to get in. There were so many applicants that slots were awarded through a lottery system. I called Goldstein's people and tried to pull the reporter card. They were unmoved. Now that I couldn't have it, I wanted it even more.

I emailed Sam Harris and asked if he could hook me up. He told me he'd put in a word, but gave no guarantees. (In the course of our email correspondence, I was surprised to learn that the hard-nosed atheist used emoticons.) Since this was the only retreat Goldstein would be leading anytime soon, I was now in the awkward position of stressing over getting into an event designed to help me manage stress, and that I was sure I would dislike intensely.

Not long thereafter, I got another chance to test my mindfulness skills under duress. Amy Entelis called to tell me that they were giving the *Nightline* job to Bill Weir. There was still no word on whether I'd gotten

226

GMA, and no date certain for a decision. So I would be in a special kind of purgatory for the foreseeable future.

The timing was interesting, though. The very next day, thanks to Sam, I was headed to California. As he put it in an email, he had "toyed with the laws of karma" and gotten me into the retreat.

CHAPTER 7
RETREAT

It was the longest, most exquisite high of my life, but the hangover came first.

Day One

Here's what I'm mindful of right now: pervasive dread.

I'm sitting in a café in San Francisco, having what I assume will be my last decent meal before I check in for the Zen Death March. As I eat, I leaf listlessly through the mimeographed information sheets sent by the people at the retreat center. The place is called Spirit Rock, which sounds like a New Age version of "Fraggle Rock," populated by crystal-wielding Muppets. The writing is abristle with the type of syrupy language that drives me up a wall:

"Retreats offer a sacred space, protected and removed from the world, intended to allow participants to quiet the mind and open the heart."

The sheets request that we "take whatever room is offered," whether it's a single or a double. (This sends unpleasant images dancing through my head of potential roommates who are all gray-haired, pony-tailed, beret-wearing, Wavy Gravy look-alikes.) The chefs will "lovingly prepare" lacto-ovo vegetarian food. We will be assigned daily "yogi jobs," either in house-keeping or the kitchen, or "ringing bells," whatever that means. There's a lengthy list of "What Not to Bring," seemingly written in 1983, which includes beeper watches and "Walkmans." The retreat will be conducted in "noble silence," which means no talking to one another and no communication with the outside world, except in case of emergencies.

The whole ten-days-of-no-talking thing is the detail that everyone I told about the retreat keyed in on. To a man (or woman), the people I had the courage to admit how I was spending my vacation asked something to the effect of, "How can you go without talking for that long?" Silence, however, is the part that worries me the least. I don't imagine there will be many people at the retreat I'll be dying to chat with. What truly scares me is the pain and boredom of sitting and meditating all day every day for ten straight days. For a guy with a bad back and a chronic inability to sit still, this is definitely a suboptimal holiday.

I call a cab for the hour-long ride to northern Marin County. As we cross the Golden Gate, I feel like a lamb leading itself to slaughter. I get an email from Sam saying he's "envious" of the experience I'm about to have. His timing is impeccable. It's an encouraging reminder that, apparently, these retreats can produce remarkable moments. In fact, I recently read a *New York Times* op-ed piece by Robert Wright, a journalist, polemicist, curmudgeon, and agnostic not known for either credulousness or mystical leanings. Wright wrote that he had "just about the most amazing experience" of his life on retreat, which involved finding "a new kind of happiness," and included a "moment of bonding with a lizard."

However, major breakthroughs — known in spiritual circles as "peak experiences" — cannot be guaranteed. What is almost certain, though — and even Sam acknowledged this — is that the first few days will be an ordeal. Classic *prapañca:* I'm casting forward to day two or three, envisioning myself marooned and miserable.

We roll up to Spirit Rock at around four

in the afternoon. As we pull off the main road and onto the campus, I spot a sign that reads YIELD TO THE PRESENT.

Jesus.

The place is beautiful, though, like something out of a French Impressionist painting. We are surrounded by hills covered in pale gold, sun-bleached scrub grass, with clusters of vivid green trees nestled throughout. The center itself is a series of handsome wood structures with Japanese-style roofs, built into the side of a hill.

As I wheel my luggage up to the main office, I catch the first glimpses of my fellow meditators. They are solidly, solidly NPR — card-carrying members of the socks-and-sandals set.

We line up for our room assignments and yogi jobs. (I'm starting to figure out that *yogi* is just another word for "meditator.") I'm told I will be a "pot washer."

Hallelujah: I get a single room, on the second floor of one of the four dorm buildings. The accommodations are spare, but not gross. There's a single bed next to a window. The walls are white. The carpet is tan. There's a mirror and a sink. The communal bathroom is down the hall.

At six o'clock, dinner — and my first big shock: the food is excellent. It's a buffet of smashed-pea dip, just-baked bread, salad with dill dressing, and soup made out of fresh squash.

I wait my turn in line, load up a plate, and suddenly find myself in one of those awkward, high school cafeteria–type situations, in which I don't know where to sit. There are around one hundred of us. The crowd consists overwhelmingly of white baby boomers. A lot of these people seem to know one another — they must be regulars on the West Coast meditation scene. Since we haven't yet been told that we have to stop talking, everyone's kibitzing happily.

I find a spot next to a kindly, older married couple, who strike up a conversation. I express my fears about the first few days being brutal. The wife reassures me, saying it's not that bad. "It's like having jet lag," she says.

As we finish eating, Mary, the head chef — a chipper, cherub-faced woman with short brown hair — gets up and makes a little presentation. There will be three meals a day: breakfast, lunch, and a light supper. There are rules: no food in the rooms; no entering the dining hall until invited in by one of the chefs, who will ring a bell; after eating, we must line up, scrape off our plates, and put them in plastic tubs for the kitchen cleaners. For hard-core vegans, there's a special side area of "simple foods." And for people who really have special dietary needs, there's a "yogi shelf," where they can keep their personal stash of wheat germ or whatever. Mary has none of the severity I was expecting. I had pictured a Buddhist Nurse Ratched. "I want you to think of this as *your* dining room," she tells us, and she seems to actually mean it.

The official opening session is held in the meditational hall, located in a stately building on an outcropping of rock set apart from the dorms by a hundred yards or so. Before entering, everyone takes off their shoes in a little foyer. The hall is large and airy, with shiny wood floors and lots of windows. There's an altar at the front with a statue of the Buddha. Arrayed before it are roughly a dozen mats in neat rows. Many people have shown up early to claim their spots and have built elaborate meditation nests out of small wooden benches, round cushions called "zafus," and thin, wool blankets. They're sitting, with legs crossed and eyes closed, waiting for the proceedings to begin. This sends my "comparing mind" aflutter. I'm clearly out of my league.

For those of us who can't hack the traditional postures, there are several rows of chairs lined up behind the mats. So, much as I'd done as a sullen punk kid in high school, I find myself sitting in the back of the room.

As soon as I'm settled, I look over to see a row of teachers walking into the hall, single file. They're all silent and stone-faced, with Goldstein bringing up the rear. I recognize him from the pictures on his book jackets. He's taller than I expected. He walks in long, slow strides. He's wearing a button-down shirt and khakis that ride high on the waist. There's a roughly three-inch strip of baldness down the center of his head, flanked by short brown hair on either side. The centerpiece of his angular face is a large, elegant protuberance of a nose. He's wearing a goatee. He looks very, very serious. The overall effect is a little intimidating.

The teachers take their seats in the front row and one of them, a fiftyish Asian woman named Kamala, welcomes us in that artificially soft, affected manner of speech that I'm now thinking they must teach at whatever meditation school these people attended. She formally opens the retreat and declares that we have now officially "entered into silence." More rules: no talking, no reading, no sex. (I've read that there's such a thing as a "yogi crush," a silent longing for one of your fellow meditators, at whom you steal furtive glances and around whom you construct feverish fantasies. As I look around the room, I realize this will not be a problem for me.)

In her contemplative purr, the teacher tells us that the goal on retreat is to try to be mindful at all times, not just when we're meditating. This means that all of our activities — walking, eating, sitting, even going to the bathroom — should be done with exaggerated slowness, so we can pay meticulous, microscopic attention.

At this point, I get my first look at the schedule we will be following for the rest of the retreat. It's even more brutal than I'd imagined. The days will start with a five o'clock wake-up call, followed by an hour of meditation, then breakfast, then a series of alternating periods of sitting and walking meditation of various lengths, lasting all the way up until ten at night, broken up by meals, rest and work periods, and an evening "dharma talk." I do some quick math: roughly ten hours a day of meditation. I honestly do not know if I can hack this.

Day Two

My alarm goes off at five and I realize, suddenly and unhappily, where I am.

I pick out one of the three pairs of sweatpants I packed in anticipation of long, sedentary days. I pad down the hall to the bathroom, perform the ablutions, and then walk outside into the chilly morning air and join the stream of yogis heading out of the dorms into the meditation hall. Everyone's walking slowly, with heads down. I realize that these people are really taking seriously the injunction to be mindful at all times.

As I walk amid the silent herd through the predawn darkness, I resolve to go balls-out on this retreat. *If I'm going to do this thing, I'm going to do it right, damn it.*

So, when I enter the hall, instead of going to the chair I'd picked out the night before, I wade into the archipelago of mats. I put two cushions on top of each other and straddle them, imitating the sitting style of some of the more experienced meditators.

I notice that as people file in, many of them stop and bow in the direction of the Buddha statue at the front of the hall. This makes me uncomfortable. I wonder how Sam deals with this.

Then another unpleasant surprise: There are pieces of legal-size paper at each of our meditation stations. They are lyric sheets. We will be expected to chant.

One of the teachers, a middle-aged white guy, takes the podium and explains that these are the "Refuges and Precepts," the chants with which yogis have, for centuries, started their day. The lyrics are in Pali, the language of the Buddha, but they're spelled out for us phonetically. He begins chanting, slow and low, and the rest of us join in, reading from our sheets. (Chanting is one of the only exceptions to the "Noble Silence" rule, along with the occasional opportunity we'll get to speak with the teachers.)

On the right side of the page is the English translation. In the first part of the chant, we're "taking refuge" in the Buddha, "the Blessed One, the Perfected One, the Fully Enlightened One." Then we take the "precepts," which are basically a series of promises: no harming (people or animals), no stealing, no lying, no substance abuse — and also, as if this might be a problem, "no dancing, singing, music, and unseemly shows." If my friends could see me perched on this tuffet, chanting, they would be laughing their asses off.

When the chant ends, we're off — we're meditating. This is it. Game on.

Almost immediately, I realize that sitting on cushions is a terrible idea. I am assailed by back and neck pain. The circulation to my feet feels like it's dangerously choked off. I try to focus on my breathing, but I can't keep up a volley of more than one or two breaths.

In.

Out.

In.

Holy crap, I think my feet are going to snap off at the ankle.

Come on, dude.

In.

It feels like a dinosaur has my rib cage in its mouth.

Out.

I'm hungry. It's really quiet in here. I wonder if anyone else in here is freaking out right now.

After a truly horrible hour, I hear a gentle ringing sound, kind of like a gong. The teacher has just tapped on what looks like a metal bowl, but apparently is a bell.

Everyone gets up and shuffles — mindfully — down the hill toward the dining hall. I follow along in a daze, like I've just had the bejeezus kicked out of me. A line forms outside the building. *Oh, right.* We're not allowed to go in until one of the chefs comes out and rings a bell. There's something a little pathetic about this.

I look around. While the word *yogi* sounds goofy — like Yogi Berra or Yogi Bear — these people all seem so grim. Turns out, mindfulness isn't such a cute look. Everyone is in his or her own world, trying very hard to stay in the moment. The effort of concentration produces facial expressions that range from blank to defecatory. The instruction sheets gently advise us not to make eye contact with our fellow retreatants, so as to not interrupt one another's meditative concentration. Which makes this the only place on earth where the truly compassionate response to a sneeze is to ignore it completely.

The outfits aren't helping this little zombie jamboree. Aesthetically, many of these people seem to be cultivating an aggressive plainness — and in some cases, a deliberate oddness. Their clothes are often mismatched or several decades out of style. One guy is wearing pleated acid-washed jeans.

Breakfast is followed by a break, and then the second sitting of the day.

Even though I've retreated to my chair, I am nonetheless besieged by screaming back pain. I still can't maintain concentration for more than one or two breaths. Perhaps because I'm having some sort of performance anxiety, the meditation is much harder for me here than it is at home. I feel like a rookie who's been called up to the big leagues and just can't cut it. I cannot believe I'm going to be sitting in this chair, here in this room, with these people, for the next nine days of my life.

During the first period of walking meditation, I'm at a loss. I have no idea what walking meditation even means, so I decide to just take a stroll. There are lots of animals here: salamanders, baby deer, wild turkeys. They come right up to you, totally unafraid. Apparently the "commitment to non-harming" memo has reached the woodland creatures. And the humans take it very seriously. Last night, I saw a guy in the meditation hall make a big show out of ushering a bug out of the room on a sheet of paper rather than squashing it.

The third sitting is even more of a nightmare. My body has now found a new way to revolt: my mouth keeps filling up with saliva. I'm trying not to move, but this situation is untenable. I can't sit here with a mouth full of spit. So I swallow. Every time I gulp it down, though, my mouth refills almost immediately. This, of course, completely derails my attempts to establish any rhythm whatsoever with my breath. My interior monologue now centers almost entirely on when the session will end.

Did I just hear the stupid bell?

Is that the bell?

No, it's not the bell.

Shit.

Shit, Shit, Shit, Shit, Shit . . . Shit.

When the bell finally does ring, Goldstein clears his voice to speak. This is the first time we'll be hearing from the Great Man himself. His voice is deep and booming, yet also has the slight nasal twang of a New York Jew, an accent apparently impervious to years of studying meditation in Asia.

Goldstein begins by setting us straight on walking meditation. "It is not recess," he intones. In other words, no strolling around and taking in the scenery. The drill is this, he explains: stake out a patch of ground about ten yards long, and then slowly pace back and forth, mindfully deconstructing every stride. With each step, you're supposed to note yourself lifting, moving, and placing. And repeat. Ad infinitum.

Excellent. So there will be no break from the tedium all day long.

And while Goldstein's laying down the law, he makes another request. When each seated meditation session is finished, he wants us to wait to leave the hall until after all of the teachers have filed out. This, he says, would be more "decorous."

Over lunch in a room filled with zombies, most of them chewing with their eyes closed, a giant wave of sadness rolls over me. I feel all alone and utterly trapped. The sheer volume of time left in this ordeal looms over my head like a mile of ocean water. It feels like the desperate homesickness I experienced every summer as a kid when my parents dropped me off at sleepaway camp.

Also, I feel stupid. Why am I here, when I could be spending this time on a beach with Bianca? She and I had had a few tense chats about this retreat. She wanted to be supportive of my "spiritual" quest, but it was hard not to be resentful of my using up ten days of vacation to go meditate, especially given how little time off I get. Furthermore, at least when I travel to someplace like Papua New Guinea or the Congo, I can call her every day, assuming I can get a signal. Here, I'm completely sequestered.

And now I'm sitting in this room full of strangers, thinking: *I shouldn't have come here. I'm such an idiot.*

As the wash of sadness and regret crests, I am able to muster some mindfulness, to see my feelings with some nonjudgmental remove. I tell myself that it's just a passing squall. It's not a silver bullet, but it does keep the demons at bay.

In the next walking meditation period, I stake out my strip of land on the stone patio in front of the meditation hall, then pace slowly back and forth, trying to note each component of my stride. *Lift, move, place. Lift, move, place.* If a civilian were to stumble upon all of us yogis out here walking in slow motion, they'd probably conclude that a loony bin was having a fire drill.

Back on the cushion, I'm waging a Sisyphean battle, trying to roll the boulder of concentration up a never-ending hill. I'm straining to focus on my breath, gripping at it like it's a rope hanging off the side of a cliff. I'm no match, though, for the pageant of pain, fatigue, and saliva. I find it humiliating — infuriating, really — that after a year of daily meditation, I cannot get a toehold here. Every instance of mental wandering is met with a tornadic blast of self-flagellation.

In.

Out.

I wonder if they'll have more of that fresh bread at dinner?

Damn, dude.

In.

Did someone actually invent and patent the

sneeze guard or, like math and language, was it devised in several disconnected civilizations, more or less simultaneously?

Idiot.

Incompetent.

Irretrievably, irrevocably, irredeemably stupid.

By the time the evening dharma talk begins, I'm feeling utterly defeated.

Goldstein and his crew process into the chamber, with Goldstein leading the way with giant, magisterial strides. He sits at the center of the altar; all the other teachers array themselves around him in their meditative positions, eyes closed.

Goldstein is trying to figure out how to put on the wireless headset. It's the kind of microphone singers wear in concert so their hands can be free as they caper around the stage. Once he has it on, he says, "I feel like a rock star."

A woman sitting behind me says reverently under her breath, "You *are.*"

As he starts his talk, I realize he's infinitely less austere than he seemed in the hothouse of the meditation session. He's actually funny, with a delivery that reminds me of those borscht belt comedians with names like Shecky.

He's talking about the power of desire in

244

our minds, and how our culture conditions us to believe that the more pleasant experiences we have — sex, movies, food, shopping trips, etc. — the happier we'll be. He reads out some advertising slogans he's collected over the years:

"Instant gratification just got faster. Shop Vogue-dot-com."

Everyone laughs.

"Another slogan says, 'I don't let anything stand in the way of my pleasure.' "

"The best one of all," he says, pausing for effect, in a wait-for-it kind of way, chuckling to himself as he lets our curiosity build.

" 'To be one with everything . . . you need one of everything.' "

The zombies erupt, as Goldstein lets out a series of gentle, high-pitched honks.

He goes on to answer one of my biggest questions, the one about Buddhism's vilification of desire. It's not that we can't enjoy the good stuff in life or strive for success, he says. The key is not to get carried away by desire; we need to manage it with wisdom and mindfulness. Quite helpfully, he adds that he is by no means perfect on this score. He tells a story about his early years of intensive meditation in India in the 1960s. "My practice was going quite well, and the mind was quite concentrated. And it's the kind of sitting where you think you're going to get enlightened any minute," he says with, I think, tongue in cheek. He explains that, at teatime at this retreat center, the yogis would be given a small cup of tea and a little banana. "So I'm sitting there, about to get enlightened and the tea bell rings." Comic pause. "Enlightenment or banana?" Another pause. He's cracking himself up again. "More often than not, go for the banana."

The humor is a relief. As is his love for the material. After a day of wondering whether sitting and watching my breath is perhaps the stupidest conceivable pursuit, Goldstein's talk is a welcome reminder of Buddhism's intellectual superstructure. His enthusiasm is palpable and infectious. He discusses verses from the Buddha like a sommelier rhapsodizing over a 1982 Bordeaux.

"In one discourse, he captured the whole game in just a few words. These lines, if you heard these lines in the right way, you could get enlightened," he says, chuckling again. "So here's your chance . . ."

He's talking about a verse where the Buddha calls everything we experience — sights, sounds, smells, etc. — the "terrible bait of the world."

"It's . . . an amazing statement," he says. "Moment after moment, experiences are arising, and it's as if each one has a hook . . . and we're the fish. Do we bite? Or do we not bite, and just swim freely in the ocean?"

I'm thinking: *Yes, right — there is a point to sitting around all day with your eyes closed: to gain some control over the mind, to see through the forces that drive us — and drive us nuts.*

As he deconstructs various parts of the Buddhist scriptures, it strikes me that Goldstein is what you get when a brainy, intense Jew like my father decides to build an entire career out of Buddhism. I assume Goldstein's parents would have preferred him to be a lawyer or a doctor, but instead he's basically become a Talmudic scholar of Buddhism. And somehow, that accent, so much like my dad's, makes me like him even more.

As the speech goes on, however, he starts to lose me. Earlier, he was joking about enlightenment, but now he's speaking without irony about rebirth, karma, "purifying the mind" and achieving "liberation." He closes by saying that the dharma "leads to calm, ease, and Nibbana." (An alternate pronunciation of Nirvana.)

Oy. Way to ruin a great talk.

247

At the end of the last sitting of the day, another unpleasant surprise: more chanting. This time, it's the metta chant, where we send "loving-kindness" to a whole series of "beings," including our parents, teachers, and "guardian deities." We wish for everyone to experience the End of Suffering.

It occurs to me that perhaps the quickest way for me to achieve the End of Suffering would be to go home.

Day Three

I have a line running through my head from *Chappelle's Show,* indisputably the funniest show in the history of television. In one of the sketches, Dave Chappelle appears in a "Hip-Hop News Break" as "Tron," a "Staten Island man" who has been brutally attacked by members of the rap group the Wu-Tang Clan. Lying in a hospital bed surrounded by reporters, he says the rappers had sewn his anus shut and "kept feeding me and feeding me and feeding me."

"It was torture — straight torture, son."

That phrase — "straight torture, son" — keeps bouncing through my skull as I rotate, with the rest of the zombies, between sitting meditation, the Ministry of Silly Walks routine, and waiting in line at the dining hall to fill our bowls with grains and greens.

I'm flat-out loathing this experience.

Late morning, I'm lingering, bored, in front of the message board in the foyer outside the meditation hall. With a frisson of excitement, I notice there's a note for me. It's from Goldstein. In neat, handwritten script on a small, white sheet of paper, he suggests we meet in about an hour. As the note explains, yogis are supposed to have regular interviews with the teachers, to discuss our practice. Since I didn't get on his schedule today, he's carving out some extra time. Around here, this is the closest you'll get to a thrill.

At the appointed hour, I'm at the main office, taking off my shoes and pushing open the screen door. I pad into the carpeted room, where Goldstein is using his unreasonably long arms to pull an office chair directly in front of the big, fluffy love seat he's planning to occupy. He pats the office chair, indicating I sit down.

One-on-one, he's even looser than he was during the dharma talk. As is my wont, I pepper him with biographical questions. Turns out he was raised in the Catskills, where his parents owned a hotel for Jews from New York City. This explains his comic timing; he literally grew up in the borscht belt.

I feel privileged to have this audience, but also mildly stressed. I have a million questions, and yet I don't want to overstay my welcome. He has a clock prominently displayed on the little table next to his chair, just like Dr. Brotman has on his desk.

I start with the most acute problem. "My mouth is filling with saliva all the time and it's messing up my ability to concentrate."

He laughs and assures me that, for some reason, this seems to happen to a lot of meditators. I find this enormously comforting. He suggests I give myself permission to swallow. Don't fixate on it, he advises, or it'll get worse. He says his mother — "a very intense woman" — used to have the same problem, except she refused to swallow, not wanting to cave to her urges, and would let it all run down the front of her dress. I am dying to hear how he convinced his Jewish mother to meditate, but I don't have that kind of time.

He asks how my practice is going, generally. Not wanting to reveal the full extent of my despair, I allow that I've had some low moments, but then add that even as I was experiencing those moments, I knew they would pass. He smiles wide, slaps his knees, and says, "That's the whole game!" It's another useful reminder of why we're here:

to learn how to not get carried away by the clatter of the mind.

After fifteen minutes, I figure I've used up all of my time. The meeting was brief, but hugely satisfying. This guy really is a gem, a mensch. He's like an emissary sent down every back alley and cul-de-sac of the mind, so that the rest of us can tell him our problems and he can say, "Oh yeah, I've been there, and here's how you deal with it."

This era of good feelings is brief. In one of the midafternoon seated meditation sessions, a teacher named Spring takes the podium and announces that today "We're going to try something different."

Spring, who appears to be in her thirties, is the embodiment of everything that most bothers me about the meditation world. She's really working that speaking-softly thing. Every s is sibilant. Every word is overenunciated. She wears shawls. She's probably really militant about recycling.

She says we're going to do metta or loving-kindness meditation, which sounds like it will fall foursquare into the category of Things I Will Definitely Hate. Here's how it works: we are supposed to picture a series of people in our minds and then, one by one, send them well wishes. You start with yourself, then move to a "mentor," a "dear friend," a "neutral person," a "difficult person," and then "all beings." Interestingly, she says not to pick someone to whom you're attracted. "Too complicated," she says. So I guess Bianca will not be on the receiving end of the good vibes.

I am immediately convinced that this exercise will never, ever have any meaning for me. Even Saccharine Spring acknowledges it might feel a little forced, although she insists it has the potential to "change your life."

The one good thing about metta meditation is that, since we're supposed to be physically comfortable while generating these good vibes, we're allowed to lie on the floor. I would treat this as a free period, except I really did promise myself to play full-on. I lie down and prepare to love hard.

We start with ourselves. Spring instructs us to generate a vivid mental picture of ourselves, and then repeat four phrases. As she says them aloud, her speaking style elevates to an entirely new level of cloying. She draws out the last syllable of every word in an almost Valley Girl–esque drawl.

May you be happy.
May you be safe and protected from harm.
May you be healthy and strong.

May you live with ease.

I get that, just like regular meditation is designed to build our mindfulness muscle, metta is supposed to boost our capacity for compassion, but all this exercise is doing for me is generating feelings of boredom, disdain, and insufficiency. It makes me question my generosity of spirit. If I was a good person, wouldn't I be suffused with love right now? If I was a good husband, wouldn't I be on the beach with Bianca? Thank you for that, Spring.

Day Four

Today is my thirty-ninth birthday. I am confident it will be the worst birthday ever.

The morning meditation is an epic battle with sleepiness. I can feel fatigue oozing down my forehead. I am overcome by the desire to burrow into this fuzzy oblivion.

The next sitting is a festival of pain, saliva, coughing, and fidgeting. My heart pounds. I feel shame and anger as I swallow, snort, and shift in my chair. Heat rushes to my cheeks. I must be driving the people near me crazy. I try to be mindful of it all, but I'm starting to forget what mindfulness even means. Straight torture, son.

Off the cushion, my misery is also intensifying. Most of my thoughts center on how I can possibly survive six more days here. I recognize that part of the goal of a retreat is to systematically strip away all of the things we use — sex, work, email, food, TV — to avoid a confrontation with what's been called "the wound of existence." The only way to make it through this thing is to reach some sort of armistice with the present moment, to drop our habit of constantly leaning forward into the next thing on our agenda. I just can't seem to do it, though.

I wonder if the others can tell that I'm struggling. Everyone else here seems so serene. I mean, there are some ostentatiously mindful people here. There's one guy staying on my floor who I have literally never seen moving in anything but slow motion.

I really thought it would be easier by now. This is way worse than jet lag. I'm starting to worry that I'm going to have to come home and tell everyone — Bianca, Mark, Sam — that I failed.

I do the last walking meditation session of the night in the upstairs area, above the meditation hall. I'm struggling to stay focused on *lifting, moving, placing,* with my mind wandering variously to thoughts of watching TV, eating cookies, and sleeping. At the end of one back-and-forth, I look up and see a statue of the Buddha. Silently, I send him the following message: *Fuck you.*

Day Five

I wake up desperate.

I'm drowning in doubt, genuinely considering quitting and going home. I seriously don't know if I can make it another day. I need to talk to someone. I need help. But I don't have an interview scheduled with Goldstein today. The only lifeline available to me is Dreaded Spring.

Since she is still technically an apprentice teacher, Spring is not assigned to directly oversee any of the yogis throughout the retreat. She has, however, posted a sign-up sheet on the message board for anyone who wants to come see her for an interview. With no small amount of hesitation, I sign up.

When my time comes, I enter the little office where she's receiving people. She's seated, smiling, with her shawl wrapped around her shoulders. She looks impossibly smug to me. I'm not even sure we are equipped to communicate with each other. We're two different species. This is going to be like a lizard trying to talk to a goat.

But whatever — I dive right in to my cri de coeur. "I'm giving this everything I have," I tell her, "but I'm not getting anywhere. I don't know if I can hack this. I'm really struggling here."

When she answers, she's no longer using her funny voice. She's talking like a normal person. "You're trying too hard," she tells me. The diagnosis is delivered frankly and firmly. This is a classic problem on the first retreat, she explains. She advises me to just do my best, expect nothing, and "be with" whatever comes up in my mind. "It's the total opposite of daily life," she says, "where we do something and expect a result. Here, it's just sitting with whatever is there."

She goes on to say that she's received a whole series of distraught retreatants, many of them in tears. This produces a very un-metta-like feeling in me: a satisfying rush of Schadenfreude. *Well, well: some of these zombies aren't as blissed-out as they seem, after all.*

I look back at Spring, sitting there with her curly locks spread out over her shawl, and I realize this nice woman was a victim of another one of my rushes to judgment. Spring is actually very cool; I'm the dumb-ass. She's right: it's not complicated; I'm just trying too hard. I feel so grateful I could cry.

For the next sitting, I decide to take a chair from my bedroom and put it out on the balcony at the end of the hallway in my dorm. I tell myself I'm going to lower the volume, to stop straining so much. I'll just sit here and "be with" whatever happens.

I can hear the others in the distance, walking back into the meditation hall for the start of the session. Then it gets really quiet. I sit, casually feeling my breath. No big deal. Whatever, man.

A few minutes in, something clicks. There's no string music, no white light. It's more like, after days of trying to tune into a specific radio frequency, I finally find the right setting. I just start letting my focus fall on whatever is the most prominent thing in my field of consciousness.

Neck pain.

Knee pain.

Airplane overhead.

Birdsong.

Sizzle of rustling leaves.

Breeze on my forearm.

I'm really enjoying putting cashews and raisins in my oatmeal at breakfast.

Neck. Knee. Neck. Neck. Knee, knee, knee. Hunger pang. Neck. Knee. Hands numb. Bird. Knee. Bird, bird, bird.

I think I know what's going on here. This is something called "choiceless awareness." I'd heard the teachers talk about it. It's

257

some serious behind-the-waterfall action. Once you've built up enough concentration, they say, you can drop your obsessive focus on the breath and just "open up" to whatever is there. And that's what's happening right now. Each "object" that "arises" in my mind, I focus on with what feels like total ease and clarity until it's replaced by something else. I'm not trying; it's just happening. It's so easy it feels like I'm cheating. Everything's coming at me and I'm playing it all like jazz. And I don't even like jazz.

Back pain.

Funny lights you see behind your eyes when they're closed real tight.

Murderous itch on my calf.

Knee. Knee, knee, knee.

Itch, knee, back, itch, itch, itch, knee, airplane, tree rustling, breeze on skin, knee, knee, itch, knee, lights, back.

Then I hear a loud rumble approaching. It's getting closer.

Now it's super loud, like the fleet of choppers coming over the horizon in that scene from *Apocalypse Now.*

Now it's right in front of me.

I open my eyes. There's a hummingbird hovering just a few feet away.

No shit.

The next sitting is even more exhilarating.

I'm back in the meditation hall now, and I'm really doing it. Whatever comes up in my mind, it feels like I'm right there with it. At times, I still find myself looking forward to the session ending. But when those thoughts come up, I just note them and move on.

It's like a curtain has been lifted. It's not that anything in the passing show is so amazing in itself; it's the sheer rapidity of it all, the objects arising and passing, ricocheting off one another with such speed. And there's something about the act of being present and awake in this way that produces a gigantic blast of serotonin.

Hands feel stiff.

Bird.

Feet numb.

Images of all those creepy baby faces in Renaissance art.

Heart pounding.

Back. Bird. Hands. Feet. Heart. Back, back, bird, feet, bird, bird, bird. Feet, hands, feet, feet, feet.

Hands. Hands. Back, back, back. Heart, bird, feet. Feet. Bird.

Feetbirdfeetbirdbackfeetfeetfeetheart.

Bird.

Bird.

Bird.

259

Old lady in the front row produces an epic burp.

It's like I'd spent the past five days being dragged by my head behind a motorboat and now, all of a sudden, I'm up on water skis. This is an experience of my own mind I've never had before — a front-row seat to watch the machinery of consciousness. It's thrilling, but it also produces some very practical insights. I get a real sense of how a few slippery little thoughts I might have in, say, the morning before I go to work — maybe after a quarrel with Bianca, a story I read in the paper, or an imagined dialogue with my boss — can weasel their way into the stream of my mind and pool in unseen eddies, from which they hector and haunt me throughout the day. Thoughts calcify into opinions, little seeds of discontent blossom into bad moods, unnoticed back pain makes me inexplicably irritable with anyone who happens to cross my path.

I'm remembering that time when my friend Kaiama stumped me by asking how anyone can be in the present moment when it's always slipping away. It's so obvious to me now: the slipping away is the whole point. Once you've achieved choiceless awareness, you see so clearly how fleeting everything is. Impermanence is no longer theoretical. *Tempus fugit* isn't just something you inscribe in books and clocks. And that, I realize, is what this retreat is designed to do.

Having been dragged kicking and screaming into the present, I'm finally awake enough to see what I could never see in my regular life. Apparently there's no other way to get here than to engage in the tedious work of watching your breath for days. In a way, it makes sense. How do you learn a sport? You do drills. A language? Conjugate endless verbs. A musical instrument? Scales. All the misery of repetition, the horror of sitting here in this hall with these zombies suddenly seems totally worth it.

Walking meditation is starting to click for me as well. I'm out on the patio in front of the retreat hall, deconstructing every step. *Lift, move, place.* My feet feel nice on the warm stones. Midway through one of the endless round-trips to nowhere, even though it's technically a violation of Goldstein's rule against using walking meditation as "recess," I stop and stare at three baby birds perched on the ledge overlooking the court-yard, screeching their heads off as their mom zips to and fro, popping food into their mouths. I'm transfixed. A few other people have joined me, gaping at this little show. I feel incredibly happy — and I keep telling myself not to cling to it.

When I walk back into the hall for the next sit, I see Spring up at the altar. *Right, it's metta time.* I lie down, and we start in, directing the four phrases at ourselves.

May you be happy. May you be safe. Etc.

Then Spring tells us to pick our benefactor. I pick my mother. I summon a mental picture of her from a few weeks ago, when she and I were taking care of my two-year-old niece, Campbell. We had just given Campbell a bath, and all three of us were lying on the bed. My mom started singing Campbell's favorite song, M. Ward's "For Beginners," which Campbell referred to as "the uh-huh song," because the chorus includes a lot of "uh-huhs." I'm able to generate a real felt-sense of my mom. I'm enjoying the sweet absurdity of a grandmother having memorized the words to an indie rock song. As I picture her, with her neatly coiffed, short gray hair, and her smart, casual clothing, something entirely unexpected overcomes me: a silent sob wells up in my chest — with all the inevitability of a sneeze.

There's no stopping this. Tears rush down the sides of my recumbent face, streaming down my temples in hot streams that get thicker with each successive wave of emotion. The water is pooling behind my ears.

"Now pick a dear friend," says Spring. She's back to using her funny voice but it's not bothering me at all.

I go with Campbell. It couldn't be more convenient; she's already right here in this scene I'm conjuring in such vivid detail. She's propped up against the pillow on the bed. I have one of her little feet in my hand and am looking at her sweet face with her mischievous eyes, which are eagerly lapping up all the attention my mom and I are giving her.

I'm crying even harder now. It's not an out-loud sobbing, but there's no way the people around me aren't noticing this, because I'm sniffling and breathing choppily.

The blubbering lasts right up until when the bell rings. As I walk out of the hall, I'm grateful for the rule against eye contact; otherwise, this would be very embarrassing. I emerge into the daylight, walk down the hill a ways, and stand in the scrub grass under the warm afternoon sun. Amid the crashing waves of bliss, I feel a gentle undertow of doubt. *Is this bullshit, or the real deal?* Maybe it's just the result of five days of unbroken agony finally relieved? Like that joke where the guy is banging his head against the wall — when asked why he's doing it, he says, "Because it feels so good when I stop."

But no, the waves of happiness just keep coming. Everything is so bright, so crisp. I feel great. Not just great — unprecedentedly great. I'm aware of the urge to cling to this feeling, to wring out every last bit of flavor, like with a tangy piece of gum, or a tab of ecstasy. But this is not the synthetic, always-just-about-to-end buzz of drugs. This is roughly a thousand times better. It's the best high of my life.

My nose is running savagely. I don't have anything to wipe it with. I blow it into my hand and walk, dripping snot, to the nearest bathroom, laughing goofily.

I take a run. I've been doing this most afternoons. I've found a little route that goes through an adjacent horse farm and out into the local neighborhood of upper-middle-class homes. I'm still high. As my feet pound, I'm crying, then laughing at myself crying, and then crying some more. I'm wondering whether this is the start of a different way of being in the world for me, one where — as Brilliant Genius Spring has described — you train yourself to have compassion rather than aversion as your "default setting."

I'd be loath to call what I'm feeling spiritual or mystical. Those terms connote — to me, at least — otherworldliness or unreality. By contrast, what's happening right now feels hyperreal, as if I've been pulled out of a dream rather than thrust into one.

After dinner, it's Goldstein giving the dharma talk. He's making an intriguing point. The Buddha's signature pronouncement — "Life is suffering" — is the source of a major misunderstanding, and by extension, a major PR problem. It makes Buddhism seem supremely dour. Turns out, though, it's all the result of a translation error. The Pali word *dukkha* doesn't actually mean "suffering." There's no perfect word in English, but it's closer to "unsatisfying" or "stressful." When the Buddha coined his famous phrase, he wasn't saying that all of life is like being chained to a rock and having crows peck out your innards. What he really meant was something like, "Everything in the world is ultimately unsatisfying and unreliable because it won't last."

As Goldstein points out, we don't live our lives as if we recognize the basic facts. "How often are we waiting for the next pleasant hit of . . . whatever? The next meal or the next relationship or the next latte or the next vacation, I don't know. We just live in anticipation of the next enjoyable thing that we'll experience. I mean, we've been, most of us, incredibly blessed with the number of pleasant experiences we've had in our lives. Yet when we look back, where are they now?"

It's so strange for me to be sitting and listening to what is essentially a sermon, complete with quotes from a sacred text, and to be genuinely moved. After all those years of being the only nonbeliever in a room filled with rapt devotees, here I am sitting and taking notes, totally engrossed, nodding my head.

I mean, he's so right. In cartoons, when the characters slurp down some delicious food or drink, they smack their lips and seem totally sated. But in the real world, it doesn't work that way. Even if we were handed everything we wanted, would it really make us sustainably happy? How many times have we heard from people who got rich or famous and it wasn't enough? Rock stars with drug problems. Lottery winners who kill themselves. There's actually a term for this — "hedonic adaptation." When good things happen, we bake them very quickly into our baseline expectations, and yet the primordial void goes unfilled.

Goldstein makes clear, as he did the other night, that he's not saying we can't enjoy pleasant things in life. But if we can achieve a deeper understanding of "suffering," of the unreliability of everything we experience, it will help us appreciate the inherent poignancy of everything in the world. "It's like we've been enchanted," he says. "We've been put under a spell — believing that this or that is going to be the source of our ultimate freedom or happiness. And to wake up from that, to wake up from that enchantment, to be more aligned with what is true, it brings us much greater happiness."

On retreat, with nothing to look forward to, nowhere to be, nothing to do, we are forced to confront the "wound of existence" head-on, to stare into the abyss and realize that so much of what we do in life — every shift in our seat, every bite of food, every pleasant daydream — is designed to avoid pain or seek pleasure. But if we can drop all that, we can, as Sam once said in his speech to the angry, befuddled atheists, learn how to be happy "before anything happens." This happiness is self-generated, not contingent on exogenous forces; it's the opposite of "suffering." What the Buddha recognized was a genuine game changer.

After the final meditation of the night, as I leave the hall, I turn around toward the Buddha, and — I can't believe I'm doing this — I bow.

Day Six
I wake up, and the world is still magical.

I'm becoming almost frighteningly alert. My senses are heightened, like in the movies when a mortal starts turning into a vampire. After breakfast, as I walk back up the hill, I can hear the mice scurrying underneath the brush alongside the path. I have a freakish attunement to the communications within the hidden society of birds in the trees.

Meditation is still easy. I start by doing a round of breath-focus, which is like filling a hot-air balloon; once the mind is fully inflated with concentration, I just let it fly into choiceless awareness.

Urge to scratch.

Image of a row of baboons sitting on bales of hay.

Thought of the illicit apple I'm hiding in my room.

Even "bad" stuff doesn't seem to really get to me. I can feel myself playing with the cape of pain draped over my back. I'm investigating it, without letting it truly bother me.

At lunch, I realize that I've now become one of these people who chews with his eyes shut. Eating mindfully, I actually put the fork down between bites rather than hunting around the plate while I'm still swallowing. As a result, I stop eating when I'm full, as opposed to stuffing my face until I'm nearly sick, as I usually do.

I spot a guy on the other side of the room who seems to be enjoying his meal immensely. I experience a sudden upsurge of what the Buddhists call mudita, "sympathetic joy." It's so strong I almost start blubbering again. It happens once more when I look up and see three women helping one another get the remaining chai out of the big metal pot in which it's served. This tableau of silent, awkward, eyes-averted cooperation fills my eyes to the rim.

But then, as quickly as it came, the rapture evaporates.

The afternoon meditation session is a humbling reversion. Sleep beckons with the unwanted seductiveness of a clingy ex-girlfriend. At times, I nod off for a nanosecond, and then come to with what feels like a jackhammer to the head. At the end of forty-five minutes, I have a massive headache. It's official: the magic is gone.

The afternoon metta session leaves me cold.

During the last sitting of the day, I am hit with a sickening jolt of restless energy so strong that it feels as if it might leave my limbs palsied. It gets so bad that I do the heretofore unthinkable. I resort to the one measure that, despite all the preceding difficulties, I have not yet employed: I give up. I open my eyes and sit in the hall, looking around guiltily.

Day Seven

Now I'm back to counting the days until I can leave. The thought crosses my mind that maybe I've gotten all I'm going to get out of this experience.

I'm still bowing to the Buddha, but mostly for the hamstring stretch.

Day Eight

I'm on the schedule to see Goldstein this morning. I arrive full of piss and vinegar; he'll be the first person I tell about my recent meditative attainments. I practically bound to my seat, and give him a full report on my breakthrough: the choiceless awareness, the humming-bird, the metta-induced weeping.

I don't know what I'm expecting. Applause, maybe? As it turns out, he's pretty much unimpressed. He smiles and gently tells me he's heard this story a million times. This is, like, First Retreat 101.

I thought I'd achieved a front-row seat in the theater of my mind. He makes it clear that I really had loge seating. "As you continue your practice," he says, "your NPMs — noticings per minute — will go way up."

Then I tell him about the horrific jolt of restlessness from the night before last. Again, his response is: Nothing special. Happens all the time.

He is massively reassuring, though, on the inevitable vexations and vicissitudes of the practice. It is, he says, not unusual at all to go from bliss to misery within the space of an hour. He assures me that as I get more advanced, the ups and downs won't be so jagged. I get up to leave, comforted by the knowledge that I am walking a well-trodden path. People have been doing this very practice for 2,500 years.

On my way to the door, he shouts after me and says I'm moving too fast. "You're not being mindful enough," he says. Like a sports coach, he exhorts me to up my game, to pay more attention as I do things like walk and open doors. "This is the stuff!"

I wonder: Is my growing reverence for Goldstein a form of Stockholm syndrome? Or is this person genuinely special? As I stand outside the office, soaking up the sunshine for a moment, the hummingbird reappears.

An hour or so later, in the morning question-and-answer period, a brassy red-headed woman in the front row asks the question that's been nagging at me this whole time: "If enlightenment is real, where are all the enlightened people?"

It gets a good laugh, including from Goldstein, who promises that at tonight's dharma talk he's going to explain everything.

This I'm looking forward to. During the course of this retreat, he has repeatedly dropped words like "liberation," "awakening," and "realization." But is this vaunted transformation actually achievable? If so, how? And what does it look like? In the Buddhist scriptures, people are getting enlightened left and right. They're dropping like flies — even seven-year-olds. The Buddha had an entire lexicon to describe enlightenment: "the true," "the beyond," "the very hard to see," "the wonderful," "the marvelous," "the island," and more. All those words, and still I have no idea what he meant.

At seven o'clock, it's time for the big show. We're all assembled in the hall. Goldstein is finally going to explain enlightenment.

He starts by acknowledging that for "householders" — non-monks — the idea of an end to craving can seem unattainable. "Can we even imagine a mind free of craving? I think most of us resonate probably more closely with the famous prayer of Saint Augustine: 'Dear Lord, make me chaste — but not yet.' "

There's laughter, but then Goldstein launches into a dead-serious description of the various steps toward achieving the "unshakable deliverance of mind, the cessation of craving without remainder." His description of the stages of enlightenment makes it sound like the most elaborate video game ever.

The process starts when the meditator becomes super-concentrated, when their NPMs reach epic velocity. It's like my *backbirdknee* experience, only on steroids. You see things changing so quickly that nothing seems stable. The seemingly solid movie of the world breaks down to twenty-four frames per second. The universe is revealed to be a vast soup of causes and conditions.

From there, the path, as Goldstein describes it, involves moments of terror, periods of sublime bliss, pitfalls, trapdoors, and detours. At the end, the meditator arrives at the true goal of Buddhist meditation: to see that the "self" that we take to be the ridgepole of our lives is actually an illusion. The real superpower of meditation is not just to manage your ego more mindfully but to see that the ego itself has no actual substance. Close your eyes and look for it, and you won't find any "self" you can put your finger on. So, for example, in my *backbirdknee* jag, if I were more enlightened, I would have been able to see that not only is reality not as monolithic as it appears, but also the "me," who was noting all the arising objects, isn't solid either. "The strong, deeply entrenched reference point of 'I' has been seen through," says Goldstein from the front of the room. "That's Nibbana." The illusion of the self is, per the Buddhists, the wellspring of all our negative emotions — specifically, greed and hatred and confusion about "the nature of reality" (i.e., that we're much more than our egos, that we are connected to the whole). Once the self is seen as unreal, these emotions are uprooted from the mind, and the meditator becomes "perfected." The mind goes from a monkey to a gazelle.

Sounds awesome, I guess, but as he concludes, I realize that he hasn't answered some of my most basic questions. If it's so rare and hard to reach enlightenment, why bother trying? Is Goldstein himself enlightened? If not, on what basis does he believe in it? What do enlightened beings look like? Is Nirvana/Nibbana a magical state? A place? Once I've achieved selflessness, do I then just return to my everyday life, or do I no longer need to put my pants on in the morning?

The Buddhists clearly figured out a workable, practical system for defanging the voice in the head, but to add on top of that the promise of a magical transformation seems to me too cute by half. I buy the thesis that nothing in an unreliable, impermanent world can make you sustainably happy, but how will a quest for an enlightenment that almost no one can achieve do so either?

When the talk is over, in a minor act of rebellion, I walk down to the dining hall and binge mindlessly on rice cakes.

Day Nine

In the morning question-and-answer session, Goldstein redeems himself with a little humor. In exhorting us not to tune out during these closing hours of the retreat, he says, "They're like the dessert. Just maybe not the dessert you ordered."

As he presses his case, he says something that bugs me. He urges us not to spend too much time thinking about the stuff we have to do when the retreat is over. It's a waste of time, he says; they're just thoughts. This provokes me to raise my hand for the first time. From the back of the echoey hall, in full-on reporter mode, with my overloud voice apparently not atrophied one bit from disuse, I ask, "How can you advise us not to worry about the things we have to do when we reenter the world? If I miss my plane, that's a genuine problem. These are not just irrelevant thoughts."

Fair enough, he concedes. "But when you find yourself running through your trip to the airport for the seventeenth time, perhaps ask yourself the following question: 'Is this useful'?"

His answer is so smart I involuntarily jolt back in my chair and smile.

"Is this useful?" It's a simple, elegant corrective to my "price of security" motto. It's okay to worry, plot, and plan, he's saying — but only until it's not useful anymore. I've spent the better part of my life trying to balance my penchant for maniacal over-thinking with the desire for peace of mind.

And here, with one little phrase, Goldstein has handed me what seems like a hugely constructive tool for taming this impulse without throwing the baby out with the bathwater.

Achieving choiceless awareness and metta-induced blubbering may have been the most dramatic moments of the retreat, but this is unquestionably the most valuable.

Day Ten

I awake to the smell of freedom.

Today is a half day. We do some meditation in the morning, and then we "break silence." The zombies reanimate, transforming from the mindful walking dead back into normal human beings. You can almost see the color return to their cheeks.

It's fascinating to engage with the people around whom I'd spun rather elaborate stories during the silence. Turns out, they're totally normal. I have lunch with a handsome German woman, who admits that she called her kids a couple of times. Also at the table is a middle-aged technology executive, who says he came on a lark and largely enjoyed it.

A young Asian guy approaches me. He's athletic and good-looking. In observing him over the past days, I had assumed he would be stern and serious. Turns out, he's super friendly. He tells me he felt "privileged" to be near me during that metta session when I cried. This produces a starburst of conflicting emotions, including gratitude and embarrassment. I mumble something and extricate myself.

The teachers warned us that the real world would seem clangorous and jangly after ten days of silence, but as I pull away from Spirit Rock in a cab, I turn on my BlackBerry and devour my email with curiosity more than dread. I visit my sister-in-law and enjoy being climbed on by her two young children. On the plane, I binge on TV shows on my iPhone. The habits of a lifetime reassert themselves with astonishing speed. It may have been one of — if not *the* — most meaningful experiences of my life, but I was nonetheless ready for it to end.

CHAPTER 8
10% HAPPIER

I knew my television career had undergone a radical shift when I found myself reading the following line off the teleprompter: "Now to the story of Irwin the paralyzed kangaroo . . ." Cut to a live shot of a woman holding a handicapped marsupial dressed up in a shirt, tie, and vest. At which point I blurted out, with forced jollity, "I like Irwin's new suit! He's looking dashing!" I was smiling onscreen, but inside, my ego was hissing, *You are a dope.*

I was in the midst of an object lesson in the Buddhist concept of "suffering," which in this case could be roughly translated into "Be careful what you wish for."

On a Friday afternoon, shortly after I'd come back from the retreat, a particularly chipper David Westin strolled into my office, stuck out his hand, and offered me the job as weekend co-anchor of *Good Morning*

America.

I was elated and relieved, light-headed with glee. It was as if I had totally forgotten all of Joseph's dharma talks about the impossibility of lasting satisfaction. I felt as if months of worrying about my place in the news division and my future in the industry could finally cease. All of my problems were solved. Deliverance!

What came next was a series of developments that could have been authored by the Buddha himself. Two days after Westin strode into my office and confidently extended the offer, I was at home when I saw the following headline on the *New York Times* website: "Chief of ABC News Is Resigning."

When I got back into work the next morning, it was quickly made clear to me by various senior executives that Westin would be staying on as president for many more months, and that the offer still stood. That meant it was time to negotiate my new contract, which produced a fresh whole set of challenges. Talks quickly got bogged down over a variety of minor issues. Both sides dug in their heels. There came a moment where the entire thing appeared to be in jeopardy.

After several weeks of stasis, in an attempt

280

to break the impasse, the executive producer of *GMA,* Jim Murphy, called me in for a meeting. Murphy (everyone called him by his last name) had been EP for several years, during which time I had grown quite fond of him. He was a tall, nattily dressed guy with slicked-back, salt-and-pepper hair, a soul patch, and a taste for cigarettes, booze, and sardonic humor.

As I sat across from him in his corner office, which had a panoramic view of Lincoln Center, I was prepared for Murphy to try to convince me that I should drop my various demands. I expected him to make the case that these issues were really not as important as I was making them out to be. Instead, he chose a more aggressive tack.

"Can I tell you something as a friend?" he asked. "Because I know," he said in his winning entre nous way, "that you, unlike other people around here, won't get overly sensitive about it."

"Sure," I said, shifting in my chair, trying to affect nonchalance.

"You're never going to be the anchor of a major weekday newscast," he said with a casual certainty that made my stomach drop. "You don't have the looks," he went on, "and your voice is too grating."

He had me in a funny spot. Having coolly

promised him that I could take whatever he had to say without getting too sensitive, I couldn't very well lash out as he killed my dreams. So I pretended not to be poleaxed as we wrapped up the meeting and I limped out of his office.

While my communication with my bosses was, to say the least, unsatisfying, I did meanwhile have a sudden epiphany about how to talk about meditation without looking like a freak.

My disappearing on retreat for ten days with no email or phone contact naturally provoked a lot of questions, which outed me as a meditator, and forced me to discuss my new practice with a much wider group.

At first, these conversations didn't go so well. At my family's annual summer pool party, just weeks after my time with Goldstein in California, my father pointedly told me a story about some people he knew who had discovered meditation and subsequently become "like, totally ineffective." Later, he warily asked me, "So, are you a Buddhist now?" To which I muttered some sort of flustered nonanswer.

Among my broader group of friends and coworkers, the retreat spurred queries as skeptical as my father's. "You did *what* on your summer vacation?" they'd ask. The subtext always seemed to be "So you've pretty much joined a cult, haven't you?" I could tell that people were thinking what I certainly would have been thinking if I were in their shoes: that I had become one of *those* people, the formerly normal guy who arrives at middle age and adopts some sort of strange spirituality.

Whenever I was asked about meditation, I would either clam up and get a sheepish look on my face, the way dogs in Manhattan do when they're going to the bathroom on the street, or I would launch into an off-putting, overly emphatic lecture about the benefits of mindfulness, how it was actually a superpower, how it really wasn't as weird as everyone thought, and didn't involve "clearing the mind," and so on. I could see the tinge of mild terror in my listener's eyes — the cornered interlocutor politely but frantically looking for any means of egress.

There were a few things I was attempting, with varying degrees of ham-handedness, to achieve in these interchanges. Mostly I was trying to defend my reputation, to make sure people didn't think I was a loon. But there was something else. The more I meditated, the more I looked around and appreciated that we all have monkey minds

— that everyone has their own Weirs and Muirs they're competing against, their own manufactured balding crises (and, of course, the kinds of more serious collisions with impermanence from which I had mercifully been spared thus far). Especially after my powerful experiences on retreat, I felt compelled to share what I had learned. I just couldn't figure out how to do this effectively. At one point, during a work meeting, for example, I mentioned to Barbara Walters that I was considering writing a book on mindfulness. She smiled and replied, "Don't quit your day job."

After several weeks of this, I had a fateful conversation with my friend Kris, a senior producer at *GMA*. She'd been a mentor of mine since my earliest days at ABC. We had a no-holds-barred relationship, which usually consisted of her making fun of me for some on- or off-air foible. One day, we were chatting at the *GMA* rim when the subject of my recent "vacation" came up. She shot me a funny look and said, "What's with you and the whole meditation thing?"

Trying to avoid another long, unsuccessful answer, I blurted out, "I do it because it makes me 10% happier." The look on her face instantly changed. What had been a tiny glimmer of scorn was suddenly transformed into an expression of genuine interest. "Really?" she said. "That sounds pretty good, actually."

Boom: I'd found my shtick. 10% happier: it had the dual benefit of being catchy and true. It was the perfect answer, really — simultaneously counterprogramming against the overpromising of the self-helpers while also offering an attractive return on investment. It vaguely reminded me of the middling 1990s comedy *Crazy People,* in which Dudley Moore plays an ad exec who decides to start employing honesty in his taglines, coming up with such gems as "Volvos — Yes they are boxy, but they're safe," and "Jaguar — For men who'd like hand jobs from beautiful women they hardly know." His company sends him to an insane asylum.

My new slogan also jibed nicely with a major behind-the-scenes ethos in TV news: reporters, it was believed, should try never to oversell their stories. You don't want to go around telling the people who run the various shows that you've got the most amazing material in the world, and then leave them underwhelmed. They'll never put you on the air again. Always best to provide room for upside surprise. (Of course, you'd never know this by watching our product.

On the air, we believe in the opposite of underselling; we slap "exclusive" labels on everything.)

I wished I'd had my 10% line at the ready when being questioned by my dad. I couldn't blame him for being skeptical, but now my new slogan was an effective kryptonite against this kind of wariness. As I started test-driving it with others, it didn't create any on-the-spot converts, but it did at least appear to prevent people from thinking I had gone completely off the deep end.

About a month or so after the retreat, I got the chance to test the slogan with Mr. Enlightenment himself. I had arranged to interview Joseph Goldstein for a new digital show on religion I'd started called *Beliefs.* On a sunny day in early September, he showed up at the ABC studios in his khakis and light blue dress shirt, wearing a Black-Berry holster attached to his belt. Outside of the retreat setting, he was looser and funnier — even charmingly goofy at times. We got along like a house on fire.

I started the interview by asking how he discovered Buddhism in the first place. As a young man, he told me, he had been quite brash — "very much in my own head," he said. He went to Columbia University with the idea of becoming an architect or a lawyer, but he ended up majoring in philosophy. He then joined the Peace Corps. East Africa had been his first choice, but "karma being what it is," he was shipped off to Thailand, where he got his first exposure to Buddhism. He joined a discussion group for Westerners at a famous temple in Bangkok, in which he proved to be a controversial presence.

"People stopped coming to the group because I came," he told me, laughing. "You've probably been to groups like that, where there's that one person who doesn't shut up. That was me. Finally, one of the monks who was leading the group said, 'Joseph, I think you should try meditating.'"

So he did. Alone in his room, he set an alarm clock for five minutes, and was instantly "hooked."

"I saw that there's actually a systematic way of becoming aware of one's own mind," he said. "It just seemed so extraordinary to me. Before one is clued in, we're living our lives just basically acting out our conditioning, and acting out our habit patterns, you know?"

He was so excited that he started inviting his friends over to watch him meditate.

"They didn't come back," he said, laughing.

"So you were slightly insufferable?" I said.

"Ah, yes — slightly insufferable. But I think the meditation over the last forty years has helped."

After the Peace Corps, he moved to India for seven years to study meditation. Eventually, by the mid-1970s, he decided to move back home to the United States, where he'd been writing books, teaching, and leading retreats ever since.

On the subject of retreats, I asked, "Most people think nine days of all vegetarian food, no talking, and six hours a day of silent meditation sounds like —"

"Hell," he said, interrupting me with an utterly nondefensive chuckle. But, he added, when people do make the leap and attend a retreat, they get "the first glimpse of what the mind is actually doing. You know, we're getting a real close, intimate look at what our lives are about."

That notion really struck me: until we look directly at our minds we don't really know "what our lives are about."

"It's amazing," I said, "because everything we experience in this world goes through one filter — our minds — and we spend very little time bothering to see how it works."

"Exactly. That's why once people get a taste of it — it's so completely fascinating, because really our life is the manifestation of our minds."

With things going well, I figured this was the moment to float my new catchphrase. "People ask me — if I dare admit to them I meditate — 'So, is your life better?' And I like to say, 'It's about 10% better.' "

"10% is good for beginning a meditation practice. 10% is huge. I mean, if you got 10% of your money —"

"Yeah, it's a good return on your investment."

"It's a good return, and it gets more — the return gets more and more."

This turn in the conversation was perhaps inevitable. By the return on investment getting "more and more," Joseph was, of course, signaling that one could not only be 10% happier, but also 100% happy.

"I will admit," I said, "I remain skeptical about this notion of enlightenment. So I want to ask you, do you feel that you have achieved it?"

"No," he said. But he very quickly went on to say something that surprised me. While he hadn't reached full enlightenment

— the complete uprooting of greed, hatred, and delusion about the nature of reality — he was, he claimed, partway there.

I'd read up on this issue a little bit since the retreat. According to the school of Buddhism to which Joseph belonged (there were many, I'd learned), there were four stages of enlightenment. The schema sounded like something out of Dungeons & Dragons. Someone who'd achieved the first stage of enlightenment was a "stream-enterer." This was followed by a "once-returner," a "non-returner," and then a fully enlightened being, known as an "arhant." Each stage had sixteen sublevels.

"So you've achieved some of the early stages?"

"Yes, and there's more work to be done."

"How do you translate that into your daily life? When you start to lose your hair, or when somebody you love dies, or when your favorite baseball team starts to not be so good anymore, you don't suffer?"

"I would say that the amount of suffering in those situations has diminished enormously. It's not that I have different feelings, but I don't identify and attach to them — or make them a huge drama. You allow your emotions to come pass through with ease."

"Are you not afraid of dying?"

"One never knows until we're at that doorway, but right now I'm not."

How was I supposed to compute this? Here I was, sitting across from a fiercely intelligent, self-deprecating guy who, like Mark Epstein, could easily have been one of my Jewish uncles. Nothing about this person screamed "crazy." And yet he was telling me that not only did he believe in enlightenment — a seemingly fantastical transformation that denudes the mind of all of the things most of us believe make us human — but also that he was partway there. Was this some sort of affinity scam?

Making things more confusing was the fact that even though enlightenment sounded about as realistic as my cats being able to control the weather, everything about Joseph's bearing signaled that he was, in fact, an uncommonly happy guy.

I'm not sure exactly why, but this enlightenment thing really stuck in my craw. Maybe it was because it made me feel like my 10% solution was insufficient. Or maybe it was because I couldn't reconcile my admiration for Joseph with the seemingly outlandish things he believed. Did those beliefs call into question the validity of the whole enterprise? If he really bought into enlightenment, could I take anything he said seriously?

Fortunately, back at the office, I was able to shelve that theoretical 10%-versus-100% debate and apply what I'd learned on retreat to the very practical challenges I was facing. I was, in fact, finding mindfulness to be extremely useful.

After an initial period of "how dare he" indignation over Jim Murphy telling me I was never going to be a big-time anchor-man, I decided to approach the problem in a Buddhist style: to lean into it, to take his views seriously, no matter how inconvenient they may have been — to respond, rather than react. I forced myself to consider an unpleasant possibility: Maybe I was like a shih tzu who thinks he's a bullmastiff? A kitten who looks in the mirror and sees a lion?

But no: I wasn't willing to fully concede — either to myself or anyone else — that Murphy's pessimistic forecast was accurate. Careers in TV news are too frequently influenced by factors like luck, timing, and executive-level caprice to ever really count anything out. However, the new mindful me, instead of automatically recoiling into denial or rage, was able to see that Murphy probably was trying to be helpful — although he was also undoubtedly aiming to put me in my place so I'd finally sign the damn contract.

On that score, he succeeded. His unsolicited dose of career perspective helped persuade me to throw in the towel and close the deal.

In signing, I told myself that at least now I would be able to officially make the jump to *GMA,* a job I was convinced would almost certainly propel my career in new and marvelous directions. Untethering myself from the rigid formalism of the evening news would, I believed, open up heretofore unseen vistas. As it turned out, being a morning TV host was not as easy as it looked.

For five years on Sunday *World News,* I had been helming a true one-man show. Ninety-seven percent of what came out of my mouth was prescripted verbiage written by me and loaded into a teleprompter. When correspondents came on the show to do live shots, I knew in advance what they were going to say. In other words, there were very few surprises. Now I would be part of a cast of four — including a female cohost, a News Reader, and a meteorologist — all of whom were free to say whatever they wanted whenever they wanted. This loss of control created some interesting challenges.

GMA was structured in a way that was loaded with opportunities for adlibbing, right from the minute we went on the air. That was the point of it, really. The audience wanted to see the hosts interacting spontaneously. The very first thing we did after the "Open" of the show — the pre-produced part where you see snippets of the morning's big stories and then the *Good Morning America* animation — was called the "Hellos," during which we would greet the viewers and preview a few of the other stories coming up that morning. Our lines were written into the prompter, but mostly that was just a guide; we were supposed to be having a conversation. However, when the chatter went down a verbal tributary for which I wasn't prepared, I would sometimes find myself tensing up, nervously shuffling my papers or letting out a forced Ed Mc-Mahon–style belly laugh.

This was frustrating for me. Off camera, I was usually able to defuse situations with humor. Part of what was holding me back now was the dawning realization that the jokes that came naturally to me were often better suited to a late-night cable show than to morning television.

Basic logistical questions could also be tricky. How did I sit on a couch — where we did some of the lighter segments toward the end of the broadcast — without slouching or spreading my legs too widely? How did I smoothly extricate the group from conversations when the producers were screaming in my earpiece that we were running out of time to hit the commercial break? No one gave me the memo.

There was also the challenge of adjusting to the content of the show. I had been around morning television for a while, so I knew when I accepted the job that we'd be peddling softer fare than the evening news. I also considered myself an info-omnivore who enjoyed crime and pop culture empty calories along with my nutritious hard news. Nonetheless, I would sometimes find myself outside of my professional comfort zone: playing judge in a live weigh-in contest to determine which Chihuahua was the world's smallest, competing in a gingerbread house–making contest with my fellow anchors, and — the coup de grace — dancing on live television with a box on my head, dressed up like the Shuffle Bot from the hip-hop band LMFAO.

Fortunately, *Nightline* and *World News* continued to provide me with opportunities to do work that put me firmly back in my comfort zone. Wonbo and I did a piece where we interviewed evangelical pastors — whose faces and voices we agreed to alter in order to protect their identities — who had secretly become atheists but hadn't yet ginned up the courage to tell their flocks. I confronted Governor Jan Brewer of Arizona about her refusal to set free an elderly convicted killer even after her own clemency board unanimously recommended his sentence be commuted. (I surprised the governor by bringing the inmate's son to a news conference. The two of us fired questions at her in tandem. She fled pretty quickly.) Most significantly, I did a full half hour on *Nightline* about the saga of an eighteen-year-old boy I'd met in Iraq and helped move to America to attend college. Much as the Bush administration had naively believed that Americans would be "greeted as liberators" after the invasion, I had assumed this young man (who, ironically, was also called Dan — a Kurdish name) would thrive upon arrival here. I had grown very attached to him, and when he got kicked out of school for misbehavior, I spent several years — and an enormous amount of emotional energy — trying to get him straightened out, only to be frustrated at every turn by his adolescent intransigence. I recorded every twist of this running drama, shooting much of it myself on a small camera. I couldn't help but view Dan's actions through the lens of the Buddhist concept of suffering. He was never satisfied where he was; he always assumed that the next big life change would solve all of his problems. Ultimately, to my profound disappointment, he ended up moving back to Iraq — a decision he regretted immediately.

Back on weekend *GMA,* I was discovering that the gig did have some upsides. Notwithstanding my occasional stiffness, our little team was getting nice feedback. Our colleagues and bosses gushed about how we had "good chemistry." I really liked the other members of the on-air team. My female cohost was a lovely young woman of Moldovan descent, named Bianna Golodryga. We had known and liked each other for several years before she became my TV wife. (The similarity of her name to that of my real-life wife was a bit delicate, though. On my first official day on the job, I said, "I am now permanently one consonant away from destruction.") The News Reader was Ron Claiborne, a drily funny former print reporter. At first, we had a rotating cast of weatherpeople, until the bosses hired a vivacious young meteorologist from Chicago named Ginger Zee. (Zee is a shortening of her real — and awesome — last name: Zuidgeest.)

I also started to appreciate that even though the morning audience was smaller than the evening audience, the relationship with the viewers was much more intimate and intense, the result of the fact that the format was looser and more personal. Morning TV, I came to see, was a potent way to convey useful and important information. Being in people's living rooms and bedrooms as they prepared for their day, and discussing current events in a more casual manner, had a unique impact — perhaps even more powerful, at times, than the intoning-from-the-mountaintop nature of evening news. I felt enormously lucky to have the job.

The intimacy with the audience was, however, a double-edged sword. While I enjoyed the opportunity to chat with viewers via Facebook and Twitter (as a broadcaster, you're always curious about people who watch), I couldn't help but notice that people felt free to share their opinions about me in ways that an evening news anchor rarely endures. I kept a file in which I saved some of my favorite messages (in their original, uncorrected form):

"will you plz unbutton ur jacket????? U look uncomfortable :)"

"Please please please tell Dan to sit squarely at the desk and QUIT leaning to his right, the viewers left towards Bianna. It is so distracting."

"make dan go away please"

"Just thought i would let you know that your tie doesnt look centered it almost looks crooked."

"Don you have a hair out place that is making you look like ALALFA !"

"please do me a favor, slow the blank down and stop trying to take over the show. it makes you look like a major clown."

"u should really dvr @gma and listen to yourself. As u give the news and the story is of a serious nature u shouldn't sound happy."

I was, in fact, DVRing myself — and my criticism of my own performance was much harsher than anything the viewers had to offer. I was not a huge fan of the guy I saw on television enthusing about the waistcoated kangaroo.

This was where meditation really paid off. Post-retreat, I was up to thirty minutes a day. Every morning, I would scan my calendar to figure out when I was going to be able to fit in work, meditation, exercise, and spending time with Bianca. Some afternoons I'd bang out my thirty minutes on my office couch as I awaited script approval from *World News* or whichever show had assigned me a story. I didn't necessarily look forward to sitting. In fact, the first thought to pop into my head after I'd shut my eyes was usually *How the hell am I going to do this for a half hour?* But then I'd see the thought for what it was: just a thought. I rarely missed a day, and when I did, I would feel not only guilty, but also less mindful.

When I got tense about work, I would watch how it was manifesting in my body — the buzzing in my chest, my earlobes getting hot, the heaviness in my head. Investigating and labeling my feelings really did put them in perspective; they seemed much less solid. The RAIN routine, plus Joseph's "is this useful?" mantra, almost always helped me snap out of it.

But while meditation made me more resilient, it certainly was not a cure-all. First, it didn't magically make me looser on *GMA*. Second, while I recovered more quickly, it didn't seem to prevent all churning. On some weekend mornings, I walked out of our studios haunted by Irwin the kangaroo.

On one such day, I left the office and headed downtown for brunch with Mark Epstein. In the two years since I'd met him, we had become genuine friends. He and his wife, a talented and successful artist named Arlene, had been to our apartment for dinner. Bianca and I had been to their airy downtown loft — and also met their two grown children. When I went to spend time with Mark solo, Bianca — who adored the guy — was just a tiny bit jealous.

I tried to orchestrate a get-together once every two or three months. Usually, it would be brunch after one of my weekend *GMA* shifts, and before Mark headed upstate to the country house where Arlene had her studio. I'd be the only one in the restaurant wearing a suit.

On this morning, having long since

branched out from the Tribeca Grand, we were meeting at one of our other regular spots: Morandi, an Italian bistro in the West Village. I arrived with a list of items in the "Questions for Mark" file in my BlackBerry. Chief among them: Even though I was rebounding more quickly, were my self-recriminations over my job performance a sign that I was somehow a JV meditator? Should mindfulness be more effective at extinguishing this kind of thing?

"How would I accurately describe how meditation is helping me here? It's just allowing me to step back and watch it all happen, nanoseconds at a time, and through that process it takes some of the fangs out of it?"

"Yes," he said.

"It's not going to make it go away."

"No. It might help it go away a little quicker. It might. It *might,*" he said, his head shaking slightly as he carefully chose his words. "To the extent that it loosens the way you would ordinarily be caught by how terrible this all is, it might loosen your own attachment to whatever melodrama is unfolding."

"My remedy these days combines some things that are non-meditative," I said. "I think to myself, 'So if this whole thing blows up, what's the worst-case scenario? I lose my job? I still have a wife who loves me — and the only person who can ruin that is me.' It works, but it has nothing to do with meditation."

"No — that's insight!" As he spoke, his voice rose an octave with insistence.

"Insight into the nature of reality?" I asked sarcastically.

"Yeah," he said, not taking the bait. "That's insight, because you're not clinging to success so seriously."

"But maybe I'm just clinging to Bianca."

"That's better. You're clinging to something that's far more substantial."

As I sat there mulling Mark's words while wolfing overpriced eggs, my new 10% happier slogan began to make even more sense. It was a reminder of the message Mark had delivered a year ago, when I was unsure about whether David Westin was going to give me the *GMA* promotion. Back then, at our Tribeca Grand beer summit, Mark had helped me see that the point of getting behind the waterfall wasn't to magically solve all of your problems, only to handle them better, by creating space between stimulus and response. It was about mitigation, not alleviation. Even after decades of practice, Mark — who, unlike Joseph, made no claims to any level of enlightenment — told me, "I still suffer like a normal person." (When I asked him what kind of suffering was most common for him, he said something about dealing with self-pity, but didn't elaborate.)

Moreover, I could now see how the mitigation Mark was pitching had real-world consequences. For example, it allowed me to acknowledge my performance issues rather than pretend they didn't exist. Perhaps most important, it made me easier to live with. Bianca said she couldn't remember the last time I walked into the apartment scowling, even when I'd had a particularly tough day. Her only beef was that she had to tiptoe around the apartment if I was meditating in the bedroom. (While she was a believer in the potential of meditation, she was not doing that much herself. On those occasions when I saw her stressed about work, it took restraint not to recommend that she start her own practice. I was pretty sure, though, that proselytizing would make her want to throttle me, and that the smarter play was just to listen sympathetically.)

Much as it had been with my Iraqi friend Dan, it was illuminating to view my own struggles as a morning-show host through the lens of "suffering." In a world characterized by impermanence, where all of our pleasures are fleeting, I had subconsciously assumed that if only I could get the weekend *GMA* gig, I would achieve bulletproof satisfaction — and I was shocked when it didn't work out that way. This, as Joseph had pointed out on retreat, is the lie we tell ourselves our whole lives: as soon as we get the next meal, party, vacation, sexual encounter, as soon as we get married, get a promotion, get to the airport check-in, get through security and consume a bouquet of Auntie Anne's Cinnamon Sugar Stix, we'll feel really good. But as soon as we find ourselves in the airport gate area, having ingested 470 calories' worth of sugar and fat before dinner, we don't bother to examine the lie that fuels our lives. We tell ourselves we'll sleep it off, take a run, eat a healthy breakfast, and then, finally, everything will be complete. We live so much of our lives pushed forward by these "if only" thoughts, and yet the itch remains. The pursuit of happiness becomes the source of our unhappiness.

Joseph always said that seeing the reality of suffering "inclines the mind toward liberation." Maybe, but all the enlightenment talk continued to feel totally theoretical and unattainable — if not downright

CHAPTER 9
"THE NEW CAFFEINE"

"Retarded."

That was how Private First Class Jason Lindemann, a twenty-something with a high-and-tight haircut and a permanently amused look on his face, described his first impression of meditation. "The first time they had us do it," he told me, "I thought, 'Oh man, here we go.' "

PFC Lindemann and I were talking in a dusty corner of the sprawling Camp Pendleton marine base in Southern California. "So no part of you thought this could in any way be useful?" I asked.

With zero hesitation, he said, "No."

Lindemann was an involuntary subject in a multimillion-dollar scientific study, requested by the marine corps brass. The military's interest in a practice that was seemingly anathema to the world of warfare was fueled by an explosion of science. Forget the blood pressure study that had made me willing to try meditation in the first place; this new research was on the next level. It was creating some surprising converts — previously hardened skeptics who were now employing mindfulness in ways that would revolutionize my approach to work, and drive a stake through the heart of the assumption that meditation made you, "like, totally ineffective."

On my travels to various Buddhist seminars, I had started to hear mentions of scientific research into meditation. It sounded promising, so I checked it out. What I found blew my mind. Meditation, once part of the counterculture, had now fully entered the scientific mainstream. It had been subjected to thousands of studies, suggesting an almost laughably long list of health benefits, including salutary effects on the following:

- major depression
- drug addiction
- binge eating
- smoking cessation
- stress among cancer patients
- loneliness among senior citizens
- ADHD
- asthma
- psoriasis

- irritable bowel syndrome

Studies also indicated that meditation reduced levels of stress hormones, boosted the immune system, made office workers more focused, and improved test scores on the GRE. Apparently mindfulness did everything short of making you able to talk to animals and bend spoons with your mind.

This research boom got its start with a Jew-Bu named Jon Kabat-Zinn, a Manhattan-raised, MIT-trained microbiologist who claimed to have had an elaborate epiphany — a "vision," he called it — while on a retreat in 1979. The substance of the vision was that he could bring meditation to a much broader audience by stripping it of Buddhist metaphysics. Kabat-Zinn designed something called Mindfulness Based Stress Reduction (MBSR), an eight-week course that taught secularized meditation to tens of thousands of people around America and the world. Having a simple, replicable meditation protocol made it easy to test the effects on patients.

Things truly got sci-fi when researchers started peering directly into the brains of meditators. A blockbuster MRI study from Harvard found that people who took the eight-week MBSR course had thicker gray matter in the areas of the brain associated with self-awareness and compassion, while the regions associated with stress actually shrank. This study appeared to confirm the whole respond-not-react superpower. The regions where the gray matter shriveled were, evolutionarily speaking, the oldest parts of the human brain, which sit right atop the spinal column, and are home to our most basic instincts. (As one person has called it, these are the "want-it-don't-want-it, have-sex-with-it-or-kill-it" zones.) Conversely, the areas that grew were the newer parts of the brain, the prefrontal cortices, which evolved to help us regulate our primal urges.

Another study, out of Yale, looked at the part of the brain known as the default mode network (DMN), which is active when we're lost in thought — ruminating about the past, projecting into the future, obsessing about ourselves. The researchers found meditators were not only deactivating this region while they were practicing, but also when they were not meditating. In other words, meditation created a new default mode. I could actually feel this happening with me. I noticed myself cultivating a sort of nostalgia for the present, developing the reflex to squelch pointless self-talk and simply notice whatever was going on around me: a blast of hot halitosis from a subway vent as I walked to work, the carpet of suburban lights seen from a landing airplane, rippling water reflecting sine waves of light onto the side of a boat while I was shooting a story in Virginia Beach. In moments where I was temporarily able to suspend my monkey mind and simply experience whatever was going on, I got just the smallest taste of the happiness I'd achieved while on retreat.

Even though scientists were quick to point out that the research was still in its embryonic stage, these studies had helped demolish neuroscientific dogma that had prevailed for generations. The old conventional wisdom was that once we reached adulthood, our brain stopped changing. This orthodoxy was now replaced with a new paradigm, called neuroplasticity. The brain, it turns out, is constantly changing in response to experience. It's possible to sculpt your brain through meditation just as you build and tone your body through exercise — to grow your gray matter the way doing curls grows your bicep.

This idea contradicted widespread cultural assumptions about happiness that are reflected in the etymology of the word itself.

The root *hap* means "luck," as in *hapless* or *haphazard*. What the science was showing was that our levels of well-being, resilience, and impulse control were not simply God-given traits, our portion of which we had to accept as a fait accompli. The brain, the organ of experience, through which our entire lives are led, can be trained. Happiness is a skill.

Among the unlikely people for whom the science was creating some open-mindedness about meditation were two hard-driving and successful women who both loomed large in my psyche.

My mother — the original skeptic in my life, the debunker of God and Santa Claus — was very impressed by the Harvard study showing gray matter thickening in meditators. After reading about it online, she asked me to give her a meditation guidebook for Christmas. A few weeks later, she sent me an excited email saying that she had read the book and had decided, during a taxi ride to the airport, to give it a try. She was able to follow her breath all the way to the terminal without breaking her concentration. She then started sitting for thirty minutes a day, something that had taken me a year to achieve. The rough breakdown of my emotional response to this information was: 80% validated, 17% humbled, 3% resentful.

A few months later, on a visit to New York, both my parents spoke enthusiastically about how meditation had stopped my mom's snoring. (When I asked by what mechanism this possibly could have been achieved, no thesis was proffered.) Despite the ebullience, my dad was still not meditating — and, like with my wife, I knew better than to push.

I was also sensing new openness to meditation from another unexpected source: the woman who, for me, represented the gold standard in professional diligence, Diane Sawyer. She was one of the most fiercely intelligent and insatiably curious human beings I'd ever met. She read every newspaper and magazine known to man. She wrote and rewrote her own stories right up until airtime. She studied for interviews or major news events for weeks, memorizing obscure yet illuminating details.

Diane was inspiring to me in many of the same ways that Peter Jennings had been. She had a deep sense of responsibility to the audience. She insisted on providing viewers with useful information and practical insights rather than just doing the same old lazy story that everybody else was doing. She had a dizzying knack for identifying the key question at the heart of every story. Unlike with Peter, though, there were no temper tantrums. I had built up a reservoir of affection for Diane ever since she visited the ABC News bureau in Baghdad when I was stationed there before the war. Shortly after anchoring *GMA* live from the roof of the Information Ministry, she came to our office and spent several hours just hanging out. Here was a woman who had worked in the White House, become the first female correspondent for *60 Minutes,* and had more journalism awards than I have teeth, casually eating bad Iraqi pizza with us.

That's not to say I didn't find her a little bit intimidating. When we went over scripts, she inevitably asked me an unanticipated and incisive question for which I had no answer.

At first, my meditation habit was a source of gentle ribbing. Diane had long teased me for being "pure." She joked about my healthful diet, frequent exercise, and abstinence from booze and caffeine. (I had recently quit both — not because I had become a straight-edge yogi or whatever, but because, as I got older, my body simply couldn't tolerate them.) I would try to defend myself, pointing to my dessert habit and taste for cheeseburgers. I did not, however, have the nerve to tell her I used to do enough drugs that it apparently contributed to my having a panic attack not ten yards away from her.

I fought through the fear that pitching Diane a story on meditation would only provoke an eye roll. I sent her an email, suggesting we do a piece about how the scientific research was inspiring people in unusual places to embrace mindfulness. To my delight, she bit.

When the PR woman in the leopard-print blouse started dropping phrases like "letting go," and "turning in to your emotions," I really knew meditation was breaking out of the Buddhist ghetto.

After Diane gave me the green light to go do some mindfulness stories, my first stop was Minneapolis, and the headquarters of General Mills, the corporate behemoth behind such brands as Cheerios, Betty Crocker, and Hamburger Helper. Everyone here was so earnest and hail-fellow-well-met, with crisp demeanors and twangy Midwest accents. Which made it all the more remarkable that there were now meditation rooms, complete with zafus and yoga mats, in every building in the complex.

The person responsible for this was a hard-charging, no-nonsense, sensible-haircut corporate attorney named Janice Marturano. She'd discovered meditation a few years prior, found it to be a massive value-add, both personally and professionally, and started spreading it virally through the executive ranks. She'd trained scores of her colleagues, including the PR woman whose job it was to shepherd us briskly through this hive of corporate busyness all day long.

A big part of Marturano's success in bringing mindfulness to this unlikely venue was that she talked about it not as a "spiritual" exercise but instead as something that made you a "better leader" and "more focused," and that enhanced your "creativity and innovation." She didn't even like the term "stress reduction." "For a lot of us," she said, "we think that having stress in our lives isn't a bad thing. It gives us an edge." I liked this — a meditation philosophy that left room for the "price of security."

Marturano had a whole slew of practical tips that extended well beyond the meditation cushion. One of her main pieces of advice was a direct challenge to me, an assault on a central pillar of my work life.

"So you're telling me that I can't multi-task?" I asked as we sat down for an interview.

"It's not me telling you," she said. "It's neuroscience that would say that our capacity to multitask is virtually nonexistent. Multitasking is a computer-derived term. We have one processor. We can't do it."

"I think that when I'm sitting at my desk feverishly doing seventeen things at once that I'm being clever and efficient, but you're saying I'm actually wasting my time?"

"Yes, because when you're moving from this project to this project, your mind flits back to the original project, and it can't pick it up where it left off. So it has to take a few steps back and then ramp up again, and that's where the productivity loss is." This problem was, of course, exacerbated in the age of what had been dubbed the "info-blitzkrieg," where it took superhuman strength to ignore the siren call of the latest tweet, or the blinking red light on the Black-Berry. Scientists had even come up with a term for this condition: "continuous partial attention." It was a syndrome with which I was intimately familiar, even after all my meditating.

Marturano recommended something radical: do only one thing at a time. When you're on the phone, be on the phone. When you're in a meeting, be there. Set aside an hour to check your email, and then shut off your computer monitor and focus on the task at hand.

Another tip: take short mindfulness breaks throughout the day. She called them "purposeful pauses." So, for example, instead of fidgeting or tapping your fingers while your computer boots up, try to watch your breath for a few minutes. When driving, turn off the radio and feel your hands on the wheel. Or when walking between meetings, leave your phone in your pocket and just notice the sensations of your legs moving.

"If I'm a corporate samurai," I said, "I'd be a little worried about taking all these pauses that you recommend because I'd be thinking, 'Well, my rivals aren't pausing. They're working all the time.' "

"Yeah, but that assumes that those pauses aren't helping you. Those pauses are the ways to make you a more clear thinker and for you to be more focused on what's important."

This was another attack on my work style. I had long assumed that ceaseless planning was the recipe for effectiveness, but Marturano's point was that too much mental churning was counterproductive. When you lurch from one thing to the next, constantly scheming, or reacting to incoming fire, the mind gets exhausted. You get sloppy and make bad decisions. I could see how the counterintuitive act of stopping, even for a few seconds, could be a source of strength, not weakness. This was a practical complement to Joseph's "is this useful?" mantra. It was the opposite of zoning out, it was zoning in.

In fact, I looked into it and found there was science to suggest that pausing could be a key ingredient in creativity and innovation. Studies showed that the best way to engineer an epiphany was to work hard, focus, research, and think about a problem — and then let go. Do something else. That didn't necessarily mean meditate, but do something that relaxes and distracts you; let your unconscious mind go to work, making connections from disparate parts of the brain. This, too, was massively counterintuitive for me. My impulse when presented with a thorny problem was to bulldoze my way through it, to swarm it with thought. But the best solutions often come when you allow yourself to get comfortable with ambiguity. This is why people have aha moments in the shower. It was why Kabat-Zinn had a vision while on retreat. It was why Don Draper from *Mad Men,* when asked how he comes up with his great slogans, said he spends all day thinking and then goes to the movies.

Janice Marturano was on the bleeding edge of what had become an improbable corporate trend. Meditation classes had infiltrated not only General Mills but also Aetna, Procter & Gamble, and Target, where, as part of my Diane-approved field trip, I sat in on a weekly session at the corporate headquarters called "Meditating Merchants." Mindfulness was also being taught in business schools and written about without derision in the *Wall Street Journal* and the *Harvard Business Review.* An article on Financial-Planning.com featured "meditation tips for advisors." High-powered executives were using mindfulness to make sure that every confrontation didn't escalate into a fight-or-flight event, and that every email, phone call, and breaking news alert didn't derail their focus. This trend had become particularly hot in Silicon Valley, where meditation was now increasingly being viewed as a software upgrade for the brain. At Google, engineers were offered a class called "Neural Self-Hacking." An article in *Wired* magazine referred to meditation as the tech world's "new caffeine."

It wasn't just corporations hopping on this bandwagon, but also schools, prisons, the U.S. Forest Service, and, of course, the marines, who were actively eyeing meditation as a way to effect a sort of psychological "regime change" among their own troops. The final stop in my field trip was Camp Pendleton, where I met the reluctant meditator, Private First Class Lindemann.

The marines were initially interested in mindfulness because they thought it might help them deal with an epidemic of PTSD, but there was also hope that meditation could produce more effective warriors. The theory was that the practice would make troops less reactive, and therefore less vulnerable to the classic insurgent tactic of provoking the types of disproportionate responses that alienate the civilian population. What a counterintuitive notion: meditation as a way to deal with asymmetric warfare. As the woman who'd convinced the marines to conduct this experiment — Georgetown professor Liz Stanley — told me, "There is nothing incense-y about that. There just isn't."

While there was resistance at first, many of the marines ended up liking meditation. Even PFC Lindemann grudgingly came around. He told me he now found it easier to calm down after stressful situations. "At first, I was kind of skeptical," he said, "but then you kinda start noticing a little bit of change. As you go further into it, you start understanding it."

After shooting all of these stories, I, too, experienced a sudden "vision." It wasn't as dramatic as Jon Kabat-Zinn's, but it did come at an unusual moment.

The producers of weekend *GMA* had decided to wire up a rental car with cameras, pack the anchors inside, punch in some GPS coordinates, and call it "America's Cheapest Road Trip." The conceit: have the cosseted on-air types drive themselves hundreds of miles to a seaside campground, pitch their own tents, and cook their own food; hilarity ensues. There was even a patina of news-you-can-use value to this ratings stunt because the economy was still in the tank, and the piece would contain a few useful nuggets of advice about how to do family vacations on a budget.

Somewhere between New York City and our final destination in Maryland, we stopped at one of those roadside plazas that have gas, greasy food, and bathrooms with fossilized filth dating back to the Mesozoic era. While I was waiting outside for Ron and Bianna to finish up inside, I decided to do a little walking meditation. About three steps into it, a family passed by and stared at me. I clammed up and pretended to check my BlackBerry.

That's when I had my vision. Nothing too elaborate; I simply flashed on a world in which doing a zombie walk in public wouldn't be slightly mortifying — where meditation would be universally socially acceptable. I felt nearly certain that this world was actually not too far off. Mind you, I wasn't predicting a Tolle-esque "shift in planetary consciousness." Nor was I forecasting that society would be overrun by "stream-entrants" and "non-returners" of the Joseph Goldstein variety. Instead, I pictured a world in which significant numbers of people were 10% happier and less reactive. I imagined what this could do for marriage, parenting, road rage, politics — even television news.

Public health revolutions can happen quite rapidly. Most Americans didn't brush their teeth, for example, until after World War II, when soldiers were ordered to maintain dental hygiene. Exercise didn't become popular until the latter half of the twentieth century, after science had clearly showed its benefits. In the 1950s, if you had told people you were going running, they would have asked who was chasing you. The difference with meditation was that if it actually took hold, the impact would go far beyond improving muscle tone or fighting tooth decay. Mindfulness, I had come to believe, could, in fact, change the world.

Of course, I hadn't gotten into the whole meditation thing to have a global impact. My interests were parochial; I wanted relief from the ego. Now, though, I found myself in the funny position of believing deeply in a cause. I began attending conferences with names like Wisdom 2.0, Creating a Mindful Society, and Buddhist Geeks. I made new friends, like the beer-drinking, backslapping congressman from Ohio who wrote a book about mindfulness, and the former JPMorgan banker (a guy so successful even my brother was impressed) who started a new venture capital fund specifically designed to "bring mindfulness to scale." I experienced a surge of excitement as I strategized with my new friends about how to expose meditation to a wider audience. We had conspiratorial meetings and meals; we exchanged emails; we hugged a lot.

In my view, the biggest impediment to Kabat-Zinn's — and now *my* — vision becoming a reality was meditation's massive PR problem. It was still mildly embarrassing to admit to most people that I meditated. This was largely because the practice was popularized in this country by Beat poets, robed gurus, and hippies — and that cultural hangover persisted. Stylistically, the presentation of the average meditation teacher struck me as a bizarre cousin of the stentorian monotone that TV reporters employ — an affectation to which I had sadly not been immune. Just as we in the news business too often relied on shopworn language — "Shock and disbelief in [fill in the blank] tonight . . ." — Buddhist teachers had their own set of hackneyed phrases. Stories were "shared"; emotions were "held in love and tenderness." While the secular mindfulness people had dropped some of this lingo, they had replaced it with a jargon of their own, replete with homogenized, Hallmark-ized, irony-free terms like "purposeful pauses," "meditating merchants," and "interiority." These people needed a Frank Luntz, that pollster who'd helped the Republicans rebrand the "estate tax" into the "death tax" and recast loosened pollution laws as "the Clear Skies Act."

I wasn't sure that I was the right Luntz for this job, but I figured it couldn't hurt to pitch in. Ever since Bangor, I'd been obsessed with finding stories I liked and figuring out how to make them interesting to other people. Mindfulness, I now realized, was the best and potentially most impactful story I'd ever covered. In many ways, it was my craziest act of gonzo journalism. If it could help a monumental skeptic like me, I could only imagine what it could do for others, and I thought that if I could find a way to make it more broadly appealing, that would be a real service.

One-on-one preaching to my friends and family was still definitely a bad idea, but finding new ways to get the word out to a wider audience somehow seemed less obnoxious. To succeed, though, would require finding fresh ways to discuss the subject. It brought to mind a former colleague of mine from local news in Portland, Maine. He was a reporter named Bob Elliot, who used to post lists on the wall of the newsroom of what he called "lose 'ems," clichéd words or phrases that were showing up too often in our newscasts. If any of the rest of us used a "lose 'em," Bob would shoot us with a rubber band.

I took my first little stab at addressing meditation's PR problem when *World News* aired my story on the increasing embrace of mindfulness in counterintuitive locales. We showed a graphic of a brain, illuminating the regions that, to use Diane's words, got "plumped up" as a result of meditation. We used a sound bite from Rivers Cuomo, the lead singer of Weezer, who credited the practice with curing his stage fright. I explained how simple meditation was — and that there was no need for robes, chanting, incense, or joining a religious group.

When I walked off the set after my live shot, members of Diane's team were abuzz. Was it really that simple? How many minutes a day did they need to do to change their brains?

The next morning I got an email from Diane herself, who expressed an interest in learning more about meditation. If I could hook someone like her, it felt like a pretty good start.

As excited as I was about the notion of popularizing the practice, the concerns of some of my old-school Buddhist friends, including Mark Epstein, did give me pause. The traditionalists did not appreciate the irony of capitalists and marines embracing a practice with a history of disdaining violence and accumulation of wealth. They worried that mindfulness would simply create better baby killers and robber barons. They pointed derisively to the proliferation of books such as *Mindfulness for Dummies, The Mindful Investor,* and *The Joy of Mindful Sex.* Critics had a term for this phenomenon: "McMindfulness." There was something important being overlooked, they argued, in the mainstreaming of meditation — a central plank in the Buddhist platform: compassion.

While I'd digested enough dharma books and lectures to know that Buddhists were always going on about compassion, I had long figured I could ignore the issue, the same way I did with karma or reincarnation. It was true that mindfulness had made me calmer and less reactive, and that I now felt the urge to spread the word as far as I possibly could, but still, my goal was not to be Mother Teresa.

Despite my powerful experience of being snot-soaked and supine while doing compassion meditation on retreat, I had not subsequently pursued metta in my daily practice. My resistance was based, in part, on the fact that compassion meditation was a little annoying — but more significantly, it stemmed from a deep-seated suspicion: that we each have a sort of kindness set point, the result of factory settings that could not be altered, and that mine may not be dialed particularly high. I was a good enough guy, yes. I loved children and animals, etc. If no one was looking, I might even get misty during a rom-com. But the Buddhist concept of boundless compassion seemed out of reach.

Once again, science — and a well-timed personal encounter — would shatter my assumptions.

CHAPTER 10
THE SELF-INTERESTED CASE
FOR NOT BEING A DICK

The international avatar of compassion marched briskly into the room and declared that he had to relieve himself.

"First duty!" said His Holiness the Dalai Lama, as he bustled off toward the bathroom. He seemed sprightly, but certainly not, as decades of relentlessly positive publicity might have led one to believe, trailing pixie dust. Moreover, the members of his entourage — often a reflection of the person they serve — were uniformly stern and unsmiling.

I came into this interview with a bad attitude. Most of my friends in the meditation world revered the Dalai Lama, but to me he represented the part of Buddhism with which I was least comfortable. What I liked about the dharma was its rigorous empiricism and unyielding embrace of hard truths. Here, though, was a guy in robes, anointed at the age of two because some government monks claimed to have seen special signs, like a rainbow in the sky near his childhood home. Fast-forward a few decades and he was buddies with the Beastie Boys and Richard Gere, invited to guest edit *Vogue,* featured in Apple ads, and the subject of adoring movies by the likes of Martin Scorsese (who reportedly said he could feel his heart beat more keenly in the Dalai Lama's presence).

My contrarian impulses were heightened by the fact that I'd just watched a bunch of scientists here at Emory University fawn all over the Dalai Lama. As the academics presented the results of their research on the effects of meditation, they leaned forward, literally on the edge of their seats, while obsequiously calling him "Your Holiness." Meanwhile, he sat there wearing an oddly inappropriate sun visor (presumably to protect his eyes from the overhead lights).

Once His Holiness had emptied his bladder, he was back in character, the smiley guy we know from gauzy hagiographies. The Emory conference had just wrapped up, and we were going to do the interview backstage. I started by asking about his long-standing support for scientific research into meditation. "There's a risk," I said. "What if scientists discover something that contradicts your faith?"

"No — no risk. If a scientist confirm nonexistence of something we believe, then we have to accept that."

"So if scientists come up with something that contradicts your beliefs, you will change your beliefs?"

"Oh yes. Yes."

Reassuring answer. I wondered to myself, though, whether this policy applied to the issue of rebirth. If scientists could prove that he wasn't the reincarnation of the previous Dalai Lama, it would erase all his religious and political power, leaving him just one more old man in a visor.

Next litmus test: "Is your mind always calm?" I asked.

"No, no, no. Occasionally lose my temper."

"You do?"

"Oh yes. If someone is never lose temper then perhaps they may come from another space," he said, pointing toward the sky and laughing from the belly, his eyes twinkling beneath his thick glasses.

"So if somebody says to you, 'I never lose my temper,' you don't believe them?"

"No. And some people say this is some miracle power — I don't believe."

Within minutes, he had already proven

himself more reasonable than either Eckhart Tolle or Deepak Chopra.

As I sat there, surrounded by cameras, my crew, the Emory PR people, and His Holiness's Tibetan retinue, it dawned on me that the Dalai Lama was yet another person I'd prematurely misjudged. After all, even if he subscribed to a metaphysical program I didn't share, he had actually played a key role in jump-starting the scientific research into meditation, providing both inspiration and funding. What's more, I realized, one should probably not overlook that whole thing where he responded to the Chinese invasion of Tibet — from which he barely escaped with his life — with repeated requests for forgiveness and nonviolence.

As the interview progressed, my posture — both internally and externally — changed. It's not that I was feeling my heart beat more keenly, à la Scorsese, but, like the academics I'd scorned at the conference, I, too, was now leaning forward in my chair, with the closest my face can come to a beatific expression. Meanwhile, I was relieved to find the Dalai Lama seemed to be pretty engaged himself. I'd read that if he leaned back in his chair, that meant he'd lost interest. But he was still inclined toward me, eyes bright.

Toward the end of our twenty-minute interview (the Tibetans, like Tolle's people, were very strict about time) came an exchange that fundamentally changed my view on compassion. I brought up something he'd posted on Twitter. (The fact that he had a Twitter feed was another reason to like the man — although I was pretty sure his staff managed the account.) "You have a quote that I love. You say, 'Most of one's own troubles, worries, and sadness come from self-cherishing, self-centeredness.' But don't we need to be somewhat self-centered in order to succeed in life?"

"Self-cherishing, that's by nature," he said (by which I assumed he meant it's "natural"). "Without that, we human beings become like robots, no feeling. But now, practice for development of concern for well-being of others, that actually is immense benefit to oneself."

A light went off in my head. "It seems like you're saying that there is a self-interested, or selfish, case for being compassionate?"

"Yes. Practice of compassion is ultimately benefit to you. So I usually describe: we are selfish, but be wise selfish rather than foolish selfish."

This was an entirely new spin for me. Don't be nice for the sake of it, he was say-

334

ing. Do it because it would redound to your own benefit, that it would make you feel good by eroding the edges of the ego. Yoked to self-interest, the compassion thing suddenly became something I could relate to — maybe even something I could do.

After the interview, the Dalai Lama placed a white satin scarf around my neck and gave me a blessing. As our crew was packing up to leave, he called me back over one more time and said that if I was really interested in Buddhism, I should read his favorite book, by an ancient sage named Shantideva. The PR people from Emory breathlessly told me this must mean he really liked me.

Ultimately, I couldn't get through the book — but that notion about being nice for selfish reasons, that I kept.

There was cutting-edge science to back up the Dalai Lama's advice about the self-interested case for not being a dick. Right there on the Emory campus, in fact, scientists had been studying regular people who were given a brief course in compassion meditation. The subjects were then placed in stressful situations in the lab, including having a TV camera pointed at them (a detail which, for me, was particularly rich). The scientists found that the meditators released significantly lower doses of a stress hormone called cortisol. In other words, practicing compassion appeared to be helping their bodies handle stress in a better way. This was consequential because frequent or persistent release of cortisol can lead to heart disease, diabetes, dementia, cancer, and depression.

You didn't even have to meditate to derive benefits from compassion. Brain scans showed that acts of kindness registered more like eating chocolate than, say, fulfilling an obligation. The same pleasure centers lit up when we received a gift as when we donated to charity. Neuroscientists referred to it as "the warm glow" effect. Research also showed that everyone from the elderly to alcoholics to people living with AIDS patients saw their health improve if they did volunteer work. Overall, compassionate people tended to be healthier, happier, more popular, and more successful at work.

Most compelling for people like me who were not naturally overflowing with loving-kindness, there was evidence that compassion meditation can actually make you nicer. The leading scientist in this area was a Jew-Bu named Richie Davidson (Harvard via Brooklyn) who now ran a large lab at the University of Wisconsin–Madison, called the Center for Investigating Healthy Minds. His team had done studies showing that people who were taught compassion meditation displayed increased brain activity in regions associated with empathy and understanding. They also found that preschoolers became more willing to give their stickers away to strangers. My favorite study, done at Emory, asked subjects to wear tape recorders for days at a time, which captured their conversations. The meditators were more empathic, spent more time with other people, laughed more, and used the word "I" less.

Compassion research was part of a larger shift in emphasis for modern psychology. For decades, scientists had focused mainly on cataloguing human pathology and cruelty, but now the positive emotions such as happiness, kindness, and generosity were getting their due. This research helped give rise to a new view of human nature itself, a move away from the prevailing paradigm that focused on the dark side of Darwin — in other words, the survival of the fittest. In the old view, man was thoroughly selfish, and morality but a thin veneer over a bottomless well of turpitude. The new view took into account a long-overlooked branch of Darwinian thinking, namely the observation that tribes who cooperated and sacrificed for one another were more likely to "be victorious over other tribes." Apparently nature rewarded both the fittest — and the kindest.

I had my qualms. I worried that in competitive career fields like TV news, compassion was not adaptive. Also, I still wasn't a huge fan of doing metta, which felt forced and artificial to me. But I wanted the aforementioned benefits. So, with some trepidation, I added a parallel track to the ongoing science experiment I'd been conducting on myself.

From a traditionalist standpoint, my approach to meditation — and that of most Western practitioners — was backward. In the Buddha's day, he first taught generosity and morality before he gave his followers meditation instructions. The logic was self-interested: it's hard to concentrate if your mind is humming with remorse over having been a shithead, or if you're constantly scrambling to try to keep various lies straight. In his typical OCD fashion, the Buddha even compiled a list of the eleven benefits to practicing metta, which promised that you'd sleep better, your face would be radiant, people and animals would love you, celestial beings would protect you, and you'd be reborn in a happy realm. As usual, the list lost impact for me as it edged toward the supernatural.

The intellectual underpinnings of the practice were compelling. We all have an innate feeling of being separate from the world, peering out at life from behind our own little self, and vying against other isolated selves. But how can we truly be separate from the same world that created us? "Dust to dust" isn't just something they say at funerals, it's the truth. You can no more disconnect from the universe and its inhabitants than a wave can extricate itself from the ocean. I couldn't imagine myself conquering these bedrock feelings of separation, but the effort seemed worthwhile.

A couple of times a week, I began adding metta into the mix of my daily meditation. Per Spring's instruction from the retreat, I'd spend the first five or ten minutes of my sessions picturing and sending good vibes out to: myself, a "benefactor" (either Matt, Mark, or my parents), a "dear friend" (my favorite cat, Steve), a "neutral person" (our overnight doorman), a "difficult person" (not a hard category to fill), and then "all living beings" (usually a *National Geographic*-style tour of the planet). On retreat, Spring had advised us not to include anyone we were attracted to, but at home I decided to add Bianca to the mix, in her own special category.

Suffice it to say, I did not enjoy the process of systematically trying to cultivate sap. I was never able to get anywhere close to the weepy catharsis of the retreat, but as the Buddhist books I read assured me, the point wasn't to make specific feelings happen on command, it was simply to try. The attempt itself was a way to build the compassion muscle the same way that regular meditation built the mindfulness muscle.

I'm not going to claim that what happened next was purely the result of doing metta. There may have been other factors, like the inevitable effects of maturation, or subtle peer pressure from my new friends in the mindfulness subculture. Whatever the cause, in the months after I started adding compassion into my meditation practice, things started to change. It's not that I was suddenly a saint or that I began to exhibit extra-virgin extroversion, just that being nice — always important to me in the abstract, at least — now became a conscious, daily priority.

I instituted a make-eye-contact-and-smile policy that turned out to be genuinely enjoyable. It was like I was running for mayor. The fact that my days now included long strings of positive interactions made me feel good (not to mention popular). Acknowledging other people's basic humanity is a remarkably effective way of shooing away the swarm of self-referential thoughts that buzz like gnats around our heads.

At work, I got better at abstaining from gripe and gossip sessions. Complaint is the background noise of news, as well as the secret handshake, like fax machines beeping at one another, or dogs sniffing each other's rear ends. While I didn't entirely swear off this kind of chatter — some discussions were too delicious — I did my best to avoid it, knowing that I'd probably want to bathe in Purell afterward.

I would see people losing their tempers — like fellow passengers at the airport going apeshit on TSA employees — and I would empathize. True, I might experience a brief burst of superiority and an urge to recommend meditation to them, but I could also, in the style of Bill Clinton, feel their pain, the toxins running through their veins. The Buddha captured it well when he said that anger, which can be so seductive at first, has "a honeyed tip" but a "poisoned root."

It's not that I never got annoyed anymore.

In fact, when you're mindful, you actually feel irritation more keenly. However, once you unburden yourself from the delusion that people are deliberately trying to screw you, it's easier to stop getting carried away. As the Buddhists liked to point out, everyone wants the same thing — happiness — but we all go about it with varying levels of skill. If you spend a half hour on the cushion every day contending with your own ego, it's hard not to be more tolerant of others.

I had to swallow hard and admit that perhaps the concept of karma did, in fact, have some validity. Not the stuff about how the decisions we make now play out in future lifetimes. In my emerging understanding, there was nothing mechanistic or metaphysical about karma. Robbing a bank or cheating at Scrabble would not automatically earn you jail time or rebirth as a Gila monster. Rather, it was simply that actions have immediate consequences in your mind — which cannot be fooled. Behave poorly, and whether you're fully conscious of it or not, your mind contracts. The great blessing — and, frankly, the great inconvenience — of becoming more mindful and compassionate was that I was infinitely more sensitive to the mental ramifications of even the smallest transgressions, from killing a bug to dropping trash on the street.

I recalled how my dad once described undergoing a shift in his professional life where the achievements of his mentees began to mean more to him than his own. I wasn't quite there yet, but I did feel an increasingly strong urge to provide for younger ABC News staffers the kind of advice and counsel that Peter Jennings and now Diane Sawyer had provided for me. I found that applying the "price of security" maxim by proxy — worrying about other people's professional challenges — was much more easeful than applying it on myself. It dawned on me that much of what had been driving me since the beginning of my "spiritual" adventure had been a not-quite-fully-conscious desire to live up to my parents and my wife, all three of whom had, for years, been putting on a clinic in metta, even without a formal practice.

Admittedly, there was a large amount of self-interest at play here. Not letting my mind get locked in negativity made space for something else to emerge. I experienced a phenomenon I had heard Joseph once describe: a virtuous cycle, in which lower levels of anger and paranoia helped you make better decisions which, in turn, meant more happiness, and so on.

There were also benefits that might have been a little too selfish for the Dalai Lama's taste. For example, being nice was a great manipulation tool. Turns out, it's pretty simple to win people over, especially in tense situations, if you're able to take their perspective and validate their feelings. And once they like you, they're much more likely to do you favors. (For example, going into script meetings with a less adversarial stance meant that my coworkers might feel comfortable enough to volunteer ideas that would ultimately make me look smarter on television.) It was weird to hear colleagues refer to me as one of the "easy" correspondents, or make offhand comments about how relatively mellow I was. It was as if my bad old days as an intramural warrior had been erased, as if the anchor who'd been reprimanded for throwing his papers on the news desk in Boston had been forgotten.

I thought it an auspicious sign that not long after I started doing compassion meditation, the pro–basketball player Ron Artest, infamous for jumping into the stands during a game and throwing punches at opposing fans, changed his name to Metta World Peace. (Less auspicious: seven months later, Mr. World Peace was suspended for elbowing an opponent in the head, giving him a concussion.)

My new compassion policy ran into a major challenge in the person of Paris Hilton. This was not the type of assignment that usually came my way, but for reasons I still don't fully understand, *GMA* asked me to fly to Los Angeles to interview Hilton about her new reality show and the recent arrest of her stalker. I barely knew anything about her, other than the obvious: the family hotel fortune, the baby voice, the sex tape. So the night before the interview, I turned to my wife — who aside from being a brilliant doctor had a near-encyclopedic memory for anything having to do with pop culture — for guidance. I asked her to do some pro-bono research for me, and she forwarded some articles she found online about the low ratings for Hilton's new reality show. Some entertainment reporters were openly opining that Hilton was in the twilight of her celebrity, having been eclipsed by her former friend Kim Kardashian. So, I figured: Why not ask her about it? I had an inkling that it could cause some fireworks, but that struck me as a good thing.

The next day, when I arrived at Hilton's mansion in a gated community built into a hillside, the crew was all set up, Hilton's as-

345

sistants were buzzing around, and the star was up in her room, primping. The house seemed barely lived-in, less a home than a product showroom. Nearly every inch of wall space was covered in glossy pictures and oil portraits of Paris. There were even throw pillows that bore her image. I did appreciate that she was an animal lover. The place was crawling with pets — seventeen of them. Out back, there was a doghouse that was a replica of the main house, complete with moldings, a chandelier, furniture, light, heat, and air-conditioning.

Soon enough, Hilton came sauntering in, wearing dressy black shorts and a sheer black top with some elaborate stitching. There was something about her that made me ill at ease. Maybe it was just that I wasn't used to interviewing celebrities. Maybe it was that she looked right through me. Maybe it was that we kept getting interrupted by various cats skulking into the camera frame.

The interview started well enough. We talked about her TV show and her stalker, as previously agreed upon. I learned that, despite her ditzy persona, she actually ran a genuinely impressive and profitable retail business with stores in thirty-one countries, selling everything from handbags to perfumes. She admitted that when she wasn't on camera, her voice dropped an octave.

The requisite topics covered, I decided it was time to trot out the tough questions. "Do you worry sometimes," I asked, "that the people who followed in your footsteps, like Kim Kardashian, are overshadowing you?"

As I posed the question, a look came over her face that said, *Where is this going?* By the time I'd finished talking, though, and it was time for her to answer, she confidently said, "No, not at all."

"There's been some talk about the ratings on the show being low. Has that upset you?"

Still holding it together: "No."

Then came the doozy: "Do you ever worry about your moment having passed?"

She paused, looked over at her publicist, and then issued a delicate snort — a sharp out-breath accompanied by a slight curling of the upper lip. Then she got up and simply walked away. The camera lingered on me, repositioning myself in my chair, my face colonized by an involuntary smirk.

In television news, the storm-off is a coveted thing. This, however, was an unusual specimen. Hilton hadn't ripped off her mic while shrieking obscenities; she'd just kind of wandered over to the safety of her publicist. Still, I knew, for better or worse, I had captured a memorable moment.

Hilton and her team knew it, too. What followed was a long, strange, and often tense negotiation. We shut off the cameras, as the celebutante, her publicist, and her manager laid into us. At one point, Hilton turned to me and said, "You're treating me like I'm Tara Reid."

Her manager tried to surreptitiously strong-arm the cameraman into handing over the tapes, but he refused. Paris herself outright demanded that we not use the material. She didn't seem to understand that I didn't work for her, that I was a reporter, not a staffer on her reality show. I stood my ground, although I was at times slightly overwhelmed by the sheer absurdity of the fact that I was having a fight with a household name.

In fact, the decision about whether to use the material was not in my hands. It was up to my bosses. As I boarded a red-eye back to New York, where I'd be live on the *GMA* set first thing in the morning, the producers asked me to write two versions of the story, which I referred to as "The Safe Version" and "The Nuclear Option."

When I landed and checked my Black-

Berry, I learned we were indeed going nuclear. Right at the top of the show, in the Open, they ran the video of Hilton walking away — and then they "teased" it going into every commercial break, right up until it was time for my story to run. After it aired, the producers and anchors expressed enthusiasm. I left the studio feeling reasonably good.

I went home to crash for a few hours. When I woke up, the story had gone viral. Every entertainment outlet on earth had picked it up. I clicked on *The View* and saw Joy Behar calling me "rude." My heart sank.

While ridiculous on a thousand levels, this incident did raise some serious questions about my compassion policy. Had I just committed an egregious violation? After all, I knew there was a possibility my pre-planned question would provoke Hilton to walk off. I was even kind of hoping that it would happen. But was I, in fact, rude to her? I tried to reassure myself with the notion that she was, after all, a public figure, and that the chatter about whether her time had passed was all over the blogs. All I did was ask her about an issue that was already in the media bloodstream. I didn't manage to entirely convince myself.

There was a larger issue at play here: Was

journalism — or any high-stakes, competitive profession, really — incompatible with metta? My job required me to ask provocative questions, to "go in for the kill," as we say — and, often, that wasn't so nice.

This question of incompatibility was about to come blazing to the fore. After all my nattering on about how Buddhism didn't make you lose your edge, how meditation was a superpower, and blah blah, I would be hoisted on my own petard.

CHAPTER 11
HIDE THE ZEN

When the email arrived, I was marinating in sitar music in the ornate, honey-lit lobby of the Intercontinental Hotel in New Delhi. It was late 2010, and I was in India to shoot an investigative story about unscrupulous back-alley doctors.

Back at the home office, an earthquake had hit. After months of fevered speculation about who would take over for David Westin, we finally received the official announcement from the head of the ABC Television Group. The name of my new boss was: Ben Sherwood.

He and I had a history. It was Ben who was in the control room as the executive producer of *GMA* when I had my first panic attack. Ben had been very supportive in that moment, immediately getting in my ear and making sure I was okay. As I stared at my BlackBerry, I began calculating what this announcement meant for me. Ben and I had always had a good relationship, I told myself. Although, with a twinge of embarrassment, I also quickly flashed back to moments when I'd mouthed off to him, in an era when I was prone to do such things. There was that time when he'd asked me to do a live shot in the aftermath of Hurricane Katrina holding up a handful of sludge from the soaked streets of New Orleans, to give viewers a visceral sense of the scope of the disaster. I was exhausted and ornery after days of round-the-clock coverage, and I got a little lippy. (I ended up holding the sludge.)

Ben was an unusual species in the broadcast news ecosystem, both in terms of pedigree and personality. A Harvard grad and Rhodes scholar, he'd held a variety of senior jobs at both ABC and NBC. Between news gigs, he would head off on his own and write a book. He had three bestsellers under his belt, one nonfiction book and two novels. (One of the novels had even been made into a movie, *Charlie St. Cloud,* starring teen idol Zac Efron.) He was extremely tall, crackling with energy, and capable of both earnestness and sarcastic candor.

I didn't know it as I sat in the lobby in India absorbing the news, but Ben's arrival would precipitate a professional crisis.

■ ■ ■ ■

He began work a few weeks later. Things started off well enough between us. He was sending encouraging emails. For example, he liked a one-liner of mine during a "live-wrap" I did on weekday *GMA*. After a story about a young man who was forced to stand for an entire flight from Chicago to Florida because he was too tall to sit in his seat, I said, "Not a problem I've ever had."

Then, when Congresswoman Gabrielle Giffords was nearly killed by a deranged, gun-toting college dropout at a "Meet Your Representative" event, Ben dispatched me to Tucson as part of the first team in. It was a round-the-clock work marathon. I'd covered mass shootings before, but the outpouring for Representative Giffords and the other victims was like none I'd ever seen. After a few days on the ground, Ben called me and we had a detailed, positive discussion about how the news division was covering the story.

It quickly became clear that Ben was going to be the most hands-on boss most of us had ever had. He personally presided over the division-wide conference call every morning, putting on a master class in TV producing, variously engaging in pointed critiques and lavish praise of our work, including details as small as the graphics and the individual shots that producers chose in their stories. The call became appointment listening.

His emails — evocative little tone poems — showed up in our inboxes at all hours. The man did not appear to sleep. He watched every minute of every show we did, and nothing escaped his attention. One day, I did a story for *World News* about a new poll showing that mainline Protestant churches were losing membership. Distracted by other work, I hadn't put a lot of time or effort into the piece — I had basically phoned it in. As soon as the story aired, I got an email from Ben saying the writing seemed flat and unimaginative. He was right and I had no defense. It was both terrifying and invigorating to have a boss who knew your job as well if not better than you did. He had served notice: no one would get away with lazy work.

As I watched the entire news division scramble to reorient to this dynamic new presence, I made a calculation: I wasn't going to crowd him or go out of my way to impress him. I didn't put in any extra effort to produce special stories that might catch his eye, and I didn't angle for face time. My motives were opaque, even to me. Maybe I thought it'd be unseemly. I was now a guy who was hanging out with the Dalai Lama; I shouldn't be striving so nakedly, right? I figured he knew me, knew my history; I'd be fine. I'd lived through these seismic events before — including Peter's death and Charlie's retirement — and always emerged unscathed, if not enhanced. I had seemingly stowed my internal cattle prod in favor of a new, creeping passivity.

Very quickly, my strategy — or lack thereof — began to backfire. When massive street protests flared up in Egypt against the dictator Hosni Mubarak, Ben flooded the zone with ABC News staffers. This was history in the making — the kind of thing I lived for. In the past, it was exactly the type of story for which I'd been first out the door, but this time I did not get the call. Instead, I watched from the discomfort of my living room couch as Terry Moran and David Muir, among others, covered the story. The old me might have made an impulsive phone call or two. But the new, metta-meditating me thought that approach, which involved making my case to the detriment of my peers, uncompassionate.

As I pondered this dilemma, the situation

at work only got worse. When a real, not figurative, earthquake and tsunami hit Japan, Ben sent David and Bill Weir over to cover it. At home on the couch with Bianca, we watched the horror play out on-screen. The images were overwhelming. My wife was in a puddle of tears, while the freshly minted brown belt in loving-kindness was feeling badly both for the victims — and himself.

Not long after Ben's arrival, I reluctantly went up to snowy central Massachusetts for a metta meditation retreat. Sharon Salzberg, an old-school Jew-Bu and new friend of mine, had invited me up several months before. It was a nice gesture, and I had accepted the invitation, but given recent developments at the office, I just wasn't in the mood for it. Even so, I drove the four hours to endure three days of straining to generate good vibes.

The setting was nice, at least. Sharon, Joseph, and another teacher named Jack Kornfield had founded the Insight Meditation Society (also known by regulars as IMS or, sometimes, "I'm a mess") back in 1976. They'd scraped together $150,000 for a down payment on a multiwing, one-hundred-room redbrick mansion that had most recently served as a Catholic monastery. They had converted the chapel into a meditation hall, although they'd left up the stained glass images of Jesus. The rest of the building was decorated with potted plants, large geodes, and ancient Buddhist artifacts, which reminded me of the living rooms of my childhood friends with progressive parents.

Sharon happened to give a very timely talk on the subject of mudita, the Buddhist term for sympathetic joy. She admitted that sometimes her first instinct when trying to summon this feeling was "Ew, I wish you didn't have so much going for you." The meditation hall erupted in laughter. Sharon said the biggest obstacle to mudita is a subconscious illusion, that whatever success the other person has achieved was actually somehow really meant for us. "It's almost like, it was heading right for me," she said, "and you just reached out and grabbed it." More laughter, as everyone in the room enjoyed one of the most satisfying of all dharma delicacies: an accurate diagnosis of our inner lunacy.

On the second day, I spotted a little note with my name on it posted to the message board in the main hallway. Sharon would see me that afternoon. As I padded into her interview room, she gave me a big hug. She was a jolly woman in her late fifties who, like pretty much every long-term meditator I knew, looked significantly younger than her chronological age. As we chatted, I mentioned that I was somewhat pre-occupied by things at work; I described my concern that I'd suddenly become more of a bench-warmer.

"When faced with something like this," she said, "often it's not the unknown that scares us, it's that we think we know what's going to happen — and that it's going to be bad. But the truth is, we really don't know."

The smart play, she said, was to turn the situation to my internal advantage. "Fear of annihilation," she said, "can lead to great insight, because it reminds us of imperma-nence and the fact that we are not in con-trol."

This got me thinking again about the "wisdom of insecurity." From the comfort and remove of the sylvan idyll of IMS, it hit me afresh that the "security" for which I had been striving was an illusion. If every-thing in this world was in constant decay, why expend so much energy gnashing my teeth over work?

I began to examine the source of my drive. Was it rooted in my privileged upbringing?

Maybe this is just what "people like me" did? Was it because I grew up in a town crawling with rich kids whose parents drove Porsches and BMWs, while my folks — academic physicians, not bankers — drove a shit-brown Plymouth Valiant and a gray Chevy Chevette? Much of my adolescence was characterized by a self-imposed feeling of lack. Now that I was a "spiritual" guy, maybe it was time to transcend my bourgeois conditioning?

I snapped out of it quickly enough. The Buddha never said it was un-kosher to strive. Right there on his Noble Eightfold Path, his list of the eight things you had to do to get enlightened, "Right Livelihood" was number five. He was proud of everything he built, including his ranks of monks and nuns. He wasn't particularly modest, either. This was a man who regularly referred to himself in the third person.

Here I was, two and a half years after I'd first discovered Eckhart Tolle, still wrestling with the same question: Was it possible to strike a balance between "the price of security" and the "wisdom of insecurity"?

Back at the office, what I viewed as a downward spiral only continued. 2011 was a huge news year: the death of Osama bin

Laden, the fall of Qaddafi in Libya, the Royal Wedding of William and Kate, and I didn't get tagged to cover any of it. (That last one fell into the didn't-want-to-do-it-but-would-have-liked-to-have-been-asked category, but still . . .)

At times, I managed to convince myself I was handling it pretty well. When I got into a rut, it didn't take long for me to jar myself out of it. I would use RAIN — watching how the feelings would show themselves in my body and then labeling them with some degree of nonjudgmental remove. It reminded me of how soldiers and police officers I'd interviewed described their reactions in emergency situations. They would almost always say something to the effect of "My training kicked in."

I also thought, with a degree of self-satisfaction, that having a calmer, more compassionate mind was allowing me to take a dry-eyed view of the situation, unclouded by unhelpful emotion. Rather than take it personally, I tried to see it through Ben's eyes. He was just doing the best he could to turn the news division around. Maybe I just wasn't his cup of tea? I comforted myself with the conclusion that I was engaged in a healthy acknowledgment of reality that would ultimately allow for the virtuous cycle of less unnecessary straining and better decision making.

My loving wife, however, thought I was being a total wuss. While she was glad I wasn't losing my cool, she was bewildered by the fact that her husband seemed so suddenly gelded. When a big story broke, she and I would often have text exchanges in which Bianca would urge me to advocate for myself. For example:

Me: "I feel I still don't have a good approach yet to asserting myself in these situations w/o reverting to my old dickish ways."

Bianca: "I understand. But you're not going to risk anything by being slightly more aggressive about it instead of a passively available team player."

I knew she wasn't trying to criticize, but I could feel defensiveness welling up anyway. I struggled not to misdirect my frustration at the one person who was trying to help me. All I wanted to do was bury my head and hope the situation went away. I just couldn't figure out the right play.

By now, the nice emails from Ben had stopped — because I wasn't doing anything to deserve them. Not only was I not getting tapped to cover the big stories, but I'd somehow lost my motivation to pitch and produce special investigative reports, my longtime specialty. I'd hear Ben praising people on the morning call, summoning rounds of applause from the attendees, and I wanted to do work that merited this reaction. And yet the more discouraged I got, the more trouble I had overcoming inertia.

After months of drift, in July of 2011 I finally decided to act.

I emailed Ben to schedule a chat, and a few days later I was in his corner office, ready to see if I could fix this thing. Between where I sat on the couch and Ben's chair was a large coffee table covered in snacks, including tall glass jars filled with pretzel sticks and licorice. There was even, curiously, a bunch of bananas. He joked that he liked to see how people managed to peel and eat a banana in front of their boss.

I assumed he'd be expecting me to come at him with a litany of complaints, so after a lot of strategizing with Bianca, I decided to take a different tack. "I'm concerned," I said, "that you do not see me as part of the A-team, and I want to know how I can change your mind."

His response was a thing to behold. I could practically see the wheels in his head turning as he calibrated, then recalibrated, his approach. After maybe five seconds of buffering, he launched into his speech.

"First of all," he said, "you're wrong. I do see you as a major player."

But, he went on, there were some real problems I needed to address. Chief among them: I wasn't hustling and getting on TV enough. He said, "I think you've fallen into that classic weekend-anchor trap where you have your little pocket of airtime on Saturday and Sunday, and then the rest of the week you're nowhere to be seen." This was unquestionably true. "You need to up your game," he declared.

The second issue was weekend *GMA*. Too often the show was going off the rails, he said, with our anchor banter devolving into silliness. I needed to play a larger role in getting this under control. "I need you to be a leading man," he said. When I put up a mild protest, arguing that I didn't want to be bossy or imperious, Ben — who knew I'd become a meditator — looked me dead in the eyes and said, in a tone that was both playful and serious, "Stop being so Zen."

In mere minutes he had pinpointed and pronounced my errors. Behind the fig leaf of being a good yogi, I had gone so far down the path of resignation and passivity that I had compromised the career I had worked for decades to build. It was just as my dad had feared; I had become ineffective. What I should have done when faced with this adversity was buckle down and work harder. Instead, I had confused "letting go" with going soft.

It was my toughest and most productive professional meeting since that encounter with my boss back at the local station in Boston who told me I was being an asshole. Except this time, ironically, the problem was almost diametrically the opposite.

Serendipitously, on the very night of my meeting with Ben, I had scheduled a dinner with Mark Epstein. In the taxi on my way downtown I called Bianca and told her how it'd gone.

"He's right," she said. Which came as no surprise; Ben had basically affirmed her thesis. "This is good. Now you know what you need to do."

Mark and I met to eat at a fussy Japanese restaurant called Brushstroke, where they only served a tasting menu and the waiters took themselves very, very seriously. Once we'd placed our orders, I told Mark what had just gone down in Ben's office. He responded with a catchy little suggestion: "Hide the Zen."

"People will take advantage of you if

they're reading you as too Zen," he said. "There's a certain kind of aggression in organizational behavior that doesn't value that — that will see it as weak. If you present yourself too much like that, people won't take you seriously. So I think it important to hide the Zen, and let them think that you're really someone they have to contend with."

But I was attached to my rep as a Zen guy. "I don't want to be an asshole at the office."

"No," he said. "That's the tricky thing about what he's saying to you. I'm sure there's a way of doing it where you don't have to be an asshole. I think it might be possible that you could give the appearance of being one of those guys while deep inside of you, you wouldn't be."

I had fallen, he said, into several classic "pitfalls of the path." People often misinterpreted the dharma to mean they had to adopt a sort of meekness. Some of Mark's patients even stopped using the word "I," or disavowed the need to have orgasms during sex. He recalled scenes from his youth when he and meditation buddies would have group dinners at restaurants and no one would have the gumption to place an order. They didn't want to express a personal preference, as if doing so was insufficiently Buddhist. Another pitfall was detachment. I thought I was being mindful of my distress when I was left out of the big stories, but really I was just building a wall to keep out the things that made me angry or fearful. The final pitfall to which I'd succumbed was nihilism: an occasional sense of, "Whatever, man, everything's impermanent."

At this point, the waiter came by to deliver an extremely long description of the dish that had just been placed in front of us. "For your next course you have the grilled *anagi,* which is freshwater eel . . ."

As he prattled on about kabocha squash and "large, translucent bits of daikon radish," the nature of my missteps became radiantly clear. The Sufi Muslims say, "Praise Allah, but also tie your camel to the post." In other words, it's good to take a transcendent view of the world, but don't be a chump. Joseph often told a story about his first meditation teacher, an Indian guy named Munindra, who used to advise all of his students to keep things "simple and easy." One day, Joseph came upon Munindra in the village marketplace, haggling fiercely over a bag of peanuts. When confronted about this apparent contradiction with his simple-and-easy mantra, his teacher explained, "I said be simple, not a simpleton."

When the waiter left, I said, "This is really humbling."

Mark, always eager to put things in the best possible light, said, "I think it's like a revolution in your understanding of this material — a deeper understanding. This makes it so much more alive."

"Right. Right," I said. "Because when everything's going well and you're being mindfully aware of stuff, that's pretty easy."

"That's easy! This is, like, a real conundrum."

The same conundrum I'd been fixated on for years, in fact — the balance between Buddhist principles and ambition. It was, I mused aloud, frustrating after all this time not to have the answer. As I sat there feeling bad for myself, it slipped right past me when Mark offered up that he actually did have an answer. It was simple, brilliant advice, but I was too preoccupied to hear it.

Nonetheless, back on the job, things began to improve. At the top of the to-do list I kept in my BlackBerry, I wrote down my marching orders from the meeting with Ben: "UP YOUR GAME," and "LEADING MAN." I'd never been one for this type of

sloganeering — I liked my mottoes to be a
touch more arch — but having these exhor-
tations blaring out at me in all-caps every
time I checked the list was extremely useful.

I started saying yes to every assignment
that came my way, no matter how small —
the way I used to do when I was an eager
cub reporter. It did not go unnoticed. A
mere three days after our meeting, the
emails started coming again, the first about
my writing in a *GMA* piece on the phone-
hacking accusations rocking Rupert Mur-
doch's British newspaper empire:

Metastasizing scandal . . .
V deft, Dan.
Good to see you on GMA (and everywhere
since our talk :)

I covered the arrest of the so-called
"Craigslist killers," who allegedly lured their
victims through a help-wanted ad; I reported from a hospital on Staten Island
where they had to send away all their
patients because Hurricane Irene was bearing down; I covered the child sex abuse allegations that brought down legendary
coach Joe Paterno at Penn State, where I
got pepper-sprayed on camera during stu-

dent riots.

Like any good coach, Ben was satisfying to please. He savored the little things — "grace notes," as he called them. When he gave a shout-out to my work on the morning call, my chest swelled more than I cared to admit.

I got back into the habit of finding, pitching, and producing special reports, which I had neglected during my long slide into professional lethargy. I chased down the CEO of Philip Morris International on the street, and confronted him about the sale of cigarettes to young children in Indonesia. I reported on suburban moms who stole Adderall from their children. I investigated con men who ran a scam that involved calling people who had illegally ordered prescription drugs online and pretending to be DEA agents. They would threaten criminal charges, and then ask for bribes to make the case go away.

But the story of which I was proudest involved my spending two days locked up in solitary confinement. The idea was to bring attention to the growing national debate over whether this kind of incarceration was torture. My producers convinced the officials at the county jail in Denver to hold me for two days in a cell wired up with

cameras. During this time, I endured boredom, bad food, claustrophobia, and the
nonstop screaming of my fellow inmates,
also in solitary, many of whom were having
full-on nervous breakdowns. I awoke on the
first morning to the animal howls of the
inmate in the cell directly beneath me. It
lasted for hours. Other inmates were holler-
ing just to let off steam, including one
troublemaker a few cells down, who, upon
seeing our cameras, yelled out to no one in
particular, "Yo, they're making a movie!
They should come suck my dick and make
it a love story!" On my last day in captivity,
as I was walking to the shower (mercifully,
they only have solo showers in solitary) my
mischievous neighbor shouted the following
advice: "You need sandals, bro. You'll catch
gingivitis!"

My time in solitary was a humbling reminder of the limits of meditation — or, at
least, the limits of my meditation abilities. I
had cockily figured I could meditate through
most of the experience, but the noise level
and the lack of privacy — with cameras
everywhere, and guards constantly peering
in — made it nearly impossible. To make
matters worse, whenever I tried to meditate,
my neighbor, who couldn't even see what I
was up to, would uncannily break into

"Karma Chameleon."

My meditation also suffered when I was out covering breaking news, arguably the time when I needed it most. During the Penn State story, for example, in between live shots and filing deadlines, I would try to meditate in my hotel room, but I was often unable to fight through the fatigue.

In the midst of these intense work sprints, when I had less time to sleep, exercise, and meditate, I could feel my inner monologue getting testier, too — and I didn't have the wherewithal to not take the voice in my head so seriously. *I looked tired in my live shot this morning. I need a haircut. I can't believe that Facebook commenter called me a "major clown."* The ego, that slippery son of a bitch, would use fatigue as an opportunity to sneak past my weakened defenses.

My increasing "story count," as we call it, may have created difficulties in my meditation practice, but it was well worth it. And this was not the only area of professional improvement. I also made some progress on weekend *GMA*.

The upturn began one morning after the show, when Bianca found me sitting on the living room couch, once again watching and puzzling over some on-air moments with which I was dissatisfied. She grabbed the remote out of my hand and spontaneously began an hour-long clinic, starting at the top of the show and deconstructing exactly how and where I went wrong. The Hellos had started well enough that morning; I was smiling and laughing alongside my cohost. (Bianna was out on maternity leave, and her seat was filled by our excellent new overnight anchor, Paula Faris.) As we were all encouraged to do, Paula made an unscripted joke a few seconds into the show. Bianca pressed pause on the remote. "Look what happens right here. You tense up. You can literally see it." It was true. Paula's quip must have deviated from the preset plan for the Hellos that I had apparently constructed in my head, and I went stiff.

"You need to stop trying so hard," said Bianca. "Just let go."

It was delicious to have my wife throw Buddhist terminology back in my face. Especially since, in this case, she couldn't have been more spot-on. I needed to approach anchoring more like meditation. If I could relax and be present enough to listen to what people were saying, it would enhance our natural camaraderie on the air.

Almost immediately, Bianca's advice

started to work. I found myself less pre-occupied with strictly following a blueprint and more focused on just being there, in a good mood, ready with a tart comment — or equally ready to react to other people's jokes with genuine, unforced laughter. So, for example, when Ron read a news item about women being happier if they had a few drinks a week, I responded by saying I would be stopping by the liquor store on my way home. I was starting to realize that by "leading man," Ben wasn't asking me to be Errol Flynn, but instead to be comfortable in my own skin.

While things were going well on various fronts at work, it was certainly not all sweetness and light. Ben's praise emails were equally balanced by notes that contained extremely precise (albeit polite) criticism. For example, he razzed me a bit for my use of the overly technical term *precip* when introducing Ginger Zee's rainy forecast on weekend *GMA*. More seriously, when I raised my hand to cover the United States' withdrawal from Iraq, I didn't get the nod. Furthermore I did not land a role in ABC's special coverage of the tenth anniversary of 9/11, the event that had been a turning point in my personal and professional life. This exclusion nearly sent me right back down to the subbasement. It was clear there was something still missing from my strategy.

During my most recent dinner with Mark, the one at the Japanese restaurant, I had, as always, placed my iPhone on his side of the table, so I could use it to record what he said for future reference. (I carried both a BlackBerry and an iPhone. Belts and suspenders.) Listening to our chats after the fact, I often found myself rooting for Mark as his thoughtful answers were continually interrupted by an amped-up interrogator, interjecting non sequiturs, half-baked theories, and partially realized insights, with a mouth filled with mindlessly consumed food.

On the tape, I could be heard lamenting the fact that after years of contemplating the balance between ambition and equanimity, I still didn't have an answer. Whereupon Mark, in his understated way, told me that he did. "The answer is in nonattachment," he said. In my defense, the term was deceptively bland. "It's nonattachment to the results. I think for an ambitious person who cares about their career — who wants to create things and be successful — it's natural to be trying really hard. Then the

Buddhist thing comes in around the results — because it doesn't always happen the way you think it should."

As I mulled this advice after the fact, I suspected there might be something to it, but I couldn't quite figure out how you could work your tail off on something and then not be attached to the outcome. I had come up through a system that venerated bootstrapping and a fierce refusal to fail. Doing this without attachment didn't seem to fit the paradigm.

A few months later, at our next meeting over eggs at Morandi, I broached the subject again. I said, "When we last spoke, you said it's okay to be ambitious, but don't be attached to the results. I cut you off, as I usually do — but what does that mean?"

"It's like, you write a book, you want it to be well received, you want it to be at the top of the bestsellers list, but you have limited control over what happens. You can hire a publicist, you can do every interview, you can be prepared, but you have very little control over the marketplace. So you put it out there without attachment, so it has its own life. Everything is like that."

For a minute, I thought he was being simplistic, giving a version of the perfunctory advice that parents give their children.

"When I was a kid," I said, "and I would get worked up about some soccer game or whatever, my parents would say, 'Just do your best.' That's basically what you're saying."

"Yeah," he said, in as snide a tone as he was capable of. "Me and your parents." But it's not the same thing, he explained. You can do your best and then, if things don't go your way, still become unconstructively upset, in a way that hinders your ability to bounce back. Dropping the attachment is the real trick.

Then it clicked. Per usual, Mark's advice was sound, even if it took me a while to absorb it. Striving is fine, as long as it's tempered by the realization that, in an entropic universe, the final outcome is out of your control. If you don't waste your energy on variables you cannot influence, you can focus much more effectively on those you can. When you are wisely ambitious, you do everything you can to succeed, but you are not attached to the outcome — so that if you fail, you will be maximally resilient, able to get up, dust yourself off, and get back in the fray. That, to use a loaded term, is enlightened self-interest.

It brought to mind a meeting we'd had at ABC a few months before the 2012 election. A small group of reporters, anchors, and executives were in a conference room, clustered around David Axelrod, who was conducting President Obama's reelection campaign. At one point, Ben asked the preternaturally even-keeled Axelrod about the existential challenges of conducting a campaign in an environment where there were so many factors out of his control — from the European debt crisis to a potential al-Qaeda plot to Israel's saber-rattling against Iran. Axelrod responded, "All we can do is everything we can do."

This was a hopeful outlook, really. I didn't need to waste so much time envisioning some vague horribleness awaiting me in my future. (Do they even have flophouses in Duluth?) All I had to do was tell myself: if it doesn't work, I only need the grit to start again — just like when my mind wandered in meditation. After years of drawing a false dichotomy between striving and serenity, unable to figure out how to square these seemingly contradictory impulses, it struck me over eggs in a bustling brunch joint: this clunky phrase "nonattachment to results" was my long-sought Holy Grail, the middle path, the marriage of "the price of security" and "the wisdom of insecurity."

■ ■ ■ ■

It was the last piece of a puzzle I'd been trying to put together since the start of this whole unplanned adventure. All along, I'd been straining for some sort of framework, a holistic answer to one of the central challenges for a modern meditator: How can you be a happier, better person without becoming ineffective? The books and teachers I'd consulted had already done the most important work: reorienting my internal life by mitigating the noxious tendencies of my mind and juicing the compassion circuitry. It was just this one area where I thought they fell short.

Since the Buddhists are always making lists (I was convinced that somewhere they had a list of the Best Ways to Make a List), I resolved to draw up one of my own. Nothing on the list I compiled was, in and of itself, mind-bogglingly brilliant. There's a reason why they call Buddhism "advanced common sense"; it's all about methodically confronting obvious-but-often-overlooked truths (everything changes, nothing fully satisfies) until something in you shifts. Likewise, with my new list, executing these precepts in tandem — and then systematizing and amplifying the whole thing with regular mindfulness practice — elevated them from platitudes to powerful tools.

I played with titles for a while ("The Ten Pillars of Cutthroat Zen" was briefly a contender), but then I heard about the ancient samurai code, "The Way of the Warrior." I decided to create a version for the corporate samurai.

The Way of the Worrier

1. Don't Be a Jerk
2. (And/But . . .) When Necessary, Hide the Zen
3. Meditate
4. The Price of Security Is Insecurity — Until It's Not Useful
5. Equanimity Is Not the Enemy of Creativity
6. Don't Force It
7. Humility Prevents Humiliation
8. Go Easy with the Internal Cattle Prod
9. Nonattachment to Results
10. What Matters Most?

Don't Be a Jerk

It is, of course, common for people to succeed while occasionally being nasty. I met a lot of characters like this during the course of my career, but they never really seemed very happy to me. It is sometimes assumed that success in a competitive business requires the opposite of compassion. In my experience, though, that only reduced my clarity and effectiveness, leading to rash decisions. The virtuous cycle that Joseph described (more metta, better decisions, more happiness, and so on) is real. To boot, compassion has the strategic benefit of winning you allies. And then there's the small matter of the fact that it makes you a vastly more fulfilled person.

(And/But . . .) When Necessary, Hide the Zen

Be nice, but don't be a palooka. Even though I'd achieved a degree of freedom from the ego, I still had to operate in a tough professional context. Sometimes you need to compete aggressively, plead your own case, or even have a sharp word with someone. It's not easy, but it's possible to do this calmly and without making the whole thing overly personal.

Meditate

Meditation is the superpower that makes all the other precepts possible. The practice has countless benefits — from better health to increased focus to a deeper sense of calm — but the biggie is the ability to respond instead of react to your impulses and urges. We live our life propelled by desire and aversion. In meditation, instead of succumbing to these deeply rooted habits of mind, you are simply watching what comes up in your head nonjudgmentally. For me, doing this drill over and over again had massive off-the-cushion benefits, allowing me — at least 10% of the time — to shut down the ego with a Reaganesque "There you go again."

The Price of Security Is Insecurity — Until It's Not Useful

Mindfulness proved a great mental thresher for separating wheat from chaff, for figuring out when my worrying was worthwhile and when it was pointless. Vigilance, diligence, the setting of audacious goals — these are all the good parts of "insecurity." Hunger and perfectionism are powerful energies to harness. Even the much-maligned "comparing mind" can be useful. I compared myself to Joseph, Mark, and Sharon, and it made me happier. I compared myself to Bianca and it made me nicer. I compared myself to Bill Weir, David Muir, Chris Cuomo, David Wright, et al., and it upped my game. In my view, Buddhists underplay the utility of constructive anguish. In one of his dharma talks, I heard Joseph quote a monk who said something like, "There's no point in being unhappy about things you can't change, and no point being unhappy about things you can." To me, this gave short shrift to the broad gray area where it pays to wring your hands at least a little bit.

Equanimity Is Not the Enemy of Creativity

Being happier did not, as many fear, make me a blissed-out zombie. This myth runs deep, all the way back to Aristotle, who said, "All men who have attained excellence in philosophy, in poetry, in art and in politics . . . had a melancholic habitus." I found that rather than rendering me boringly problem-free, mindfulness made me, as an eminent spiritual teacher once said, "a connoisseur of my neuroses." One of the most interesting discoveries of this whole journey was that I didn't need my demons to fuel my drive — and that taming them was a more satisfying exercise than indulging them. Jon Kabat-Zinn has theorized that science may someday show that mindfulness actually makes people more creative, by clearing out the routinized rumination and unhelpful assumptions, making room for new and different thoughts. On retreat, for example, I would be flooded with ideas, filling notebooks with them, scribbling them down on the little sheets of paper between sitting and walking. So, who knows, maybe Van Gogh would have been an even better painter if he hadn't been so miserable that he sliced off his ear?

Don't Force It

It's hard to open a jar when every muscle in your arm is tense. A slight relaxation served me well on the set of *GMA,* in interpersonal interactions, and when I was writing scripts. I came to see the benefits of purposeful pauses, and the embracing of ambiguity. It didn't work every time, mind you, but it was better than my old technique of bulldozing my way to an answer.

Humility Prevents Humiliation

We're all the stars of our own movies, but cutting back on the number of *Do you know who I am?* thoughts made my life infinitely smoother. When you don't dig in your heels and let your ego get into entrenched positions from which you mount vigorous, often irrational defenses, you can navigate tricky situations in a much more agile way. For me humility was a relief, the opposite of humiliation. It sanded the edges off of the comparing mind. Of course, striking the right balance is delicate; it is possible to take this too far and become a pushover. (See precept number two, regarding hiding the Zen.)

Go Easy with the Internal Cattle Prod

As part of my "price of security" mind-set, I had long assumed that the only route to success was harsh self-criticism. However, research shows that "firm but kind" is the smarter play. People trained in self-compassion meditation are more likely to quit smoking and stick to a diet. They are better able to bounce back from missteps. All successful people fail. If you can create an inner environment where your mistakes are forgiven and flaws are candidly confronted, your resilience expands exponentially.

Nonattachment to Results

Nonattachment to results + self compassion = a supple relentlessness that is hard to match. Push hard, play to win, but don't assume the fetal position if things don't go your way. This, I came to believe, is what T. S. Eliot meant when he talked about learning "to care and not to care."

What Matters Most?

One day, I was having brunch with Mark and Joseph, forcing them to help me think about the balance between ambition and equanimity for the umpteenth time. After the entrées and before dessert, Joseph got up to hit the bathroom. He came back smiling and pronounced, "I've figured it out. A useful mantra in those moments is 'What matters most?' " At first, this struck me as somewhat generic, but as I sat with the idea for a while, it eventually emerged as the bottom-line, gut-check precept. When worrying about the future, I learned to ask myself: What do I really want? While I still loved the idea of success, I realized there was only so much suffering I was willing to endure. What I really wanted was aptly summed up during an interview I once did with Robert Schneider, the self-described "spastic" lead singer for the psych-pop group, Apples in Stereo. He was one of the happiest-seeming people I'd ever met: constantly chatting, perpetually in motion — he just radiated curiosity and enthusiasm. Toward the end of our interview, he said, "The most important thing to me is probably, like, being kind and also trying to do something awesome."

I proudly presented my list to Bianca. Her response was to flash an impish grin and say, "But you're not actually practicing these." Specifically, she was referring to the first one about not being a jerk.

"This is aspirational, not operational," I assured her.

While imperfectly applied, my precepts were having salutary effects at the office. Nine months after my initial meeting with Ben, I requested another meeting — this time to ask him a specific question related to this book. I wanted to make sure he was okay with my including old stories of drug abuse. It was the first time I was telling anyone in power about the real story behind my panic attacks. It was fascinating to watch the twitch of recognition on his face as he recalled and reevaluated the event. We discussed the pros and cons of disclosure. Ultimately, he said he would have my back, whatever I decided.

Then, unprovoked, he raised the subject of the two mantras he had created for me in our last meeting, and declared that I had, in his eyes, fully succeeded in both "upping my game" and becoming a "leading man."

For good measure, he also pointed out that while he had enjoyed a recent story I'd done for *Nightline* on a squad of teenage girl exorcists, he thought I could have used a cleaner shave.

EPILOGUE

As I write this, in the fall of 2013, it's been five years since I first read Eckhart Tolle, four years since I started meditating, and more than two years since I had my pivotal meeting with Ben Sherwood.

I have three significant updates since the end of the last chapter. These include: a flip-flop, a promotion, and I guess what you might call a moment of clarity.

Let's start with the volte-face. To my profound surprise, I've pulled something of a reversal on enlightenment. As with most of my changes of heart, this one was rooted in science. During my travels in the mindfulness subculture, I heard about a group of young neuroscientists taking a bold, public stance. Unlike their Jew-Bu predecessors, who, like Jon Kabat-Zinn, have bent over backward to distance themselves from traditional Buddhism, these young guns are unabashedly interested in "liberation," rather than just stress reduction. They've been doing fMRIs of advanced practitioners. While they haven't proven that enlightenment is real by, say, finding the brain signature for stream-entry or arhanthood, they are interested in trying.

I was, to say the least, intrigued. I made friends with one of these scientists, Dr. Jud Brewer, a compact thirty-eight-year-old with short brown hair, perfect teeth, and an ebullient manner that reflects both his earnest Indiana roots and Ivy League pedigree. In the course of his research at Yale, he had invented something potentially revolutionary: a real-time neuro-feedback mechanism that allows meditators to see when they're shutting down the Default Mode Network (DMN) of their brains, the so-called "selfing regions" that are active during most of our waking, mindless hours. From inside the narrow tube of the scanner (which I was too claustrophobic to get inside of, by the way), the meditator can see, via a mirror, a small computer monitor. When the DMN is deactivated, the screen goes blue. When the ego is chattering, the screen goes red. Essentially, Jud's invention tells people whether they're meditating correctly. He's had a dozen or so people who claimed to be highly attained practitioners hop in the scanner; many of them made the machine go deeply blue. Jud's vision for his technology is that it could teach average Joes how to meditate so well that they wouldn't waste their time doing it incorrectly, which would then put them on a speedier path toward enlightenment.

Over plates of pasta one day, I pressed Jud on the whole notion of liberation. "Why am I wrong to think enlightenment is this weird piece of bullshit baked into this otherwise really helpful program?" He explained that the brain is a pleasure-seeking machine. Once you teach it, through meditation, that abiding calmly in the present moment feels better than our habitual state of clinging, over time, the brain will want more and more mindfulness. He compared it to lab rats that learn to avoid an electric shock. "When you see that there's something better than what we have," said Jud, "then it's just a matter of time before your brain is like, 'Why the fuck am I doing that? I've been holding on to a hot coal.' " If you give your brain enough of a taste of mindfulness, it will eventually create a self-reinforcing spiral — a retreat from greed and hatred that could, Jud insisted, potentially lead all the way to the definitive uprooting of negative emotions (in other words, enlightenment). "Why would it stop?" he said. "Evolutionarily, it doesn't make sense that it would stop. Does water seek out the lowest level?"

This was the first rational explanation I'd heard for enlightenment yet. I found myself sitting there, nodding my head in agreement, stunned by the fact that I was doing so. I could barely believe it, but I was actually thinking, *Should I be gunning for stream-entry?* Perhaps this was another arena in which I needed to up my game?

To make sure I wasn't losing my mind, I called the most skeptical person I knew, Sam Harris. Lo and behold, he, too, said enlightenment was real, although he used a different analogy. Just as it's possible for humans to train to be fast or strong enough to compete in the Olympics, he argued we can practice to be the wisest or most compassionate version of ourselves. In fact, he said he had personally achieved something roughly analogous to stream-entry, the earliest stage of enlightenment — that he had "seen through the ego in a way that is decisive." Although he quickly added, "That's not the same thing as being a Buddha, where you're no longer capable of being a schmuck."

To top it off, Sam told me he thought it

391

was entirely possible that some people could become suddenly enlightened with no meditation at all. Specifically, he was referring to Eckhart Tolle. "I don't have any reason to doubt his story," he said. He added that there's something more "authentic" about people like Tolle, who have accounts of breakthroughs that come out of the blue without any formal training — "because they're not getting it from anywhere else." This was a bitter pill to swallow. Mockery of Tolle had been my one true north on this journey. Now, as the Buddhists say, maybe I had to let it go. I went back and read that first Tolle book, the one that kicked off my whole "spiritual" odyssey, and while it still struck me as flowery and bizarre, it made a lot more sense to me now than it did five years ago. When I first read *A New Earth,* I had rolled my eyes when Tolle rather immodestly promised that his book would "initiate the awakening process" in the reader. Now I had to admit that, in my case, the weird little German man was, in a sense, right.

Here's where I've come down on this, for now: I don't know if it's possible to be enlightened, either through meditation, or through a Tolle-style sudden awakening. I'm agnostic — but not with the deadening incuriosity that characterized my stance before I began this whole trip. I now realize that on the issue of enlightenment I was blinded by my own skepticism. All the poetic language about the Buddha sitting under a tree and reaching "the beyond," "the deathless," "the very hard to see," and so forth had provoked a sort of intellectual gag reflex. I had, in essence, inverted the normal quandary that spiritual seekers face. Instead of a Meat Puppets–esque "open your mind, in pours the trash," I had closed my mind prematurely. This whole experience had been a process of my seeing over and over that many of my assumptions were wrong. Enlightenment was perhaps the latest example.

I do know one thing for sure: there's much more for me to do. Whether or not 100% happy is achievable, I can definitely be more than 10% happier — and I'm excited to try. I often think about a quote from a writer I admire named Jeff Warren, who called meditation "the next frontier of human exploration." It's insanely encouraging to see that my Jew-Bu friends, all a full generation older than me, are still as excited about this stuff as when they were in their twenties. Mindfulness, happiness, and not being a jerk are skills I can hone the rest of my life — every day, every moment, until senility or death. And the payoff is less reactivity, less rumination, and — who knows? — maybe stream-entry. I have willingness and curiosity. I have confidence and trust. I guess another word I could use is . . . faith.

The next update is more down-to-earth.

The other day — on October 7, 2013, at eleven A.M., to be exact — Ben asked me to meet him on the set where we shoot most of our major broadcasts. He stuck out his hand and offered me a job as one of the co-anchors of *Nightline.* I said yes, and then he gave me a hug. My face only came up to his solar plexus. (It's worth mentioning here that Ben recently started meditating and loves it. Diane Sawyer is also now meditating. So is George Stephanopoulos. Even Barbara Walters recently tried it, although it apparently didn't stick.)

True to the Buddhist principle of suffering, by the time I got the job I'd coveted for years, the show had been moved back to a later time slot. However, as my colleague David Wright, the correspondent I used to compete against when we were both younger and more uppity, wrote me in an email, "It's still the best perch in network news." I heartily agree. Nowhere else in television do journalists have the kind of freedom and airtime that we enjoy at *Nightline.* A few days after Ben gave me the job, the news was announced in front of the show's full team. As I stared out at the faces of my friends on the staff — which I consider to be among the best in all of news — I was engaging in a positive version of *prapañca,* picturing all the adventures we could have, stories we could tell, and bad guys whose days we could ruin. Meanwhile, I convinced the bosses to let me keep doing weekends on *GMA,* a job I am enjoying more than ever. On most mornings, I'm actually excited when the alarm goes off at four A.M.

So, now that I have these two amazing gigs, am I finally fully satisfied? Have I truly arrived? Am I like a shark that no longer needs to keep moving? I don't know — probably not. But for now, at least, I'm not thinking about what I can do next, only about how I can keep my current circumstances from changing.

In any event, while the promotion was a huge deal for me, a more significant moment actually came a few months before.

I was in Rio de Janeiro, shooting a piece about police efforts to clean up the city's drug-ravaged slums before the 2016 Summer Olympics. One night, my crew and I found ourselves in a small concrete structure, down a dark and filthy back alley, filming members of a drug gang as they prepared marijuana for sale. All of a sudden, a tank of a man came charging in, with an entourage of teenaged henchmen. This guy was carrying a semiautomatic rifle and wearing layers of gold chains in a style reminiscent of Mr. T. When he shook my hand, it actually hurt. He was the leader — or "don" — of the gang, and he was willing, he said, to grant us a rare interview, as long as we promised not to show his face. We hastily set up our cameras, with the don's heavily armed lieutenants looming over my producer's shoulder, peering into the viewfinder to make sure we didn't compromise the boss's anonymity.

When the interview got under way, I asked him, "Would you describe your work as dangerous?"

"*Your* job is dangerous," he said. "What if I decided to kill or kidnap you right now?"

Awkward silence.

I was 97 percent sure the don was kidding, but the remaining 3 percent was enough to throw me into a funny headspace. What followed was what I'm calling, for lack of a better term, a moment of clarity. Again, nothing mystical — just a series of thoughts, realizations, and entreaties that arose in a flash.

It began with an internal plea: *Dear Drug Lord, please don't kill me just when I've finally gotten my shit together.*

This was followed by a sort of stock-taking, a review of how far I'd come since my bad old days of mindlessness — the days when I might have come face-to-face with a drug dealer under entirely different circumstances. It struck me that the voice in my head is still, in many ways, an asshole. However, mindfulness now does a pretty good job of tying up the voice and putting duct tape over its mouth. I'm still a maniacally hard worker; I make no apologies for that. I still believe firmly that the price of security is insecurity — that a healthy amount of neuroticism is good. But I also know that widening my circle of concern beyond my own crap has made me much happier. Paradoxically, looking inward has made me more outward-facing — and a much nicer colleague, friend, and husband to the wonderful Bianca (who, when she hears that I've gotten myself into this situation with the drug lord is probably going to threaten to kill me herself). And while I still worry about work, learning to "care and not to care," at least 10% of the time, has freed me up to focus more on the parts of the job that matter most — such as covering great stories like this one.

Then I sent one more little mental plea to the drug lord: *Meditation (which — and I say this with nothing but respect — you should really try) has made me much less reliant on unstable and constantly changing external circumstances. My happiness is much more self-generated. In other words, I'm increasingly comfortable with impermanence — but not so comfortable that I am okay with you erasing me right this very moment.*

As I said, this all happened very quickly. Seconds after he issued his threat, the drug lord's ample belly began to shake with laughter. "Tell him I'm joking," he said to my translator. The gangster then reached out and put his bear claw on my shoulder, in what was either supposed to be a gesture of reassurance or intimidation — or a little of both — while I chuckled nervously and gulped down saliva.

I had one more thought. Ironically, it was the exact same thought I had had more than a decade prior, at the beginning of this odyssey, on the top of that mountain in Afghanistan when I was shot at for the first time:

I hope we're rolling on this.

ACKNOWLEDGMENTS

In the immortal words of Jay Z, "First of all, I want to thank my connect." Huge gratitude to my wife, Dr. Bianca Harris, for making me 100% happier before I became 10% happier. Thank you for introducing me to the work of Dr. Mark Epstein, for tiptoeing around our little apartment when I'm meditating, for putting up with my going on retreats, and for helping me every step of the way with this book — even though you were uncomfortable with my repeatedly gushing about your brilliance and beauty. I love you.

Speaking of the amazing Mark Epstein, I want to thank him for agreeing — for reasons I'll never fully understand — to make friends with an obnoxiously inquisitive stranger. (Meanwhile, a big "you're welcome" to Mark's wife, Arlene Shechet, who, when she heard that I'd made fun of her husband's clogs, said, "Oh, thank you

— I hate those shoes!")

I want to thank *all* of my Jew-Bu friends, including Mark, Joseph Goldstein, Sharon Salzberg, Daniel Goleman and Tara Bennett-Goleman, Jon Kabat-Zinn, and Richie Davidson. You guys changed my mind.

I can't forget my other contemplative co-conspirators, whose writings, friendship, and advice have benefited me enormously: Sam Harris, Stephen Batchelor, Robert Thurman, Jud Brewer, Jack Kornfield, Matthieu Ricard, Jay Michaelson, Jim Gimian, Barry Boyce, Melvin McLeod, David Gelles, Josh Baran, Representative Tim Ryan, Jeff Walker, Jeff Warren, Daniel Ingram, Tara Brach, Spring Washam, Emiliana Simon-Thomas, Chade-Meng Tan, Mirabai Bush, Vince Horn, Elizabeth Stanley, Janice Marturano, Soren Gordhamer, and Gyano Gibson.

I was lucky enough to have a volunteer army of first readers, who dedicated truly unreasonable amounts of their personal time, and saved me from embarrassing myself in countless ways. Chief among them are: Matt Harris, Regina Lipovsky, Karen Avrich, and Mark Halperin, four of my favorite people on earth, to whom I am now forever indebted. Other game-changing first readers included: Jessica Harris, Susan Mercandetti, Kris Sebastian, Amy Entelis, Kerry Smith, Andrew Miller, Nick Watt, Ricky Van Veen, Wonbo Woo, Glen Caplin, Zev Borow, and Hannah Karp. This book would not have happened without their guidance, or without the early encouragement of my hilarious and supportive book agent, Luke Janklow, as well as my excellent and patient editor, Denise Oswald, both of whom talked me off of countless ledges. (Not incidentally, I also want to thank the whole team at It Books: Lynn Grady, Michael Barrs, Sharyn Rosenblum, Tamara Arellano, Beth Silfin, and ace copy editor Rob Sternitzky.) Also, I must acknowledge William Patrick, who swooped in late in the game and made some hugely valuable contributions.

There are many past and present colleagues at ABC News who contributed in various ways to this book: Ben Sherwood, Diane Sawyer, James Goldston, Barbara Walters, David Muir, George Stephanopoulos, Bill Weir, Chris Cuomo, Dr. Richard Besser, Jake Tapper, David Wright, Bob and Lee Woodruff, Jeffrey Schneider, Alyssa Apple, Julie Townsend, Barbara Fedida, Felicia Biberica, Almin Karamehmedovic, Jeanmarie Condon, Bianna Golodryga, Ron Claiborne, Ginger Zee, Sara Haines, John

Ferracane, Tracey Marx, Cynthia McFadden, Dan Abrams, Alfonso Pena, Diane Mendez, Nick Capote, Miguel Sancho, Beau Beyerle, Wendy Fisher, David Reiter, Joe Ruffolo, Simone Swink, Andrew Springer, and Jon Meyersohn.

A few personal friends I'd like to mention who also hooked me up along the way: Willie Mack, Josh Abramson, Jason Harris, Jason Hammel, Kori Gardiner, Meg Thompson, Stephan Walter, and Kaiama Glover.

In the book, I borrowed or modified some lovely turns of phrase from several authors I admire: Gary Shteyngart seems to have invented the word *blightscape* in *The Russian Debutante's Handbook;* Benjamin Kunkel writes about "reality . . . gathering in the corners of the room" in an ecstasy scene in *Indecision;* Ben Sherwood uses the term "honeyed light" in *The Survivors Club.*

Finally, to Jay and Nancy Lee Harris, the two truly indispensable "causes and conditions" (to use some Buddhist phraseology) for this book. This seems like a good place to note, for the record, something my dad recently said that surprised me: the "price of security is insecurity" line was not, in fact, his personal motto, but instead something he concocted to make his anxious young son feel better about worrying so much. So apparently, the advice was not strategic, but rather compassionate. It only took me four decades to figure out how to put it to use wisely. Thanks to both of you for being as close to perfect as parents could possibly be, for letting me write about you honestly, and for not freaking out when I finally told you (nearly a decade after the fact) about the whole drug thing. Also, I forgive you for sending me to that yoga class.

APPENDIX: INSTRUCTIONS

There are a lot of bad reasons not to meditate. Here are my top three:

1. "It's bullshit." I get it. As you may remember, I used to feel this way, too. But there's a reason why businesspeople, lawyers, and marines have embraced meditation. There's no magic or mysticism required — it's just exercise. If you do the right amount of reps, certain things will happen, reliably and predictably. One of those things, according to the research, is that your brain will change in positive ways. You will get better at not being carried away by your passing emotional squalls; you will learn — maybe 10% of the time, maybe more — to respond, not react. We now know that happiness, resilience, and compassion are

skills, susceptible to training. You don't have to resign yourself to your current level of well-being, or wait for your life circumstances to change; you can take the reins yourself. You brush your teeth, you take the meds your doctor prescribes, you eat healthfully — and if you don't, you probably feel guilty about it. Given everything modern science is telling us, I think it's now safe to put meditation in this category.

2. "It's too hard for me." I call this the "fallacy of uniqueness" argument. People often tell me, "I know I should meditate, but you don't understand: *my* mind just moves too fast. *I* can't possibly do this." News flash: Welcome to the human condition. Everybody's mind is out of control. Even experienced meditators struggle with distraction. Moreover, the idea that meditation requires you to "clear your mind" is a myth. (More on this misapprehension below.)

3. "I don't have the time." Everybody has five minutes. My advice is to start with five minutes a day and to tell yourself you'll never do more. If

you increase your time gradually and organically, great. If not, totally fine.

Basic Mindfulness Meditation

1. Sit comfortably. You don't have to twist yourself into a cross-legged position — unless you want to, of course. You can just sit in a chair. (You can also stand up or lie down, although the latter can sometimes result in an unintentional nap.) Whatever your position, you should keep your spine straight, but don't strain.

2. Feel your breath. Pick a spot: nose, belly, or chest. Really try to *feel* the in-breath and then the out-breath.

3. This one is the key: Every time you get lost in thought — which you will, thousands of times — gently return to the breath. I cannot stress strongly enough that forgiving yourself and starting over is the whole game. As my friend and meditation teacher Sharon Salzberg has written, "Beginning again and again is the actual practice, not a problem to overcome so that one day we can

407

come to the 'real' meditation."

Pro Tips

- To stay focused on the breath, try making a soft mental note, like "in" and "out." (Don't get too mesmerized by the note itself, just use it to direct your attention to the actual sensory experience of the breath.)
- "Noting," as it's called, can also be useful when something strong — such as itches, pain, worries, or hunger — comes along and drags your attention away from the breath. The act of applying a label — "planning," "throbbing," "fantasizing" — can objectify whatever's going on, making it much less concrete and monolithic. (Don't get too caught up in thumbing through your internal thesaurus for the right word. Make a note and move on.)
- Another trick for staying focused is to count your breaths. Start at one, and every time you get lost, start over. When you reach ten — if you ever reach ten — start back at one.
- Try to meditate every day. Regularity is more important than duration.
- Set a timer so that you don't have to check your watch. There are apps for

this. (I use something called the Insight Timer.)

- Find friends who are also interested in meditation. It's not a must, but sitting with a group — or merely having people with whom you can discuss your practice — can have an HOV lane effect.
- Find a teacher you trust. Meditation can be a lonely and subtle business. It really helps to have some personal guidance. If you live in a remote area, there are teachers who offer lessons over Skype.
- Beginning meditators are sometimes advised to sit at the same time and in the same place every day. If, like me, your schedule is unpredictable and involves a lot of travel, don't worry about it. I sit whenever and wherever I can fit it in.
- Every once in a while, do a little reading about meditation or Buddhism. Even though the basic instructions are simple, hearing them repeatedly can be useful. It's the opposite of airplane safety announcements. Also, since the practice itself often feels stupid ("in," "out," ad nauseam), glancing at even a few passages of a good book can be a

helpful reminder of the intellectual underpinnings of the practice, which are extremely compelling. Here are some books I like:

On meditation
Real Happiness, Sharon Salzberg
Insight Meditation, Joseph Goldstein

On Buddhism and mindfulness in general
Going to Pieces Without Falling Apart, Dr. Mark Epstein
Buddhism Without Beliefs, Stephen Batchelor

FAQS
Remind me, what's the point of this?
Meditation is the best tool I know for neutralizing the voice in the head. As discussed, the ego is often a hatchery of judgments, desires, assumptions, and diabolical plans. The act of simply feeling the breath breaks the habits of a lifetime. For those short snatches of time when you're focused on the rise and fall of the abdomen or the cool air entering and exiting the nostrils, the ego is muzzled. You are not thinking, you are being mindful — an innate but underused ability we all have, which allows us to be aware without judging.

When you repeatedly go through the cycle of feeling the breath, losing your focus, and hauling yourself back, you are building your mindfulness muscle the way dumbbell curls build your biceps. Once this muscle is just a little bit developed, you can start to see all the thoughts, emotions, and physical sensations that carom through your skull for what they really are: quantum squirts of energy without any concrete reality of their own.

Imagine how massively useful this can be. Normally, for example, when someone cuts you off in traffic or on line at Starbucks, you automatically think, *I'm pissed.* Instantaneously, you actually *become* pissed. Mindfulness allows you to slow that process down. Sometimes, of course, you're right to be pissed. The question is whether you are going to react mindlessly to that anger or respond thoughtfully. Mindfulness provides space between impulse and action, so you're not a slave to whatever neurotic obsession pops into your head.

My mind keeps wandering. Am I failure?
This question gets back to the whole "clear your mind" misconception. The relationship between thinking and meditating is a funny one. Thoughts are simultaneously the biggest obstacle to meditation,

and also an unavoidable part of it — like the opposing team in basketball, or the hurdles in track. The goal is not to erase the obstacles, but to play as well as possible.

So, again: this entire endeavor revolves around moments of mindfulness, interrupted by periods of distraction, then gently catching yourself and returning to the breath. Over time, the mindfulness may grow longer and the wandering shorter. Not incidentally, the ability to begin again and again has significant "off the cushion" benefits. It creates a resilience that can be enormously useful when confronting the ups and downs of everyday life.

How come I don't feel relaxed? This really sucks.

First of all, when you learn any new skill — Urdu, French horn, krumping, whatever — it is often awkward and difficult at the beginning.

Second, write down this quote from Jon Kabat-Zinn and put it up on your wall: "Meditation is not about feeling a certain way. It's about feeling the way you feel."

It's amazing how many times I can hear this message and yet forget it when I sit down to meditate. You don't need to achieve some special state; you just need to be as aware as possible of whatever's happening right now. This is what the Buddhists mean by "letting go" — better translated as "letting be."

Meditation became much easier for me when I stopped holding myself responsible for what was happening in my head. To this day, as soon as I start meditating, the first thoughts are usually: *How the hell am I going to make it until the timer goes off? Why am I even doing this?* But I haven't summoned those complaints. They just come out of the void. So rather than lapse into what Sharon Salzberg calls a "judgment jag," I just note the thoughts as "complaining" or "rushing" or "doubt." Yet again, there are massive off-the-cushion consequences to cultivating this attitude. Just because your wife or your kids are driving you nuts does not mean you are a "bad person." You can't control what comes up, only how you respond.

You keep talking about this notion that "you can't help what we feel, only how you respond," but I want to feel different things. Won't meditation do that for me?

In my experience, yes, it will. Not right away, of course — and not entirely. But as you learn to stop feeding your habitual thought and emotional patterns through

413

compulsive mental churning, you will make room for new things.

If I'm in physical pain, should I change position?

I know this stinks, but the advice is to sit still and investigate the discomfort. If you look closely, you'll see the pain is constantly changing. Try to note it: "stabbing," "throbbing," "pulling," etc. You may find that it's not the pain that is intolerable, but instead your resistance to it. Of course, if you think you're in real danger of injury, definitely shift position.

I keep falling asleep.

This is not a new problem. The Buddhists, perhaps unsurprisingly, have lists of things you can do to fight fatigue.

- Meditate with your eyes open. (Just enough to let a little light in. Try to fix your gaze on a neutral spot on the wall or the ground.)
- Do walking meditation. (More on this later.)
- Investigate the feeling of fatigue. Where do you feel it in your body? Is your head heavy? Your forehead buzzy?
- Do metta. (More on this later, too.)

- Pull your ears, or rub your hands, arms, legs, and face.
- Splash water on your face.
- If all else fails, go to bed.
- Also, consider the possibility that you're constipated. (Seriously, they say that.)

This is so unbelievably boring.

Boredom: also not a new problem. The advice here is similar to how you should handle pain and fatigue: investigate. What does boredom feel like? How does it manifest in your body? Whatever comes up in your mind can be co-opted and turned into the object of meditation. It's like in judo, where you use the force of your enemy against him.

Another trick for overcoming boredom is to increase the level of difficulty in your meditation. Try feeling the breath more closely. Can you catch the beginning and the end of an in- or out-breath? Can you see yourself subtly leaning forward into the next breath instead of being exactly where you are? Can you note the intervals between breaths? Maybe, if those periods are long enough, you can designate a few "touch points" — quickly bring your attention to your butt or your hands or your knees before the next breath resumes.

I keep trying to feel the breath as it naturally occurs, but every time I focus on it, I involuntarily start to control it, so it feels artificial.

Doesn't matter. As Joseph Goldstein says, "This is not a breathing exercise." You don't have to breathe a certain way. If you want, you can even take sharper breaths so that it's easier to feel them. What matters here is the mindfulness, not the breath.

What if I feel panicky and hyperventilate every time I try to watch my breath?

This is not uncommon. Fortunately, there are many variations of mindfulness meditation.

Body Scan

1. Sit, stand, or lie down.
2. Start at one end of your body and work up or down. Bring your attention to your feet, your calves, your knees, your butt, and so on. When you get to your head, what can you feel? Anything? After reaching the top, work your way back down.
3. Every time your mind wanders,

gently bring it back.

Walking meditation

1. Stake out a stretch of ground roughly ten yards long. (That's somewhat arbitrary — whatever length you've got will work.)
2. Slowly pace back and forth, noting: *lift, move, place* with every stride. Try your best to feel each component of every stride. (Don't look at your feet, just look at a neutral point in the distance.)
3. Every time your mind wanders, gently bring it back.
4. There is a temptation to denigrate walking meditation as less serious or rigorous than seated meditation, but this is wrong. Just because your legs are crossed doesn't mean you're meditating more effectively. As a noted teacher once said, "I've seen chickens sitting on their eggs for days on end."

Compassion meditation (aka metta)

At first blush, most rational people find the below off-putting in the extreme. Trust me

— or, better, trust the scientists — it works.

1. This practice involves picturing a series of people and sending them good vibes. Start with yourself. Generate as clear a mental image as possible.

2. Repeat the following phrases: *May you be happy, May you be healthy, May you be safe, May you live with ease.* Do this slowly. Let the sentiment land. You are not forcing your well-wishes on anyone; you're just offering them up, just as you would a cool drink. Also, success is not measured by whether you generate any specific emotion. As Sharon says, you don't need to feel "a surge of sentimental love accompanied by chirping birds." The point is to try. Every time you do, you are exercising your compassion muscle. (By the way, if you don't like the phrases above, you can make up your own.)

3. After you've sent the phrases to yourself, move on to: a benefactor (a teacher, mentor, relative), a close friend (can be a pet, too), a neutral person (someone you see often but don't really ever notice), a difficult

418

person, and, finally, "all beings."

Open awareness

1. Sit, stand, or lie down. (You can actually do open awareness while walking, too.)
2. Instead of simply watching the breath, try to watch everything that arises. Set up a spy cam in your mind and just see what is there to see. To maintain your focus, try noting whatever comes up: *burning, hearing, itching, breathing,* etc.
3. Every time you lose your focus, just forgive yourself and come back. (It's pretty easy to get distracted doing this type of meditation, so you might want to use your breath as an anchor that you return to when you get scattered. It's like filling up the hot-air balloon of the mind with enough concentration so that you can fly.)

More questions:
Isn't noting just a form of thinking?

Yes, but it's what the Buddhists call a "skillful" use of thinking, designed to direct the mind toward connecting with what is

419

actually happening, as opposed to getting caught up in a storm of unproductive rumination. As with all thinking, it's possible for noting to lapse into judgments. For example, I often find myself noting: *You're wandering again, you gigantic moron.*

Is being mindful the same thing as being in the moment?

Being in the moment is necessary but not sufficient for mindfulness — which involves being in the moment, but also being aware of what's going on. Joseph has a term I like: "black Lab conscious." Black Labs are always in the moment, but they're probably not nonjudgmentally aware of the contents of their consciousness as they eat sweat socks or take a dump on the rug.

I keep hearing about Transcendental Meditation. Lots of celebrities do it. What's the difference between TM and the stuff you're talking about here?

TM involves a mantra — a word or a phrase that you repeat silently to yourself. It's a style of meditation that comes out of Hinduism and is focused mainly on generating a deep sense of concentration, which can feel terrific. The practices we're discussing here come out of Buddhism and are

420

focused more on developing mindfulness. (The dividing lines aren't so neat. You definitely build up concentration in Buddhist meditation, and you can also develop some mindfulness in TM.) The two schools tend to look down their noses at each other. However, even though I'm in the Buddhist camp, I've done enough poking around in the TM world to be convinced the practice has plenty of benefits.

Is meditation good for everyone?

If you have severe depression or trauma, it might be best to practice in close consultation with a mental health professional or a very experienced teacher.

You're not a teacher. What business do you have providing meditation instructions?

Fair question. You should be wary of teachers who lack deep experience. I had everything here vetted by people who actually know what they're talking about.

Can I meditate if I'm a believing Christian (or Jew or Muslim, etc.)? Will it erode my faith?

There's some controversy around this question. Dr. Albert Mohler, the head of the Southern Baptist Theological Seminary, has criticized both yoga and meditation as being based on Eastern spirituality, and therefore not good for Christians. Before he became Pope Benedict XVI, Cardinal Ratzinger specifically slammed Buddhism as an "auto-erotic spirituality."

There's equally strong pushback from devout Christians (and Jews and Muslims) who point out that meditation has been a part of the mystical traditions of all the great faiths. Furthermore, they argue, mindfulness meditation — especially the secularized MBSR technique pioneered by Jon Kabat-Zinn — is simply a tool for improving mental hygiene. In fact, they argue, quieting the voice in the head has helped them feel closer to God.

What is the least amount of time I can sit and still get the benefits the scientists are always talking about?

No one's figured out the dosage question yet. I don't have any evidence for this, but I think if you can manage five minutes, you'll start seeing changes in your own life, particularly as it pertains to your level of emotional reactivity.

In sum

Forget your preconceived notions. Forget the dopey packaging and the unfortunate cultural baggage. Meditation is worth the work — even if you're too embarrassed to admit to your friends that you're doing it.

Under the sway of the ego, life becomes a constant low-grade crisis. You are never sated, never satisfied, always reaching for the next thing, like a colicky baby. Meditation is the antidote. It won't fix everything in your life, make you taller, or (most likely) land you in a state of bliss on a park bench. But it can make you 10% happier, or maybe much more.

There used to be a sign on the wall of Newbury Comics, my favorite record store in Boston. Above the list of upcoming releases, it read, ALL DATES CAN CHANGE, SO CAN YOU.

ABOUT THE AUTHOR

Dan Harris is a co-anchor of *Nightline* and the weekend edition of *Good Morning America* on ABC News. Previously, he was the anchor of the Sunday edition of *World News.* He regularly contributes stories for such shows as *20/20, World News with Diane Sawyer,* and weekday *GMA.* Harris has reported from all over the planet, covering wars in Afghanistan, Israel/Palestine, and Iraq, and producing investigative reports in Haiti, Cambodia, and the Congo. He has also spent many years covering America's faith scene, with a focus on evangelicals — who have treated him kindly despite the fact that he is openly agnostic. He has been at ABC News for fourteen years. Before that, he was in local news in Boston and Maine. He grew up outside of Boston and currently lives with his wife, Bianca, in New York City. This is his first book.